ECONOMIC DEVELOPMENT
The History of an Idea
H. W. Arndt

Economic development is one of the great themes of our time. It is the dominant objective of national policy in the majority of countries, those of the Third World. But anyone who might ask what, precisely, people mean by economic development would get very different answers—and the answers have changed over the years, at least in emphasis, and are still changing.

Here, H. W. Arndt traces the history of thought about economic development as a policy objective. In nontechnical terms, he shows readers what the development objective has meant in various times and places, to political and economic theorists, policymakers, and politicians from Adam Smith to Ayatollah Khomeini. In a chapter on the pre-history of "economic development," before the term came into general use after World War II, Arndt outlines the Western origins of the idea of material progress. He uncovers antecedents of modern thought about development in the writings of nineteenth-century colonial theorists and leaders of nationalist movements in Asia, in Marxist thought, and finally in the 1940-45 literature on war aims.

Next, Arndt gives an account of the phase during the 1950s and 1960s when economic development was largely identified with economic growth, and the emphasis shifted from physical capital formation to human capital and trade as the presumed main engines of growth. He then deals with the changes that began in the late 1960s when economic growth came to be widely downgraded as an objective, relative to social objectives such as employment, equity, or basic needs. In his last two chapters, Arndt turns to radical thought about development: on the left, neo-Marxist, Maoist, and Latin American structuralist approaches; on the right, skepticism about development targets or outright condemnation of modernization on the Western model.

Economic Development focuses on the ends, not the means, of policy. It is a fascinating and readable account of what people have thought—and still think—about one of the most important and contentious issues that divide us: the trade-offs between economic growth, social justice, personal freedom, and national independence as policy objectives. It will have a wide appeal among thoughtful readers interested in public and world affairs, as well as to students of development.

H. W. Arndt is professor emeritus of economics at The Australian National University. His book *The Rise and Fall of Economic Growth: A Study in Contemporary Thought,* is also published by the University of Chicago Press.

ECONOMIC
DEVELOPMENT

ECONOMIC DEVELOPMENT
THE HISTORY OF AN IDEA

H. W. Arndt

The University of Chicago Press

Chicago and London

H. W. ARNDT is professor emeritus of economics at The Australian National University. His book *The Rise and Fall of Economic Growth: A Study in Contemporary Thought,* is also published by the University of Chicago Press.

The University of Chicago Press, Chicago 60637
The University of Chicago Press, Ltd., London
© 1987 by The University of Chicago
All rights reserved. Published 1987
Printed in the United States of America

96 95 94 93 92 91 90 89 88 87   54321

Library of Congress Cataloging-in-Publication Data

Arndt, H. W. (Heinz Wolfgang), 1915–
    Economic development.

    Includes index.
    1. Economic development. 2. Developing
countries—Economic policy. I. Title.
HD82.A66   1987   338.9   86-25108
ISBN 0–226–02720–1

Contents

CONTENTS

Preface

Some years ago, I published a book entitled *The Rise and Fall of Economic Growth*. It told the story of how economic growth came in the 1950s to be regarded as the single most important objective of economic policy in the rich industrial countries, and how in the 1960s it came under attack from various quarters. This book attempts a similar treatment of economic development as a policy objective in the poorer countries of the world.

The book has been long in the making and in the process I have become an intellectual debtor many times over. During some decades of study of economic development, I have learned most from the work of Arthur Lewis and Hla Myint and, in practice, from my work and friends in Indonesia. In recent years, I have been stimulated by two books, both invaluable though very different in approach, I. M. D. Little's *Economic Development* and R. M. Sundrum's *Development Economics*. I am conscious of two debts I should have incurred but did not—to authorities on the politics and sociology of development and to writers on development in languages other than English. Had I attempted to fill these two gaps, the book would have never been finished. I can only hope other studies will complement this one in both respects. Even within the narrower confines of writings in English on economic development—a vast literature—I cannot pretend to have read and digested more than a fraction. Readers will miss some of their favourite authors, even if they remember that my concern has been with statements about policy objectives, not with economic analysis. But I believe the sources on which I have drawn adequately represent the main strands of thought about the development objective.

Parts of chapters 2, 3, and 5 were originally published elsewhere. For the use of this material, I am grateful to the following sources: (chap. 2) *Newsletter*, Economic Thought Society of Australia, no. 2 (Autumn 1982); (chap. 2) "Development Economics before 1945," in J. Bhagwati and R. S. Eckaus, eds., *Development and Planning: Essays in Honour of Paul Rosenstein-Rodan* (London: Allen and Unwin, 1972); (chap. 3) "Trade as the Engine of Growth," *Wirtschaft und Gesellschaft* 8, no. 2 (Vienna, 1982); (chap. 5) "The Origins of Structuralism," *World Development* 13, no. 2 (February 1985), published by Pergamon Journals Ltd., Oxford.

1

Introductory

The world has become accustomed to thinking of itself as divided into developed and developing countries. That the developing countries should develop further is almost universally desired by their own peoples and considered desirable by almost everybody else. But anyone who asked articulate citizens in developed or developing countries what they meant by this desirable objective of "development" would get a great variety of answers.

Higher living standards. A rising per capita income. Increase in productive capacity. Mastery over nature. Freedom through control of man's environment. Economic growth. But not mere growth, growth with equity. Elimination of poverty. Basic needs satisfaction. Catching up with the developed countries in technology, wealth, power, status. Economic independence, self-reliance. Scope for self-fulfilment for all. Liberation, the means to human ascent. Development, in the vast literature on the subject, appears to have come to encompass almost all facets of the good society, everyman's road to utopia.

This has not always been so. The term "economic development" as denoting a process which societies undergo was hardly used before World War II, although the use of "economic development" in the sense of an activity applied, especially by governments, to a country's land and natural resources is at least a hundred years older. The English term previously most commonly used for the process was "material progress." It was "the progress of England towards opulence and improvement" which Adam Smith hoped would continue in all future times, and it was "economical progress" about which John Stuart Mill was one of the first to express a jaundiced view. For people in Britain and France

1

and later in Germany, the United States and other Western countries, material progress was what they were experiencing all around, with all the benefits and costs of capitalist development. In the aspirations of people in Asia, Africa, and Latin America, the quest was for modernisation, industrialisation, even Westernisation, as much for national survival, power, or independence as for enjoyment of the material fruits of Western civilisation. During and immediately after World War II, the adoption of economic development as a policy objective in and for the "underdeveloped" countries of the world coincided almost fortuitously with the elevation of economic growth to the status of prime economic policy objective in the developed countries. A humanitarian response to statistical evidence of the gap between rich and poor countries lent support to the political pressures for economic development exerted by movements for national independence in colonial territories and by rivalry with Japan in east Asia and with communism the world over. At the same time, the achievement of full employment during the war and its unexpectedly easy maintenance through the postwar years shifted the emphasis in economic policy in Western countries from the preoccupation with instability and underemployment of the interwar years to a new preoccupation with economic growth. It was this coincidence which largely accounts for the fact that, at least in Western postwar thinking and writing, economic development was interpreted as virtually synonymous with economic growth. The first comprehensive study of the process and problems of economic development was entitled *The Theory of Economic Growth*. Economic development was defined as "a rise in the levels of living of the common people" and measured by growth of per capita income.

Initially, the pioneers of the new academic discipline of development economics in Western countries and the planners in what was coming to be called the Third World, in the classical tradition but under the particular influence of current growth theory—Keynesian macroeconomics dynamised by Harrod and Domar—put the stress on fixed capital formation as the most important source of economic growth and/or development. The main policy implications appeared to be a need to raise the domestic saving rate in the poor countries and an opportunity for capital aid by the rich countries. During the 1960s it become increasingly evident that different rates of capital formation did little to explain why growth rates differed, either in developed or in developing countries. Among the residual factors left after differences in growth rates of the quantity of capital and labour had been allowed for, quality differences, especially those resulting from technical progress and education, seemed to deserve much more attention. Human capital, and with it education and manpower planning, transfer of technology, and technical assistance, assumed a new importance in thinking about development. During the 1960s, also, disappointment with the results of industrialisation based on import substitution, in Latin America and elsewhere, led to a renewed belief that trade could serve as an engine, or at least a helpful handmaiden, of economic growth in developing countries; more outward-looking industrial development came into favour.

Changing perceptions about the relative importance of physical and human capital or about the relative merits of inward and outward oriented industrialisation involved, at most, shifts of emphasis about means, not ends, about the best strategy for accelerating economic development in the sense of growth of total or per capita GNP. But such perceptions shifted the prism through which people looked at development. Seeing economic development as a more complex process modified perspectives about development as a policy objective. Education, technical progress, integration into the world market economy—all these had implications beyond their contribution to economic growth.

A more pronounced change of course came towards the end of the 1960s. Statistics showed that many developing countries had indeed enjoyed quite rapid economic growth, more rapid than Western countries had generally experienced during the nineteenth century, yet growth in per capita income had not eliminated poverty or underemployment and had frequently been accompanied by a widening gap between rich and poor within developing countries. The meaning of development, it was said, had been misconceived. Economic growth was not enough. More important criteria were what happened to poverty, to unemployment, to equality. At the very least, development policies must aim at growth with equity. Better still, in the view of some, priority should be accorded to the satisfaction of basic needs.

This call for much greater attention to distributional equity and other social objectives evoked little response in Third World countries, where political and social elites were understandably apt to view it as a threat to their own positions, or at any rate as unwarranted interference in their internal affairs, a new sort of cultural imperialism. But it fitted in well with, indeed probably in part reflected, the current intellectual climate in Western countries where, after twenty years of unprecedented economic growth, growth itself had come under attack from several quarters— from sceptics and critics increasingly conscious of the costs of affluence for the quality of life, from students and others alienated and radicalised by the Vietnam War, and from voices warning about dangers to the environment, about pollution and exhaustion of non-renewable natural resources. This call also connected mainstream thinking about economic development with some of the currents of heterodoxy that had been flowing and continued to flow alongside it, in developed and developing countries.

On the left, Marxism gave rise to widely divergent doctrines about the means and ends of economic development, doctrines which had in common only a belief in the need for revolutionary overthrow of Western capitalism-imperialism. Marx's own magnificent dynamics, which had presented capitalism, with its capacity to release colossal productive forces, as an inevitable though temporary stage in the dialectic process of economic development, did not meet the political needs of socialist revolutionaries in precapitalist societies. Lenin, preoccupied with the achievement of power, and Stalin, preoccupied with its military and industrial consolidation, did not explicitly challenge the classical Marxist conception. But Mao Tse-tung first adapted Marxism to the requirements of Chinese nationalist-agrarian radicalism and then, in the Great Cultural Revolution, superseded it with his own millenarian vision of mass mobilisation for the transformation of human nature. Meanwhile, in the Latin American countries which had gained political independence a century earlier, neo-Marxists used the notion of economic "dependence" of the underdeveloped countries of the "periphery" on the developed "centre" to expound the thesis that underdevelopment was itself caused by imperialism. The neo-Marxist view of the world as embroiled in class war between the underdeveloped Third World and the imperialist West had its reformist counterpart in the campaign for a New International Economic Order which held the stage in international debate during the 1970s.

On the right, there were in the first decade or two after World War II few prominent echoes of Gandhi's passionate denunciation of Western civilisation and modernisation, although there were sceptics who questioned the prevailing consensus about the desirability or practicability of rapid economic development of traditional societies. But in the 1970s, the Islamic fundamentalism of the Ayatollah Khomeini shared the Gandhian view of Western civilisation as morally evil, and, like both these religious leaders, spokesmen of the Christian churches rejected capitalist economic development as inconsistent with social justice. In this belief that distributional equity must have priority over economic growth, there was in fact little that divided the religious leaders on the "right" from some of the neo-Marxists on the "left."

My purpose in this book is to trace in some detail the history of thought about economic development as a policy objective that has just been sketched in outline, to explain how and why people's ideas changed or differed with circumstances in different parts of the world. Like my earlier book *The Rise and Fall of Economic Growth*, this one is a history of thought, but not strictly of *economic* thought. It is concerned with views about the ends, not the means, of policy. It does not attempt to make any new contributions to economic analysis, or even to give an account of the history of development economics. The focus is on changes in people's ideas about objectives, as reflected in academic writing and public discussion.

Of course, the distinction between ends and means—between final and instrumental objectives—is not always clear-cut. The choice of means may unintentionally affect the resulting trade-off between ends, and the desired trade-off necessarily governs in some degree the choice of means. Some sections, especially in chapter 3 of this book, go some way into the discussion of alternative development strategies. But they do so only because different strategies seem in part to reflect and promote different values.

This book has turned out to be a more difficult enterprise than its predecessor. Economic growth in the developed countries was unambiguous in its meaning. The question merely was why people thought such growth increasingly desirable for some years and then became doubtful. Development, in contrast, has meant almost all things to all men and women. This story has no simple plot. If there is a central theme, it is, as we have already seen, one of increasing complexity and divergence. Today, a variety of interpretations remains, each competing with others for allegiance. To show how and why these interpretations arose may help readers to clarify their own ideas, perhaps to make up their minds as to where they stand on one of the great issues of our time, or at least to become more aware of the dilemmas. Students of economics, immersed in the study of means, may derive benefit from being stimulated to think about the ends—what it is all for.

The claim that this book explains how and why people's ideas about development have changed in the span of a few decades may seem presumptuous. This is not a history of science in which thought progresses in large measure guided by immanent logic and new empirical knowledge. Nor is it a history of political and social thought over centuries in which it may be possible, along Marxist lines, to relate changing ideas to changes in the political, economic, and social structure of society. The changes in thinking about development traced in this book will at times seem mere changes in intellectual fashion, the products of a burgeoning academic industry. But some of them also, not unlike changes in the history of science, represent the response of intelligent observers to the failures and successes of specific national policies—uncontrolled but not unilluminating experiments, as it were, in the laboratory of the Third World. Others are in the nature of political statements, articulating the viewpoints and interests of combatants in national and international struggles. Whatever their origin, they constitute collectively an aspect of the intellectual history of our times which may interest others besides development economists.

Some readers may come away from the book saying to themselves, with Ecclesiastes, there is no new thing under the sun. This should cause neither surprise nor disappointment, for embedded in the concept of development are all the dilemmas about the human condition and human hopes. It is probably true that almost everything that has been said in the last thirty years about development as a policy objective can be found somewhere in the writings of Adam Smith, John Stuart Mill, Giovanni Battista Vico, Karl Marx, Gandhi, Sun Yat-sen, or Schumpeter. Finding it is one of the pleasures of the historian of thought. But it will be found only because it has been rediscovered, presented in terms relevant to our time, discussed, and made familiar.

2

The Prehistory (to 1945)

Gunnar Myrdal, in his book *Economic Theory and Under-Developed Regions*, published in 1957, wrote that "the emergence in underdeveloped countries of this common urge to economic development as a major political purpose, and the definition of economic development as a rise in the levels of living of the common people, the agreement that economic development is a task for government . . . all this amounts to something entirely new in history."[1]

As I have indicated, my primary purpose is to examine what people have meant by economic development as a policy objective for the Third World and to trace changes and divergences of opinion about the idea since it came to the forefront at the end of World War II. Before we embark on this task it is desirable to set the stage, to say something about the prehistory.

What was new was not economic development as a historical process. This had gone on for centuries in the West. The new departure was an almost universal acceptance of the view that the countries that had hitherto been left behind in this process should seek to participate in it and be assisted in doing so. Even as a policy objective for these countries, economic development had long been in the minds of some of their leaders of opinion, though under different labels, "modernisation" or "Westernisation" or quite often "industrialisation." And even in the West economic development, in some senses, had long been the subject of a large, specialised literature, about colonial theory and policy, and a theme in the counterculture of Marxist theory.

This chapter will look at each of these three antecedents of the post-1945 history of economic development as a policy objective and at the emergence of the idea in the years just before and during World War II.

CHAPTER TWO

Western Origins

W. W. Rostow has, more explicitly and successfully than anyone else, tried to explain *How It All Began*.[2] It certainly began
in Western Europe, though just where and when, whether in
eighteenth, seventeenth or sixteenth century Britain or in the
city states of Renaissance Italy or in monasteries from the
tenth century onwards, depends on which aspect of the
emergence of modern civilisation one regards as crucial, the
Industrial Revolution, the Newtonian view of the physical
world, the rise of capitalism and the Protestant ethic, or the
very notion of rational and empirical enquiry.

Industrialisation may later have become "the hallmark of
modernity,"[3] but it has plausibly been argued that "in Western Europe the machine had been developing for at least
seven centuries before the dramatic changes that accompanied the 'industrial revolution'."[4] If "what distinguishes
the world since the industrial revolution from the world before is the systematic, regular, and progressive application of
science and technology to the production of goods and services,"[5] seventeenth-century Britain, with Francis Bacon and
Isaac Newton, clearly played a major role. Bacon, insisting
that the real and legitimate goal of the new sciences is "the
endowment of human life with new inventions and riches,"[6]
was one of the first to link science with material progress; and
in Newton's synthesis, as Rostow has put it, "man was put in
a position to understand, to predict, and to manipulate nature. . . . By changing the way man looked at the world
around him, the Newtonian perceptions increased, in ways
impossible to measure, the supply of inventions and the will-
ingness of entrepreneurs to introduce innovations."[7] But in
the century before Bacon and Newton, the Protestant Refor-
mation had sanctioned a new ethic, turning "the asceticism
countenanced by religion into a device for concentration
upon worldly goods and worldly advancement,"[8] and Coper-
nicus and Galileo had taken the first giant steps in the scientific revolution, "driven by an inner impulse to make sense of
the universe."[9]

Indeed, it is arguable that the real origins go still further back. "Before the new industrial processes could take hold on a great scale, a reorientation of wishes, habits, ideas, goals was necessary."[10] Two essential steps were the emergence of the modern categories of time and space and the discovery of nature. The former, it has been suggested, arose in part out of the routine of the monastery, the discipline of the rule: in the seventh century the pope decreed that the bells of the monastery be rung seven times in twenty-four hours. Thinking in modern categories of time and space was a huge break with the past, for to medieval man "the dropping of a ship below the horizon no more needed an explanation than the dropping of a demon down the chimney. . . . Objects swam into vision and sank out of it. . . . In this symbolic world of space and time everything was either a mystery or a miracle."[11] The symbol of a new belief in an independent world of mathematically measurable sequence was the mechanical clock, which, invented a good deal earlier, came into use in thirteenth-century cities. In this sense, "the clock, not the steam engine, is the key-machine of the modern industrial age."[12] The second major change was "in the direction of interest from the heavenly world to the natural one. . . . By a slow gradual process, the world of nature breaks in upon the medieval dream of hell and paradise and eternity. . . . The discovery of nature as a whole was the most important part of the era of discovery which began for the Western World with the Crusades and the travels of Marco Polo (1250–1320) and the southward ventures of the Portuguese."[13]

However we date the origins of Western civilisation—of which material progress or economic development was but one facet though perhaps the most important in its consequences—there is no doubt that it increasingly differentiated Western European society from anything that had gone before and existed elsewhere. The economic historian R. H. Tawney, in a book on China, delineated the contrast between modern and traditional society: "Rapid economic change as a fact, and continuous economic progress as an ideal, are the notes, not of the history of the West, but of little more than its last four centuries . . . [Before then, in the West, as still in the East] the common man looked to the good days of the past, not to the possibilities of the future, for a standard of conduct and criterion of the present; accepted the world, with plague, pestilence and famine, as heaven had made it; and were incurious as to the arts by which restless spirits would improve on nature, if not actually suspicious of them as smelling of complicity with malign powers."[14]

Rostow has pointed out that premodern societies were not static. Not only had there obviously been a long evolution of man and civilisation for millennia, but even on a shorter time scale, in peasant society and in the great empires, there were good times and bad. In good times there were surpluses. "Culture and tradition prescribed how these surpluses should be used: to build public monuments, for private luxury or, occasionally, to ease the burden of revenue payments on the peasantry. . . . There were positive norms for good rulers and good societies but they did not include the notion that surplus, when it existed, should be invested to yield a progressive expansion in per capita income."[15]

In traditional society, the abiding tasks of government were security, welfare, and constitutional order: "To preserve or advance their interests against other political systems; to provide an acceptable standard of welfare for the people in terms of the cultural norms of their day; and to conduct their constitutional business, notably the maintenance of unity and the provision of justice." The norms for security and order were not greatly different from those of modern times. "With respect to welfare, the situation was different. There were norms for good times, often drawn from the memory of golden eras of the past when the frontiers were quiet, crops ample, taxes modest, state granaries full, the roads free of bandits, and, where relevant, the irrigation works well maintained. Rulers were assessed, in part, against such standards, but the society was not expected to yield a regularly rising standard of living for the people as a whole. This was not because people lacked interest in material things. . . . But the expectation for the society as a whole was that, although it might suffer good times or bad at the whim of harvests, the vicissitudes of war, or the quality of rule, there would not be regular overall progress."[16]

It is not easy to see in what sense economic development represented a policy objective during the embryonic and infant stages of capitalism, between (say) 1200 and 1500 A.D. Whose objective? For most of this period, it was a spontaneous process in which government played a marginal role. "Whatever other human motives may have been at work— creative striving, search for prestige, fame, etc.—a straightforward interest in financial gain was clearly present and important."[17] With the emergence from feudalism of the modern nation-state, the promotion of economic development can be said to have become an objective of state policy. "The European rulers perceived . . . that their interests in revenue for military purposes required an expansion in production. . . . Not merely to maximise revenue from a static production base but to stimulate an increase in output."[18] "With the passage of time the idea was formulated and spread gradually into political life and policy that the expanded wealth of a nation was not merely an objective to be pursued as a means to a larger military end, but that increased production and welfare were in themselves legitimate objects of state policy."[19]

By the middle of the eighteenth century, material progress had, at least in Britain, come to be regarded as both possible and desirable. Adam Smith articulated this widening consensus when he referred to his fellow citizens' "universal, continual, and uninterrupted effort to better their own condition" and expressed the hope that "the progress of England towards opulence and improvement" would continue "in all future times."[20] From England modernisation spread, first to other countries of Western Europe and, through the European expansion, to overseas areas of European settlement and then, before the end of the nineteenth century, to Russia and Japan. Thus, in one sense, "modernisation in an interconnected world is a single case of modernisation."[21] But in each country, after Britain, modernisation was "initiated by some intrusion from abroad"[22] and motivated by what Rostow has called "reactive nationalism."[23]

Even in Europe, the economic history of every country illustrates in varying degree "the primacy of reactive nationalism over other motives which have led nations to modernise their economies."[24] Rostow's generalisation that only at a later stage does the primary motive of nationalistic reaction "merge with the interests and motives of others who, for reasons of profit, domestic power or status—or whatever—are prepared to act or press for the modernisation of the economy,"[25] though drawn from European experience, is no less valid for the rest of the world. The prehistory of economic development as a policy objective in the minds of Third World leaders and writers is very largely a history of "reactive nationalism."

Reactive Nationalism

The clearest case is Japan. In the modernisation of Japan, which as a conscious national policy began with the Meiji restoration of 1868, the objective of higher living standards played little, if any, part. The purpose was national survival. "The steady aggrandizement of Western commercial and political power in the Far East threatened nothing less than the dissolution of the Japanese polity and the reduction of the society to colonial status. All efforts, therefore, had to be applied to enhancing the country's national power, so that Japan could treat with the 'barbarians' on equal terms."[26]

Japan's first reaction to Western intrusion, two hundred years earlier, had been to shut itself off. Even during the Tokugawa period of exclusion of all foreign trade and contact which began in 1640, Western ideas and technology continued to seep in and contributed to a quickening of economic growth.[27] But it was the experience of China, "its humiliation and defeat by the West,"[28] which convinced the initiators of the Meiji restoration that isolation was no longer possible. The immediate objectives of the new regime were the establishment of a strong central government and the acquisition of modern military technology. But the Meiji leaders realised that more was needed. "If Japan were to match strength with the great Western Powers, she would have to accomplish a metamorphosis. Modern armed forces could be equipped and sustained only by a modern economy, and this in turn required an educated, mobile, motivated population."[29]

National power was the dominant, but not the only, motive. Closely allied with it was an intense desire to stand on an equal psychological footing with the advanced nations of the West. The material and cultural achievements of Western countries made a profound impression on Japanese who travelled abroad. Just as the first great moderniser, Peter the Great, while wanting above all guns to fight wars, had also sought for Russia "something of the civilised amenities and quality of life he experienced in his travels,"[30] so Japanese leaders "were determined to bring 'civilisation' and 'enlightenment' to Japan."[31] Modernisation appears to have yielded a steady rise in average consumption per head,[32] but this was incidental. The ruling group, as Reischauer has put it, "was interested in developing a powerful nation rather than a prosperous people."[33] Indeed, by 1900, influential voices warned about the "growing emphasis on personal and material benefits among the people."[34]

Its origins in a patriotic revolution from above gave the modernisation of Japan, and modern Japan, a flavour which was, and to this day remains, unique. "The integration of economic development in a general program of national enhancement had important consequences for the course and rate of economic growth. . . . It conferred a patriotic nimbus on the everyday virtues of diligence, thrift, perseverance, and the like, while making a virtue of acquisitiveness."[35] Similarly, "nationalism played an important role . . . in that it provided a ready-made rationale for government aid to private business, and for the rejection of . . . laissez faire."[36] "For a generation [those] who might have been expected to become apostles of *individual betterment* and freedom [acted as] . . . exponents of *national* betterment and rights."[37] But if Japan's modernisation was in some respects unique, both in its origins and in its subsequent course, its basic motivation conformed to a common pattern already established in Europe and later repeated elsewhere.

In China, too, the mid-nineteenth century officials who advocated modernisation as a means of "self-strengthening" had in mind a "policy of building up China's military potential, chiefly by adopting Western technology, so as to meet the challenge of external aggression."[38] "Learn the superior techniques of the barbarians to keep them in check."[39] It was no accident that China's first modern factory was a state-owned arsenal.[40] Reform from above, which succeeded so spectacularly in Japan, failed in China. From the turn of the century the impetus to modernisation came from below, from the intellectuals, led by Sun Yat-sen, who sought the revolutionary overthrow of the Manchu dynasty.

His starting point, like that of the Meiji leaders in Japan, was that "China has been under the political domination of the West for a century. To ward off this danger, we must espouse Nationalism and employ the national spirit to save the country."[41] But Sun Yat-sen's Three Principles, which he first proclaimed in 1905, included, besides nationalism and democracy, "The Principle of the People's Livelihood."[42] Ten years earlier he had become convinced that the West's power had a broader base than military might. People in the West, he pointed out, were able to develop their talents; the greatest yield was obtained from the land; natural resources were fully exploited; goods flowed freely from place to place.[43]

While expounding a socialism that owed more to Henry George than to Marx, Sun Yat-sen, well before World War I, set his heart on, and pleaded for, a plan for the economic development of China that, more than anything else written before 1939, anticipated post-1945 thinking.[44] A campaign in 1913 to raise funds in the United States and Japan for railway development in China came to nothing. In 1918 he tried again, this time using as a selling point the need for markets to employ the vastly expanded productive capacity of the American war economy—in much the same way as did those who advocated the establishment of the World Bank twenty-five years later. His book *The International Development of China*, written in English in 1918 though not published until 1922, was almost certainly the first to advocate economic development in something like the modern sense and use of the term.[45]

While impressed by the October Revolution in Russia, Sun Yat-sen's thinking was influenced much more by what he had seen of the achievements, and the flaws, of capitalist development in the United States and Japan. "China must not only regulate private capital, but she must also develop state capital and promote industry— . . . build means of production, railroads and waterways, on a large scale. Open new mines . . . hasten to foster manufacturing . . . Our economic rights are leaking away [to other powers] . . . If we want to recover these rights, . . . we must quickly employ state power to promote industry, use machinery in production, and give employment to the workers of the nation." Marxists "fail to realize that China now is suffering from poverty, not from unequal distribution of wealth"; the country needs a plan that will forestall the social problems of capitalism: "the development of state industries." China cannot generate enough capital at home for massive industrialisation. "So we shall certainly have to borrow foreign capital to develop our communication and transport facilities, and foreign brains and experience to manage them."[46] Fear in the West of potential Chinese competition is unfounded. The proposed scheme is big enough "to absorb all the surplus capital as quickly as the Industrial Nations can possibly produce."[47]

In all this Sun Yat-sen was a generation ahead of his times. It was almost certainly the influence of his book which during the interwar period made the economic development of China a pet theme among Western economists with a special interest in the Far East, such as J.B. Condliffe and others who met at conferences of the Institute of Pacific Relations.[48]

In Japan and China, there was, from the late nineteenth century onwards, little dissent from the view that modernisation was necessary for the maintenance of national independence. In India, the leaders of the movement for national independence were much less of one mind. All were agreed on the objective of freedom from colonial rule, and some saw in modernisation a means to that end or at least a necessary part of a wider program for national regeneration. But few, if any, of these leaders put improved living standards for the masses high among their objectives, while those most aware of the poverty of the Indian people, most conspicuously Gandhi, passionately opposed modernisation.

There were those, best represented by Dadabhai Naoroji, who blamed all of India's problems on the British. "It is not the pitiless operations of economic laws, but it is the thoughtless and pitiless action of the British policy; it is the pitiless eating of India's substance in India, and the further pitiless drain to England; in short, it is the pitiless *perversion* of economic laws by the sad bleeding to which India is subjected, that is destroying India."[49] Others rejected the "drain" theory. Ranade, the Indian disciple of Friedrich List, saw the cause of India's economic and social problems in the disparity in technological development between India and England and advocated infant industry protection."Convinced that industrialisation was the key to India's economic progress, and also that in India it required the initiative and active help of the government,"[50] he painted an unvarnished picture of India's underdevelopment. "Our habits of mind are conservative to a fault. . . . Labour is cheap, but unsteady, unthrifty, and unskilled. Capital is scarce, immobile, and unenterprising. . . . Commerce and Manufactures on a large scale are but recent importations. . . . The desire for accumulation is very weak. . . . The religious ideals of life condemn the ardent pursuit of wealth. . . . These are old legacies and inherent weaknesses . . . Stagnation and dependence, depression and poverty—these are written in broad characters on the face of the land and the people."[51]

The intellectual orientation of the "Moderates" among India's nationalists was a product of the Western impact on Indian intellectuals. "Their liberalism was grounded in a firm faith in progress through science."[52] Even Naoroji was all in favor of economic development—capital must come in instead of being taken out: "If sufficient capital is brought into the country and carefully and judiciously laid out, all the present difficulties and discontent will vanish."[53] For Ranade, as we noted, poverty was an aspect of the problems of India. But his belief in the importance of industrialisation was not wholly or even mainly economic in its motivation. To him, as to many

European intellectuals, including Marx, what mattered more was urban civilisation. "Manufactures are, if possible, more vital in their bearing on the education of the intelligence and skill and enterprise of the nation."[54] The prime objective was to reclaim "India from the ancient bondage of Feudalism and Status, and bring it into line with modern civilisation."[55]

It is hard to imagine a more extreme contrast than the one between this outlook and that of Gandhi. As a young man, pointedly dissociating himself from Naoroji, Gandhi wrote: "It is my deliberate opinion that India is being ground down, not under the English heel, but under that of modern civilisation." "Civilisation is not an incurable disease, but . . . the English people are at present afflicted by it. . . . Its true test lies in the fact that people living in it make bodily welfare the object of life. . . . This civilisation is irreligion." His special detestation—like that of critics of economic growth of a later generation for the motor car—was reserved for the railways, which, he declared, "accentuate the evil nature of man," and which he believed to have been responsible for increasing the frequency of famines in India and for spreading bubonic plague.[56] Deploring the damage that Manchester had done to India by displacing handicraft, he denounced machinery as "the chief symbol of modern civilisation; it represents a great sin."[57] He greatly cared for the poor. But, like many religious leaders before him, he discounted the value of material comfort. "A man is not necessarily happy because he is rich, or unhappy because he is poor. . . . Millions will always remain poor."[58]

Jawaharlal Nehru, for most of his life, until he became prime minister of independent India, agreed neither with Gandhi's antimodernisation views nor wholly with the pro-modernisation stance of the liberal moderates. He regarded himself as a socialist. He had learned his politics as a student at Cambridge and for most of the interwar period his views were not very different from those of left-wing English intellectuals of his generation.

Like Gandhi, he was concerned about poverty in India, but for long, as a socialist, he saw the answer not in economic development but in the overthrow of capitalism. "The only way to right [injustice and exploitation] is to do away with the domination of any one class over another. . . . We have to decide for whose benefit industry must be run and the land produce food."[59] In 1927 he visited Moscow and for some years he became a great admirer of the Soviet Union, where, like Sidney and Beatrice Webb, he detected "some glimpse of a new civilisation."[60] In India, as in England and other capitalist countries, the poor could not be made better-off without the rich being worse-off—"at every stage some have to be sacrificed for others," just as "a currency policy may be good for creditors or debtors, not for both at the same time"[61]—although he thought the case of England was a little different since "the exploitation of India and other countries brought so much wealth to England that some of it trickled down to the working class and their standard of living rose."[62] None of this was very different from contemporary editorials in the *New Statesman*.

By 1936, largely under the influence of the Soviet example, he came to "believe in the rapid industrialisation of the country . . . only thus I think will the standard of the people rise substantially and poverty be combated."[63] But if the end was now economic development very much in the post-1945 sense, the means was still a change of the economic system: "I see no way of ending the poverty, the vast unemployment, the degradation and the subjection of the Indian people except through socialism. That means the ending of private property, except in a restricted sense, and the replacement of the present profit system by a higher ideal of cooperative service."[64] All that stood in the way of adequate feeding, clothing, and housing for everybody, through the application of science and technology, was "vested interests."[65]

A decade or so later, as prime minister, he was to express very different views. Distribution is important, he said in a speech in 1947, but "there must obviously be something to distribute before we can start the process of distribution. Therefore, we come to the problem of production. Production becomes the first essential."[66] And two years later: "It is not a question of theory; of communism or socialism or capitalism. . . . The method which delivers the goods and brings about the necessary changes and gives satisfaction to the masses will justify itself. . . . Our problem today is to raise the standard of the masses, supply them with their needs, give them the wherewithal to lead a decent life, and help them to progress and advance in life not only in regard to material things, but in regard to cultural and spiritual things also."[67] By 1949 this was the conventional wisdom throughout the Third World.

The role of reactive nationalism as the catalyst of modernisation in Japan, China, and India had its later echoes elsewhere in Asia and Africa, both in countries like Thailand and Egypt, which had maintained a precarious independence, and in colonial territories. One large part of what is now the Third World, Latin America, represents, in this respect, an exception. Through most of the nineteenth century, the countries of Latin America were much more like the non-European countries of what is now the First rather than the Third World, like Australia, New Zealand, and Canada. They had neither colonial status nor external threat to react to. Their economies developed as part of the liberal international economic order. Their "traditional systems of mining and agriculture . . . were sufficient to supply a growing international market with the primary commodities and agricultural products that Latin America appeared to produce almost effortlessly."[68] Their elites "possessed a modern view of things. . . . In this period, the miracles of economic liberalism, of free enterprise capitalism, were quite apparent."[69] Even radical politicians favoured free trade: "We are neither industrialists nor navigators, so, for centuries to come, Europe will supply us with manufactures in exchange for our primary commodities; and we will both profit from such an exchange."[70] In 1891 a left-wing Buenos Aires newspaper attacked the "pernicious protectionist system" as a "tremendous capitalist barbarity" which "raises the prices of essentials and is designed to free the upper classes from paying taxes by shifting these to the shoulders of the workers."[71]

In the next fifty years, for reasons which may have had something to do with their different ethnic composition, especially their much larger indigenous populations, the countries of Latin America fell in their economic development behind Australia, New Zealand, and Canada. Thus, "as the most progressive elements in Europe and North America were concerned with the inequities and injustices of the Industrial Revolution, with the fact that the benefits of modernisation had been imperfectly distributed . . . , so this new generation of Latin Americans were obsessed by the contradiction between the modern enclave in their own societies and the way of life of the rest of the nation."[72] By 1945, Latin America had become, economically and even more so emotionally and ideologically, part of the Third World. In the following decades, reactive nationalism began to play a part also in Latin America, in the guise of populist anti-imperialism, resentment of *dependencia*, and demands for a New International Economic Order.

Colonial Theory and Practice

Long before Asian national leaders opted for or against economic development as the road to national survival or independence, problems of underdevelopment and development strategy, as they would now be called, had presented themselves in theory and practice to Western colonial policymakers and administrators.

"Colonies," one of the Encyclopedists said, "were made by and for the mother country."[73] Francis Bacon, a century earlier, had been no less candid: "It cannot be affirmed, if we speak ingeniously, that it was the propagation of the Christian faith that was the [motive] . . . of the discovery, entry, and plantation of the new world; but gold and silver, and temporal profit and glory."[74]

There is no doubt that, throughout the centuries of European colonialism, the metropolitan governments' primary concern was their countries' national interests, as they saw them, and that among these interests economic ones were never absent and often dominant. It is therefore tempting to dismiss all motives which ostensibly had the welfare of native populations in mind—the salvation of souls in the sixteenth century, restoration of law and order in the eighteenth, and the blessings of Western civilisation and economic progress in the nineteenth—as mere rationalisations. This would certainly be simplistic. There was always a mixture of motives. Charles Grant, a former chairman of the East India Company and member of the evangelical Clapham Sect, was without doubt completely sincere when, in his treatise on India, he posed the rhetorical question: "In considering the affairs of the world as under the control of the Supreme Disposer, and those distant territories . . . providentially put into our hands, . . . is it not necessary to conclude that they were given to us, not merely that we might draw an annual profit from them, but that we might diffuse among their inhabitants, long sunk in darkness, vice and misery, the light and benign influence of the truth, the blessings of well-regulated society, the improvements and comforts of active industry?"[75] When he added that "in every step of this work, we shall also serve the original design with which we visited India, that design still important to this country—the extension of our commerce,"[76] he was indulging in the common practice of the Evangelicals of seeking "to carry their aims by harnessing their cause to the most powerful political force of their time, the interests of British Commerce,"[77] much as do-gooders of the foreign-aid lobby in our time think it necessary to sell their message by stressing export promotion as a by-product of development assistance. Similarly, "the material urge for commercial expansion and the moral urge to eradicate slavery . . . were unexpected yet logical bedfellows" in the 1830 expedition that led to the first British settlement in Nigeria, "for the great philanthropic faith was in the civilizing blessing of what was regularly referred to as 'legitimate trade' and was regarded as the antidote and substitute for the obnoxious 'slave-trade'."[78] Half a century later, the partisans of French imperialism, "for the most part strong nationalists and republicans . . . sought to enlist support for their cause by using the appeal of the economic argument."[79]

There is ample evidence of genuine concern for the welfare of the subject people of the colonies in the writings of many Western colonial theorists and administrators. It is another question whether any of them envisaged a process of economic development for the native populations, in the sense of generally rising living standards, the sort of material progress that was going on in their own countries. The general conclusion suggested by a large literature is that, until very near the outbreak of World War II, the benefits which Western colonial policies sought for the indigenous populations rarely explicitly included economic progress in this sense. Insofar as they aimed at economic development, it was primarily development of the natural resources of the colonies for their own countries' benefit or at best that of the world at large.

For three centuries the main economic motive of Western expansion was the lure of gold and silver and profit from trade in tropical products, and the main noneconomic motive, "the proselytising spirit inherent in Christian teachings."[80] The two went hand in hand. In the words of a historian of the Portuguese empire, "I do not pretend that our sole aim was to preach, if others will allow that it was not only to trade."[81]

Even when propagation of the faith or, in the Protestant version, "the evangelisation of India's heathen millions,"[82] was no longer the dominant theme, Western colonisers, with few dissenting voices, were sublimely convinced that they were the bearers of civilisation,[83] that they were bringing to Indians, and later to other Asians and Africans, "the pacific triumph of reason over barbarism."[84] When William Wilberforce referred to "the vast superiority even of European laws and institutions, and far more of British institutions, over those of Asia,"[85] he was merely trumpeting forth what most of his contemporaries quietly took for granted. The belief that they had a "civilising mission," which imbued the emissaries of Victorian England, played an even greater role in French colonial theory. From the days of Louis XIV when a royal decree laid it down that "the natives, once converted to Catholicism, were to be considered 'citizens and natural Frenchmen',"[86] la mission civilisatrice, born of the conviction that French culture represented the acme of human achievement and a priceless gift to all who could be helped to share it, continued as the central idea of French colonial thought and practice. Meanwhile, however, at least in British writings about India and the colonies, claims had begun to be made that

British rule would bring material as well as moral and intellectual benefits.

By the end of the eighteenth century, the mercantilist justification of British rule in India, tribute, had disappeared, as the East India Company's administrative expenses absorbed all its revenue.[87] When the closure of the Continental market by Napoleon encouraged British merchants to extend their trade to Asia, India began to be seen as a potential market for British manufactures. Manufacturers and traders acquired a direct interest in Indian welfare, but the only inference for economic policy drawn from this was, in the spirit of laissez-faire doctrine, to reduce the role of government. Free-traders even began to question the need for colonial rule. As Macaulay put it in a famous passage: "The mere extent of empire is not necessarily an advantage. . . . To the great trading nation, to the great manufacturing nation, no progress which any portion of the human race can make in knowledge, in taste for the convenience of life, or in the wealth by which those conveniences are produced, can be a matter of indifference. It is scarcely possible to calculate the benefits which we might derive from the diffusion of European civilisation among the vast population of the East." One day, "having become instructed in European knowledge, [Indians] may demand European institutions. Whenever it comes, it will be the proudest day in English history. To have found a great people sunk in the lowest depths of slavery and superstition, to have so ruled them as to have made them desirous and capable of all the privileges of citizens, would indeed be a title to glory all our own."[88]

Meanwhile, however, while there was no doubt an unspecific belief that free trade would benefit India as well as Britain, specific benefits were much more clearly visible for the latter. If India becomes open to free trade, wrote an enthusiast, "under a mild, liberal, and effective government, . . . what a sudden change we might not anticipate? We should not only see the palaces of the Rajah, . . . furnished and decorated with the produce of English arts and manufactures, but the Ryots, who form so large a part of the Indian population, may, like the British farmers, have a taste for foreign produce, as soon as they can acquire property enough to procure it."[89] How they were to acquire property enough the author did not go on to consider.

Laissez-faire liberalism did not have the field to itself. The utilitarians who exercised great influence on British policy towards India in the first half of the nineteenth century believed that "the vices and defects of the masses of mankind arose not from a lack of schooling but from poverty."[90] But since they also believed that "poverty is the effect of bad laws, and bad government," their remedy, "no less easy than sure," was good government. "Light taxes and good laws; nothing more is wanting for national and individual prosperity all over the globe."[91] Others, especially among those who had experienced the problems of administering a huge country of different culture, were much less confident that they had the answers. One, in the spirit of Edmund Burke, warned: "The ruling vice of our government is innovation. . . . It is time that we should learn that neither the face of the country, its property, nor its society, are things that can be suddenly improved by any contrivance of ours, though they may be greatly injured by what we mean for their good."[92] Even James Mill, who, in the peroration of his monumental *History of British India*, felt able to claim that British rule had given Indians the benefit of "exemption from the fatal consequences of native mis-rule," added a prophetic reservation about "the evils which are inseparable from the nature of the connexion that subsists between the Government of India and its subjects—the unnatural rule of foreign masters . . . whose only sympathy with the natives of India arises from a sense of duty."[93] But such doubts did not significantly impinge upon the predominant climate of opinion or on the course of colonial policy.

The last three decades of the nineteenth century brought a marked change in colonial theory and policy, from laissez-faire liberalism to imperialism. Again, economic and noneconomic factors intermingled in bringing about the change. Among the economic ones the most important was the emergence of new opportunities for profitable investment in mining and plantation enterprise to meet the West's growing demand for food and industrial raw materials, and in supporting public works in transport and irrigation financed by loan capital. While

Manchester manufacturers—and Macaulay—could view with detachment the prospect of an independent India because it would still provide a market for British manufactures, "capitalists engaged in western enterprise in the tropics and concerned for their supplies of raw materials demanded a more active and intensive colonial policy."[94]

Whether, as Hobson and Lenin argued, rival economic interests of this kind provided the impetus or whether every self-respecting imperialist believed, as one of the French imperialists of the time put it, that his country "had to possess an overseas empire as a condition of national freedom and greatness"[95] and looked for economic reasons to justify empire, the 1870s and 1880s brought the scramble for colonies in which the Western powers carved up among themselves all hitherto unclaimed territories.

The fact that colonial policy, in the era of imperialism, sounded a new note of responsibility for the welfare of the subject people—notions of "the White Man's Burden" and "trusteeship"—has been attributed partly to a need for self-justification. Since men like to justify their activities on moral grounds, colonial policy "must now be justified to world opinion with reference to world welfare."[96] It has also been linked with "social and political evolution in Western society."[97] As labour entered politics and governments responded with social legislation at home, "the earlier policy of *laissez faire* was gradually transformed into a policy of actively promoting economic progress, and this was slowly permeated by ideas of social justice and concern for the welfare of the people."[98] Growing fears of cheap labour competition probably also played a part: "The condition of labour in the tropics became a matter of economic interest, and welfare measures began to assume a new importance in colonial policy."[99]

The objective of native welfare, it is important to note, was throughout this period regarded as quite distinct from that of economic progress or development. As a historian of French colonial policy has expressed it, the new colonial theorists demanded "a policy by which the conqueror would be most able to develop the conquered region economically, but also one in which the conqueror realized his responsibility to the native's . . . mental and physical well-being"[100]—the "dual mandate" of British colonial theory.[101]

Economic development meant what Lilian Knowles, the historian of *The Economic Development of the British Overseas Empire*, meant by it when she referred to "the remarkable economic achievements within the Empire during the past centuries . . . the hacking down of the forest or the sheep rearing or the gold mining which made Canada, Australia and South Africa into world factors . . . or the struggle with the overwhelming forces of nature which took shape in the unromantic guise of 'Public Works' in India"[102] or, in J. S. Furnivall's words, in his *Introduction to the Political Economy of Burma*, "the development of the material resources of Burma through trade and economic enterprise."[103] It was certainly not synonymous with native welfare, though it could be expected to contribute to it indirectly, as was suggested in a resolution of the French Colonial Congress of 1904 that "colonial governments concentrate their efforts on the economic development most likely to assure [the natives'] well-being along with that of the colonists."[104]

In 1929, the British Parliament passed a Colonial Development Act. Ten years later it was replaced by a Colonial Development and Welfare Act. W. K. Hancock commented on the latter: " 'Development and welfare' will probably be the cry of the generation which follows the present one. . . . In the nineteenth century development occurred as a by-product of profit." The new concept is quite different. "It gives a positive economic and social content to the philosophy of colonial trusteeship by affirming the need for minimum standards of nutrition, health and education."[105]

Not only were economic progress and native welfare distinct, but, in the view of some experienced colonial administrators, the former was frequently unconnected with, or even destructive of, the latter. The Dutch scholar, J. H. Boeke, on the basis of his study of the Netherlands East Indies, formulated the theory of dualistic development according to which "the most important and immediate result of the steadily increasing intrusion of Western technique . . . is that native production is pushed more and more into the background. . . .

The mass of the [native] population take an ever more modest and slighter share in the economic development of the country."[106] Furnivall, on the basis of his experience in Burma, took an even more pessimistic view. He questioned whether the economic progress which the British had brought to Burma "was a sufficient guarantee of general welfare. . . . There is good reason to believe that the cultivators, as individuals, were vastly better off from a material standpoint under British than under Burmese rule."[107] But "the mere maintenance of law and order set free economic forces which dissolved the village into individuals. . . . The annexation destroyed the Burmese social order and probably nothing less catastrophic would have cleared the way for reconstruction; but the destruction of a civilisation is in itself an offence against humanity."[108]

During World War II, the British government published an economic plan for Jamaica prepared by the economist F. Benham, written very much in the spirit of Hancock's slogan of "development and welfare." It was severely criticised by W. Arthur Lewis, who acknowledged that it implied recognition that "positive measures to raise the standard of living in the colonies should have high priority" but argued that it is necessary to distinguish between "social welfare" and "economic development." "The principal object of colonial policy should be to enable the colonies to stand on their own legs as soon as possible. This can be done only through their rapid economic development."[109] Here "economic development" no longer meant mere development of natural resources but much more nearly what it came to mean in the post-1945 years.

Mainstream Economics

So far, we have reviewed two specialist literatures, that of the leaders of national movements in non-European countries and that of the colonial theorists and practitioners. What, before 1945, did the mainstream of Western economists have to say about underdevelopment outside Europe and development economics? The answer is, very little. As educated men, they no doubt shared the varied views of their contemporaries about India and the colonies, about the development of economic resources and native welfare beyond the seas and later about national independence movements. But as professional economists, they had, until World War II, almost nothing to say about what we now call the Third World, its problems and its future.

The classical economists, from Adam Smith to J. S. Mill and Marx, were intensely interested in economic development. But their concern was naturally with the capitalist development of their own Western world.

Adam Smith liked to illustrate his argument by occasional references to China and India, well aware that he had to rely largely on accounts "generally drawn up by weak and wondering travellers, frequently by stupid and lying missionaries."[110] To illustrate his proposition that "it is not the actual greatness of national wealth but its continual increase which occasions a rise in the wages of labour," he cited the case of China, "one of the richest, one of the most fertile, best cultivated, most illustrious, and most populous countries of the world." Yet, because "it has long been stationary," the wages of labour are so low that "the poverty of the lower ranks of people far surpasses that of the most beggarly nations in Europe."[111] To illustrate the advantage for export trade of a large domestic market for manufactures, he referred, surprisingly for modern readers, to India. "The great extent of Hindostan rendered the home market of the country very great, and sufficient to support a great variety of manufactures. . . . Bengal, accordingly, has always been more remarkable for the exportation of a great variety of manufactures, than for that of its grain."[112] But all this was little more than the encyclopedic stock-in-trade of the eighteenth-century philosopher.

Ricardo and his contemporaries kept their eyes firmly on Britain, Western Europe, and North America, mentioning other parts of the world only in the context of British commercial, migration, or colonial policy—though on the last, as we have seen, some of them had a great deal to say—and this remained substantially true of English economists and, *mutatis mutandis*, of Western economists, at any rate until 1914. J. S. Mill, who was for over thirty years an official of the East India

Company and knew a good deal about India, committed himself to the statement that "it is only in the backward countries of the world that increased production is still an important subject. In those most advanced, what is economically needed is a better distribution."[113] But what concerned him was not the need for greater production in the backward countries but for better distribution in his own.

It was J. S. Mill, according to Hicks, "who killed the old Growth Economics and paved the way for the Static Epoch which was to follow."[114] From about 1850 onwards, most Western economists took growth for granted and worried about other aspects of economic welfare—allocative efficiency, distribution, and stability. Marshall has what Hicks calls two "really rather perfunctory" chapters on economic progress, Wicksell a chapter on capital accumulation "just tacked on at the end." "But the spotlight is not on them. And in Walras, Pareto and the Austrians there is even less."[115] If there was little interest in growth, there was even less in underdevelopment.

Hicks's comment on Marshall is not perhaps quite fair. In what became Appendix A to the *Principles* he reflected on the forces that had propelled economic change in Europe, and in this context he referred to India and other parts of the East, though his chief motive, as he once explained, was the belief that much can be done "in applying contemporary observation of the East to explain the economic past" of Europe.[116]

During the interwar years, the problems of long-term economic growth and development all but disappeared from the mainstream of economics and, to a degree which is astonishing in retrospect, Western economists ignored the underdeveloped world. In all the works of the leading economists of the period, there is hardly a reference to the problems of the underdeveloped regions. Marshall, in his last work, *Industry and Trade* (1919), refers to them only in the course of "some slight speculations as to future homes of industrial leadership,"[117] though he also, and more interestingly, looks forward to a future when the rich countries would acknowledge an obligation to share their wealth with the poor. "This and every other western country can now afford to make increased sacrifices of material wealth for the purpose of raising the quality of life throughout their whole populations. A time may come when such matters will be treated as of cosmopolitan rather than national obligation; but that time is not in sight."[118] Pigou, in his great work *The Economics of Welfare* (1920), never once referred to poverty outside Europe, while pointing out that "in a great number of ways, and for a variety of reasons, poor people in civilized countries are given help, in the main through some state agency, at the expense of their better-to-do fellow citizens."[119] In Taussig's *Principles of Economics,* non-Europeans make an appearance only in the chapter entitled "Some Cause Affecting Productiveness." "The Hottentot cannot use tools even of a comparatively simple kind because his brain power is not sufficiently developed. . . . Many of the operations of agriculture require nothing beyond delving and ditching. But the fruitful agriculture of advanced people calls for care, discrimination, intelligence and could not be practised by Indian ryots or Russian peasants."[120] Irving Fisher refers once to differences between rich and poor countries but only to play down their importance: "although a whole nation may be rich or poor relatively to another nation, the widest differences between nations are small compared with the differences *within* any one nation."[121]

Keynes, of course, as a young man, wrote *Indian Currency and Finance.* But in all his later works, one searches almost entirely in vain for any signs of interest in or concern for the poor outside Europe. When, in 1930, to counter the "bad attack of economic pessimism" from which "we are suffering just now," he dazzled himself and his readers with "the power of accumulation of compound interest," he predicted, with a Europocentrism that strikes us as grotesque, that "assuming no important wars and no important increase in population, the *economic problem* may be solved, or be at least within sight of solution, within a hundred years. This means that the economic problem is not—if we look into the future—the permanent problem of the human race."[122] Schumpeter, for all his interest and insight into the process of economic development, shared Keynes's tastes and limitations in this respect.

In the treatises and textbooks of the period references to the underdeveloped countries occur most often in the chapters on population. Cannan, noting in 1931 the decline in the birth rate in Western countries, optimistically predicted that "the cause of it—birth control—will doubtless in time affect the rest of the world, so that while we may expect considerable increase . . . to take place among the more backward peoples for another half-century at least, there is no reason whatever for expecting the population of the world 'to tread close on the heels' of subsistence in the future."[123] Benham's single reference to the underdeveloped countries in his *Economics* (1938) is in the context of international migration: "emigration has had very little effect on the dense populations of Eastern countries. . . . Their populations remain much larger, relative to their resources, than those of Western countries, and this is perhaps the main reason why their standards of living are so low."[124]

The point may be driven home with two striking illustrations from the end of the interwar period. In 1938, James Meade wrote the best of the League of Nations *World Economic Surveys*. The focus was on the state of world "business activity." Developments in the United States, Western Europe, and Japan were covered in some detail in twenty-six pages; the "primary producing countries" (Australia, Canada, New Zealand, Argentina, Brazil, Chile, Hungary, Rumania, Yugoslavia) rated one paragraph and a table; the Balkans, the Dutch East Indies, one sentence each; South America one paragraph; all the rest, including all of Asia (except Japan), Africa, and the USSR, were completely ignored.[125]

In 1948, Paul Samuelson published the first edition of his *Economics*. Of the theme of underdevelopment, which in the latest edition (1980) runs from the front flyleaf through chapter 5, "Income and Living Standards," to many of the last 100 pages, there are only three traces: a sentence comparing the steady improvement in Western living standards with "more backward nations, two-thirds of whose inhabitants are badly undernourished";[126] a statement, in a paragraph on the World Bank, that "South America, the Orient and other regions of the world could profitably use our capital for their industrial development";[127] and a reference to Chinese coolies in a rebuttal of the "cheap labour" argument for protection.[128]

Apart from the literature on colonial economics which has already been considered, there were two other specialist fields in which Western economists concerned themselves with underdeveloped countries. One of these consisted of studies of special aspects of underdeveloped economies of interest to the developed countries, such as commodity problems, international investment, migration, and industrialisation. The other was statistical work, which was beginning to throw light on the facts of underdevelopment.

The former need not detain us long. World commodity problems were of interest as part of the wider problem of economic stability; Brazil, Malaya, West Africa, and the East Indies were studied because and to the extent that they were exporters of coffee, rubber, cocoa and sugar and, as such, part of the international trading system.[129] Similarly, studies of the collapse and chances of revival of international investment were generally undertaken from the point of view of the investing countries,[130] studies of international migration from that of the countries of Western emigration.[131]

Of greater interest are a series of studies of industrialization, expecially in Asia. For, although they were a response to Western fears of Eastern competition, these studies contain some of the most important scholarly analyses of this aspect of economic development and its effects on world trade written before 1945.[132] Although the theme of Eastern competition was prominent also in the early biennial conferences of the Institute of Pacific Relations,[133] the motivation of most of the participants was idealistic. Through these conferences and the monographs it sponsored, the IPR contributed greatly during the interwar years to scholarly study of problems of economic development in the Pacific region and did something to awaken Western public opinion to these problems.

More important contributions to Western appreciation and study of the problems of underdeveloped countries were made in the interwar years by social scientists who provided statistical data in various fields.

One of these, associated especially with the name of Colin Clark, emerged, almost as a by-product, from the compilation of national income estimates. As such estimates became available for an increasing number of countries, the way was opened towards quantification of international comparisons of living standards. It was Colin Clark who, on the suggestion of Bowley, embarked on the task with indefatigable energy and imagination, and in 1939 produced his monumental *Conditions of Economic Progress*.[134] The book not only gave a considerable stimulus to the subsequent development of growth theory and models but also had an important effect on Western thinking about the underdeveloped world. For the first time, the gulf between living standards in the rich and the poor countries of the world was brought home in hard statistical terms. Well into the postwar years, until United Nations data became available, almost every writer on development economics quoted Colin Clark's estimates.

A similar contribution was made by the international surveys on nutrition conducted by the League of Nations. Initiated by the League's health organisation in the 1920s, the study of nutrition standards was given a new impetus by a group of enthusiasts, including the British agricultural scientist, Boyd Orr, and two Australians, the former prime minister, Stanley Bruce, and his economic adviser, F. L. McDougall. They induced the League to appoint a committee under Lord Astor, whose report in 1935 gave the first systematic account of the extent of hunger and malnutrition in the world.[135]

Finally, mention should be made of the work of the International Labour Office. Charged with the task of promoting industrial peace and social welfare through international cooperation, the ILO not only sponsored studies of social and industrial conditions throughout the world, including dependent and other less developed territories,[136] but during the 1930s began to parallel the nutrition studies of the League of Nations by systematic international comparison of levels of consumption in such fields as food, clothing, housing, medical care, and education.[137] It is no accident that several of the most influential voices in the awakening concern about world poverty during World War II were those of former members of the ILO secretariat.

Before giving an account of this awakening, however, we must turn aside to note another important specialist, or at any rate special, literature which we have so far neglected, Marxist thought about economic development as a policy objective.

Marx and Marxism

All through the "static period" among mainstream economists, the classical tradition of interest in the "magnificent dynamics" of capitalist development was carried on by Marx and his followers. Marx was the first to aim explicitly at a theory of economic development—the final purpose of *Capital* was, he said, to "reveal the economic law of motion of modern society"[138]—and indeed the first to use the term "economic development" in this sense.[139] Moreover, though of course primarily interested in Europe, Marx wrote a good deal about Asia.[140] Marx and Marxism might therefore be expected to figure prominently in the pre-1945 history of the development objective. For various reasons, this expectation is only very partially fulfilled.

Marx, the quintessential European intellectual, was as convinced as any of his Victorian contemporaries of the superiority of European over Asian civilisation, let alone the civilisations of other "barbarian or semibarbarian countries."[141] Marx never doubted that the emergence of capitalism from the feudal society of medieval Europe, with all its horrors and iniquities, had been a giant step in human progress. Capitalism represented progress not because it raised living standards—Marx was not very interested in the greatest happiness of the greatest number—but because it had created "more massive and more colossal productive forces than have all preceding generations together."[142] For Marx, as for many Victorians, the essence of progress was the Promethean conquest of nature by man, "the development of the productive power of man and the transformation of material production into a scientific domination of natural agencies."[143] This, as he saw it, was "the progress of society which the bourgeoisie involuntarily and passively promotes."[144] His focus was on the role of the bourgeoisie in creating urban civilisation, in rescuing "a considerable part of the population from the idiocy of rural life."[145] Hence his ambivalence about capitalism: from one point of view "an instrument of civilised and refined exploitation," but from another "a historical advance and a necessary developmental factor in the economic evolution of society."[146]

It is hardly surprising that, to someone with this outlook, viewing the mid-nineteenth-century world from London, the non-European countries presented a picture of not greatly differentiated backwardness. What seemed to Marx most striking about Asia, in contrast to Europe, where "the bourgeoisie cannot exist without incessantly revolutionising the instruments of production, and consequently the relations of production and therefore the totality of social relations,"[147] was "the mystery of the unchangeableness of Asiatic society."[148] What Marx had read about Indian society horrified and repelled him. The destruction of traditional village communities by the British in India may be "sickening to human feeling," but one must not forget that these village communities were the "solid foundation of oriental despotism," characterised by "undignified, stagnating and vegetative life" and by "wild, aimless, unbounded forces of destruction, murder as religious rite." "They restrained the human mind within the smallest possible compass, making it the unresisting tool of superstition, enslaving it beneath traditional rules, depriving it of all grandeur and historical energies."[149]

Westernisation was the only way out of this dismal condition. "The question is, can mankind fulfill its destiny without a fundamental revolution in the social state of Asia?" The answer he gave is well known. "Whatever may have been the aims of England, she was the unconscious tool of history in bringing about the revolution. . . . England has to fulfil a double mission in India: one destructive, the other regenerating—the annihilation of old Asiatic society, and the laying of the material foundation of Western society in Asia."[150] Marx took it for granted that the economic development of the backward countries would come through the expansion of Western capitalism, as "all the people of the world are enmeshed in the net of the world market, and therefore the capitalist regime tends more and more to assume an international character,"[151] and that it would follow the same course as in Europe. "The natural laws of capitalist production [determine] . . . the tendencies which work out with an iron necessity towards an inevitable goal. A country in which industrial development is more advanced than in others simply presents those others with a picture of their own future."[152]

Marx's view that the backward countries would necessarily have to pass through a capitalist phase before they could turn to socialism, because no society "can overleap the natural phases of evolution,"[153] became an embarrassment to his followers when, first in Russia and later in China and elsewhere, Marxists found themselves leading, or trying to take over, agrarian radical or revolutionary movements in preindustrial societies. Protagonists of the new orthodoxy later discovered a passage written by Marx near the close of his life which could be read as a partial retraction.[154]

The tremendous influence which Marx was to exercise in the less developed countries of the world in the century following the publication of *Capital* did not rest to any great extent on his theory of economic development, but rather on his condemnation of capitalism as unjust, his interpretation of social relations as dominated by class war, his promise of the inevitable victory of socialism, and his call for revolution to "shorten and lessen the birth-pangs."[155] The slogans which inspired Marxists throughout the world were not those embodying Marx's views on the "development of the productive power of man" but those which attributed poverty to exploitation and prophesied the day when "the knell of capitalist private property sounds" and "the expropriators are expropriated."[156] By a singular irony, the author of the first and still one of the grandest and most sophisticated conceptions of economic development inspired some of the crudest forms of "zero-sum game" thinking (as it would now be called) about the problems of the less developed countries.

Marx's European followers displayed at international socialist congresses before World War I a range of views about colonialism and the future of the backward countries almost as wide as that among their establishment contemporaries. There were anticolonialists, such as the British socialist Hyndman, who deplored the destruction by Britain of India's greatness— "a hideous crime"—and the German socialist Karski, who denied Europeans the right "to praise our civilisation so much and to impose it upon the Asiatic peoples who possess a culture much more ancient than ours and perhaps much more refined."[157] But there were also others, such as the French socialist Rouanet, who could not see why "the peoples of the civilised European and American countries [who] find themselves before enormous expanses . . . should not use these expanses to better the economic existence of their countries"[158] and the German socialist Bernstein, who objected to demands for national independence for the colonies on the ground that "the final consequence of this conception would be to give the United States back to the Red Indians."[159]

In all the voluminous writings of Lenin, until his very last years, there is very little discussion of the means and ends of economic development, even in Russia, let alone in less developed countries. What he has to say about such countries is almost invariably incidental to problems of revolutionary tactics or strategy. It has been said, not altogether unfairly, that "from the rich and complex thought of Marx, Lenin extracted above all certain recipes for the conquest of power."[160] Thus, the economic theory of imperialism, which was for decades to give Third World radicals valuable ammunition against the West, was first borrowed by Lenin from Hobson to serve as polemic against his social-democratic enemies in Britain and other Western countries. It was revolutionary tactics that led Lenin, after the evidence of spontaneous agrarian uprisings during the abortive Russian revolution of 1905, to envisage a revolutionary role for the peasantry as well as the industrial proletariat. Similarly, it was his need for allies in the struggle for survival of the USSR in the first years after the 1917 Revolution that led him to revise Marxist doctrine, agreeing with Asian revolutionaries that, once Soviet power was established, Asian countries could avoid the capitalist stage of development.[161]

When Lenin did, occasionally, advert to objectives, he spoke, in much the same terms as development economists after 1945, about alleviating poverty and raising living standards. Usually, the cause of poverty under capitalism was, in conformity with most socialist doctrine, assumed to be that too large a share went to the owners of capital. "As long as capitalism remains capitalism, surplus capital will never be used for the purpose of raising the standard of living of the masses, for this would mean a decrease in profits for the capitalists."[162] But at times he took a more dynamic view. "If capitalism would develop agriculture, which today lags far behind industry everywhere, if it would raise the standard of living of the masses which are still poverty stricken and half-starved everywhere in spite of the amazing advance of technical knowledge, there would be no talk of a surplus of capital."[163]

A little more than a year after this was written, Lenin found himself head of the Bolshevik government of Russia. Immediate problems were almost overwhelming. "Dire necessity is knocking at the door of the entire Russian people." For a while, he favoured large-scale farms. "Individual husbandry on individual plots . . . offer no way out of the terrible crisis. . . . It is essential to go over to joint production on large model farms."[164] But when the peasants took over the land, the idea of large-scale units of cultivation was quietly abandoned.[165] For a while, too, in 1918, Lenin conjured with grand plans for the construction of railways, canals, roads, power stations, grain elevators, for irrigation and land reclamation, but the realities of civil war pushed such plans into the background. Nonetheless, even while, to get the economy moving again, he took a very large step back with the New Economic Policy, he made plans for the long-term economic development of the Soviet Union, for Russia "to catch up with other nations."[166] Unlike Trotsky, he had no time for planning—"idle talk," "boring pedantry."[167] But when he drew up proposals "to reorganise the whole of industry on the principle of large-scale collective production and on the most modern technical basis" because only thus could help be brought by the town to the "backward and dispersed countryside" and the productivity of peasant labour raised,[168] and when in his last year he defined Communism as "Soviet power plus electrification of the whole country,"[169] Lenin was giving economic development a thoroughly twentieth-century meaning.

The same urgent exigencies of practical policy-making motivated the participants in the great "Soviet Industrialisation Debate" of 1924–28.[170] But there is no doubt that what they were all concerned with was economic development strategy. As the historian of the debate has said, all contestants "were now at one in their refusal to romanticize Russian backwardness; to all of them industrialization was both the synonym of economic progress and an indispensable basis for a fully socialist society in the future."[171] Bukharin, in particular, argued a developmental view against the zero-sum-game of War Communism, criticising "its emphasis upon the redistribution of the given real income rather than upon securing its continuous reproduction on an expanded scale" and, with an eye to the urgent need to accelerate capital formation, advocated telling "the whole peasantry, all its strata: get rich, accumulate, develop your country."[172] While the debate over the pace of industrialisation was still going on, it was completely overtaken, and its participants destroyed, by Stalin's "second revolution."

That Stalin aimed at economic development cannot be questioned. How far, however, he was concerned, even in the long run, to raise the living standards of the masses is debatable. One view is that, for Stalin, "the rapid-fire industrialization and the sweeping collectivization were not merely devices of economic policy, but means of extending the direct control of the totalitarian state over the largest possible number within the shortest time. . . . The way in which this extension was brought about had, from the viewpoint of the 'controllers,' a high value of its own. The lightning speed of the drive pulverized the will to resist."[173] But there is at least one striking pronouncement by Stalin from those years which shows him motivated by much the same "reactive nationalism" as the modernisers of late nineteenth-century Japan and China: "The pace must not be slackened. On the contrary, we must quicken it as much as is within our power and possibilities. . . . To slacken the pace would mean to lag behind; and those who lag behind are beaten. . . . [Throughout] the history of old Russia . . . she was ceaselessly beaten for her backwardness. She was beaten by the Mongol Khans . . . Turkish Beys . . . Anglo-French capitalists . . . Japanese barons, . . . for military backwardness, for cultural backwardness, for political backwardness. . . . We are fifty or a hundred years behind the advanced countries. We must make good this lag in ten years. Either we do it or they crush us."[174]

The same theme, not surprisingly, is prominent in the thinking of Asian and African Marxists and their radical precursors, but with more than one special twist. Mao Tse-tung gave Stalin's "nationalisation" of Marxism an Asian stamp: "Marxism must take on a national form before it can be applied."[175] Li Ta-chao, one of the first Chinese Marxists, fitted Ho Chi Minh's thesis that "Europe is no longer the centre of the revolution"[176] into a traditional Chinese pattern of thought about the rise and decay of civilisations: Western Europe had reached the limit of expansion, Russia and China still had reserves of energy for future development.[177] Similarly, the Indian Marxist, N. Roy, argued at the first congress of the Comintern (1919) that now "the fate of European revolution depended entirely on the revolution in Asia."[178] This was partly a reaction to the failure of revolution in Western Europe, but also an inference from Lenin's theory of imperialism, with its assumption that Western capitalism could not survive the overthrow of colonialism because "world capitalism draws its main resources and income from the colonies, principally from those in Asia."[179]

A second twist given to Marxism was the notion that, in Asia and Africa, it was the entire nation that was engaged in the class struggle against the Western oppressors. As one of the Moslem delegates to the Baku (1920) congress of the Comintern, Sultan Galiev, put it: "The Moslem people are all proletarian people."[180] Li Ta-chao made the same point when he said China as a whole was a "proletarian nation" which must be prepared to enter a class struggle with other races of the world.[181] But Sultan Galiev went still further. Like other Moslem delegates he resented the attitude displayed at the congress by some of the Russian comrades, the "con-

temptuous attitude on the part of the privileged classes towards the indigenous masses" which he seemed to detect
among "the communists who retain a mentality of oppressors
and regard the Muslims as their subjects."[182] He drew the
inference that "the replacement of the Western bourgeoisie by
the Western proletariat as the dominant class would not lead
to any change whatever in the relations of the latter class with
the oppressed countries of the East, for the Western proletariat
mechanically inherited the attitude of the class to which it had
succeeded as far as national questions were concerned."[183]

There were among the early Asian and African Marxists, as
among the middle-class nationalist leaders, some who de-
tested Western civilisation and some who admired it. Some
could see only "the essential barbarism of the 'civilising'
hordes," a civilisation imposed by the Europeans "à coups des
canons, à coups d'alcool et à coups de spirochète."[184] Others
saw that behind the European usurpation was "science that
everywhere manifests its greatness and power,"[185] that the
task was to turn poverty-stricken indigenous millions, "this
mass of starvelings, into a modern society, . . . to educate
them to human dignity."[186] Among those who sought to har-
monise the transformations of modern times with the values
inherent in Islam was the first advocate of "Islamized communism,"Hanafi Mussafar.[187] Mao Tse-tung's aims at that time
have been described similarly as having been "to assimilate
certain essential elements of Western civilization, in particular
its Promethean will to master nature, but in the political context of a radical transformation of the existing society in order
to resist Western domination."[188] Another part of Mao which
came to the fore during the Great Cultural Revolution was his
"passionate desire to transform man, with its curious mixture
of humanistic and totalitarian motives."[189] But this belongs to
a later chapter.

War Aims and Postwar Plans

Economic development in the Third World as a major interest
of Western governments, of economists, and of public opinion
generally, was born during World War II. It was the need of

the Western Allies to formulate war aims, not least to counter Hitler's New Order and Japan's Co-Prosperity Sphere, and the characteristic reaction of British and American public opinion to the horrors of war through a wave of idealism about plans for a better postwar world, which in the span of a few years promoted development economics from the most neglected to the most written-about branch of the discipline. At the same time, by demonstrating the power of government action in mobilising economic resources, the war itself generated a climate of optimism about what could be done to make a better world, abroad as much as at home.

Within a few days of the outbreak of the war in Europe, Cordell Hull, then secretary of state, appointed an advisory committee in the State Department to deal with postwar problems.[190] The subcommittee on postwar international economic problems and policies did not at first go beyond the problems of the 1930s, such as regional blocs and international commodity markets, and appraisal of the economic capacity of various countries.[191] But a new note was injected into official thinking in the next few months. In January 1941, in his message to Congress, President Roosevelt proclaimed the Four Freedoms, including freedom from want, as the Allies' peace objectives; and in August 1941, Churchill and Roosevelt signed the Atlantic Charter, which, among its eight principles, promised equal access to trade and raw materials to all states and the "assurance that all men in all the lands might live out their lives in freedom from fear and want."[192] These broad aims, as well as the departure from orthodox international finance in the Lend-Lease arrangement between the Allies, became signposts to a new era, of which governments were reminded again and again in the following years.

For two years after Pearl Harbor, postwar problems received little official attention in Washington. But as the tide of war turned, planning for postwar reconstruction was resumed. In 1943, the same group of "nutrition fanatics" who had stirred the League of Nations in the 1930s to investigate the world nutrition situation induced President Roosevelt to call the Hot Springs Conference on Food and Agriculture, which led to the establishment of the Food and Agriculture

Organisation (FAO). In the following year, the Bretton Woods Conference created the International Monetary Fund and the World Bank (then called the International Bank for Reconstruction and Development); and at Dumbarton Oaks a draft charter for the United Nations was agreed upon which, in the final version adopted at San Francisco, included among its objects the promotion of "higher standards of living, full employment, and conditions of economic and social progress and development." By 1945, economic development of underdeveloped countries had become an accepted objective of national and international policy of the developed countries. A major contributing factor was the sustained emphasis on this objective in unofficial discussion of peace aims in Britain and the United States almost from the moment of outbreak of the war.

"The average citizen has been thinking a great deal about how to win the peace. . . . The commonest symptom of this attitude of mind has been a strong demand for, and much controversy about, the formulation of 'peace aims'. Groups and societies for the study of the problems of the peace sprang up like mushrooms overnight. Pamphlets, broadsheets . . . burgeoned from every printing works."[193] This, though written about Britain, was as true of the United States. Indeed, the traditional American readiness to espouse causes, led by Cordell Hull's Wilsonian idealism and less hampered by the immediate pressures of the war, ensured that the public discussion of peace aims started in the United States earlier than in Britain. The first phase did not advance much beyond the proclamation of liberal generalities. A symposium of distinguished names published in *The Annals* in July 1940 did not get closer to the issues of economic development than a statement by Gustav Cassel that "the fundamental problem before us is to create such conditions as will secure the greatest possible progress," and such policy objectives as the principle of the "open door" in trade, loosening the fetters on migration, and condemnation of autarky.[194]

The man who more than any other brought the theme of economic development into the American discussion was Eugene Staley. In 1939, the Council on Foreign Relations had published his report *World Economy in Transition*. Its central theme was the conflict between technological opportunities and political barriers to greater human welfare. Much of the book was inspired by a broad liberal concern for world welfare in the International Labour Organisation (ILO) tradition, for "world federal union," and for freer trade. But in one chapter Staley moved from international investment to a discussion of a "world development program" which echoed the idea first thrown out by Sun Yat-sen and carried on by Condliffe and others during the interwar years, but gave it a thoroughly postwar flavour. Keynes's "economic millennium . . . will not be brought about by hoping for it."[195] "In some areas, like China and India, the people live so near the margin of subsistence that rapid capital accumulation could take place only at a great cost in human deprivation."[196] What is needed is "an international long-term investment bank for financing world public utilities" and "international transfer of knowledge and its industrial application."[197] "A beginning is already being made in the Americas."[198] This must be extended by "bringing roads and schools and technical institutes and machinery to China and India and Borneo . . . education must go along with capital investment."[199] When in 1941 the Commission to Study the Organization of Peace published a preliminary report, Staley developed this theme, demanding educational and technical assistance, as well as capital investment, organised through international agencies. "International assistance for this purpose should be a fundamental goal of the development programmes."[200]

In the next two years, these ideas were taken up by many others.[201] A Canadian, R. B. Bryce, summed them up well in a 1943 symposium organised by Seymour Harris: "If indeed in the postwar world we are to apply the lesson the world has now learnt at so heavy a price, that no nation can live unto itself alone, then we must have substantial loans from the richer States to the poorer States of the United Nations. . . . These conclusions follow from the fact that most of the world and its inhabitants are woefully short of capital and unable to provide it from current income. . . . Billions upon billions of dollars must be invested in Asia, Polynesia, South America and Africa, if the great masses in these lands are to be made productive and eventually brought up to minimum standards of health and decency, let alone comfort."[202]

In Britain, one of the first statements of similar ideas was the report of a conference organised by the National Peace Council. Once again, it was a member of the ILO secretariat, Wilfred Benson, author of a prewar report *Social Policy in Dependent Territories*, who expounded the case for "The Economic Advancement of Underdeveloped Areas."[203] He was powerfully backed up by Evan Durbin, in perhaps his last published statement: "Despite a very strong left-wing prejudice . . . the fact remains that international lending has been one of the most powerful engines of economic progress throughout the world, and that an immense task remains for it to do. Consider the position of the poorer part of the earth—the position of China, India or of our Colonies in Africa. What they require in order to raise their standard of living is the sort of changes in the techniques of production that we called the 'Industrial Revolution' in our history, and that Russia calls a series of 'Five-Year Plans'—that is, a wider programme of industrialization . . . [and] modernization of agriculture."[204]

From 1941 onwards, various organisations, among them the Royal Institute of International Affairs, Nuffield College, the Oxford Institute of Statistics, and Political and Economic Planning (PEP), embarked on programs of research on postwar problems.[205] Partly because of the presence in London of several refugee governments and economists from Czechoslovakia, Poland, and Yugoslavia, research on underdeveloped countries concentrated on Eastern and Southeastern Europe. PEP published a preliminary report "Economic Development in South-Eastern Europe" in 1944.[206] The Oxford program produced a planning model for the region in K. Mandelbaum's *The Industrialization of Backward Areas.*[207] At Chatham House, P. N. Rosenstein-Rodan in 1941 became secretary to a Committee on Postwar Reconstruction and in a private study group with Eastern European economists discussed "Problems of Industrialization of Eastern and South-Eastern Europe." An article with this title and a more popular lecture, "The International Development of Economically Backward Areas,"[208] may well be regarded as the beginning of modern development economics.

3

Development as Growth (1945–1965)

When World War II ended, there was a well-established consensus among official and articulate public opinion in Western countries on the need to do something about the "urgent problems of economic development of underdeveloped countries."[1] Some were prepared to go so far as to declare that "the development of the less advanced countries may be regarded as the major need of the decades following the war."[2]

In the first few postwar years, thinking aloud about economic development was largely confined to the United Nations and other international organisations. But from 1949 onwards, a huge literature began to pour forth, some of the earliest contributions coming from economists such as Singer, Rosenstein-Rodan, Nurkse, Prebisch, Myrdal, and Lewis, who as experts in and for these international organisations had tried to come to grips with some of the problems. Their books and articles, and some by public men in the less developed countries themselves, crystallised what, for the next decade or two, became the conventional wisdom on economic development.

The reasons why the economic development of less developed countries, which had hardly received a passing thought at the end of World War I, was almost universally acknowledged as a major national and international policy objective at the end of World War II are not difficult to identify. The war had changed the balance of world power. The former colonial powers emerged greatly weakened, the national independence movements greatly strengthened. The ascendancy of the Soviet Union and the consequent spread of communist influence gave the less developed countries the status of a Third World progressively able to take advantage of the Cold War between the superpowers to press their demands. In the

West, the exigencies of power were reinforced by the commitment of influential public opinion to liberal and humanitarian principles which found colonial rules and the glaring contrast between life in rich and poor countries no longer acceptable. As the first economic textbook to treat the subject, P. T. Ellsworth's *The International Economy*, put it, "one of the outstanding social trends in the past twenty years or more has been mounting unrest in the economically backward nations of the world. Its principal manifestation has taken the form of an increasingly insistent demand for economic development to improve the lot of these less fortunate countries."[3]

"To improve the lot." In the most general terms, there was little doubt in anyone's mind about the meaning and purpose of economic development. In the words of an early postwar ILO document, "the improvement of standards of living is to be regarded as the principal objective in the planning of economic development."[4] Raising living standards could mean many different things. It could be interpreted as an all-encompassing objective, as when Myrdal said that "development means improvement of the host of undesirable conditions in the social system that have perpetuated underdevelopment."[5] Or it could focus specifically on the poor, as in an Indian official statement of 1947: "The main objective of the National Planning Committee was to ensure an adequate standard of living for the people and to overcome the appalling poverty and illiteracy of the masses."[6] Frequently, especially but not only in Latin America, economic development was still equated with industrialisation; Rosenstein-Rodan's 1943 article, for example, referred to problems of industrialisation, not economic development, of the countries of Eastern Europe.[7]

But economists soon sharpened and narrowed the interpretation. From a proclamation that the "ultimate *aim* in economic development is to raise the national welfare of the entire population[8] and the explanation that "essentially the *problem* of economic development is that of raising the level of national income through increased per capita output so that each individual will be able to consume more,"[9] it was only a step or two to speak of "the *definition* of economic development as a rise in the levels of living of the common people"[10] or to say, more precisely, that " 'economic development' may be defined as a sustained, secular improvement in material well-being . . . reflected in an increasing flow of goods and services"[11] or, still more technically, to "define economic development as the process by which an economy is transformed from one whose rate of growth of per capita income is small or negative to one in which a significant self-sustained increase of per capita income is a permanent long-run feature."[12] From about 1950 and through most of the next two decades, this interpretation dominated the literature, so that economic development was often virtually equated with economic growth, although the former term tended to be used mainly for poor, the latter for rich countries. When W. A. Lewis in 1955 published the first comprehensive book on economic development in all its aspects he called it *The Theory of Economic Growth* and nobody at the time seems to have thought this odd.[13]

In recent years it has become fashionable to scoff at this narrowly economic notion of economic development. It is therefore worth pointing out that, at least as a sort of short-hand, the notion made a good deal of sense and that few serious writers about economic development employed it without emphatic qualification.

People were unquestionably concerned to raise material living standards in the less developed countries, and economists had in the previous decade or two learned for the first time how, in however rough a fashion, to measure material living standards statistically. As Hicks had explained, "when the national income has been converted into real terms . . . it provides us with the best single measure of the nation's economic well-being, or economic progress, which we are likely to be able to get," although, as he had hastened to add, "of course no single measure can tell us all we should like to know."[14] Colin Clark, as we noted before, had published international comparisons of real per capita income which for the first time indicated the magnitude of the gap in material living standards between rich and poor countries. In the early postwar years, the United Nations secretariat prepared such estimates from official national statistics and used these figures to illustrate the magnitude of the problem of underdevelopment.[15]

Even if full weight was given to the inadequacy of per capita income as a measure of living standards, there was a more fundamental case for treating growth of real GNP as an essential ingredient; a necessary if not a sufficient condition, of economic development. "There is basically only one way in which 'all the men in all the lands' can approach freedom from want, namely, through vastly increased production. It cannot be too often repeated that improvement in living standards depends fundamentally on improvement in the capacity of a people to produce," particularly in contrast to prevailing popular notions that "steadier use of existing productive capacity and more even distribution of its fruits would yield fairly satisfactory living standards."[16] In this sense, it was not unreasonable to think of economic development as primarily "a combination of methods by which the capacity of a people to produce (and hence to consume) may be increased."[17] In the same spirit, Singer, in one of the first expositions of his views on economic development, insisted that "the important thing now must be to raise national income, to raise the level of resources, as quickly as possible."[18]

In Western countries, the tendency to think about economic development mainly as economic growth was undoubtedly strengthened by the fact that in the postwar decade economic growth became a major objective of economic policy in the developed countries and a major interest of economic theorists.[19] There was therefore a tendency to approach the study of problems of economic development with the toolkit designed by economists for the analysis of economic growth in advanced countries. The very fact that economists had a theory, or theories, of economic growth seemed to give them a head start over other social scientists as experts on economic development.

Even with all these reasons for thinking about economic development as chiefly a matter of economic growth, there was hardly an economist writing about economic development who did not go out of his way to warn his readers that economic development "means more than growth in national product."[20] Some emphasised change in economic structure, particularly "a relative shrinkage of the agricultural sector,"[21] or change in social structure[22] as essential ingredients of the process of economic development. Others stressed that "growth, if associated with an increasing inequality in the distribution of income, is consistent with an increase both in the absolute numbers and in the percentage of the total population which is living in squalid and diseased poverty."[23] "Raising per capita income is not enough. . . . Unless the higher income per capita means a higher standard of living for the majority of people, . . . the result will only be to widen the gap between the rich minority who have grown richer and the poor majority."[24] The United Nations Economic and Social Council at its first session proclaimed the need for a long-term and balanced program of development which should include not only economic aspects but also "the social, scientific, health, educational and cultural aspects of community life."[25] Many made it clear that as economists they were focusing on but one aspect of a complex process which, under the name of modernisation, embraced among both its necessary conditions and its objectives profound changes in social attitudes. "Progress," Arthur Lewis argued more than once, "occurs only when people believe that man can, by conscious effort, master nature. . . . Even when people know that a greater abundance of goods and services is possible, they may not consider it worth the effort. Lack of interest in material things may be due to the prevalence of an other-worldly philosophy which discourages material wants."[26] The objective, said Myrdal, is much more than higher material living standards; it is "new men," "modern men."[27]

Nonetheless, until around 1960, these tended to be qualifications of the central theme of the economic development literature. The touchstone, if not the essence, of economic development was taken to be growth in output and income per head in the less developed countries. There were, even among Western economists, some who right from the start were highly sceptical about this whole approach to economic development. But the consideration of the views of these critics is best deferred to chapter 6.

Most of the literature, of course, was about means rather than ends, about the economics of development, and that is not what I am concerned with in this study. But the division between means and ends is never clear-cut. Ends determine means and means colour ends. The main strands in thinking about development *economics* are therefore of some relevance because they influenced the way people conceived the development *objective*. In the rest of this chapter, I shall describe the three main strands which can be identified during the period when economic development was very largely equated with economic growth. The first stressed capital formation as the most important factor, the second sought to correct this emphasis by stressing the importance of human capital, the third revived interest in trade as the engine of growth.

Capital Formation

The cornerstone of modern development economics in its first phase was capital formation. Nurkse was expressing a very generally accepted view when he said in 1952 that "this subject lies at the very centre of the problem of development in economically backward countries."[28] He, like others, was careful to add that capital formation is not the whole story. "Economic development has much to do with human achievements, social attitudes, political conditions—and historical accidents." Capital alone is not enough. But it is "a necessary condition of progress."[29] Arthur Lewis, in a famous passage, pointed to the saving rate as the key difference between an underdeveloped and a developed country: "The countries which are now relatively developed have at some time in the past gone through a rapid acceleration in the course of which their rate of net investment has moved from 5 per cent [of national income] or less to 12 per cent or more. . . . The central problem in the theory of economic growth is to understand the process by which a community is converted from being a 5 per cent to a 12 per cent saver."[30]

There is nothing surprising about this starting point. If economic development is mainly a matter of economic growth it obviously requires "diversion of a part of society's currently available resources to the purpose of increasing the stock of capital so as to make possible an expansion of consumable output in future."[31] This had been the centrepiece of classical economics, from *The Wealth of Nations* to *Das Kapital*, and it had recently again become central to the growth theory which Harrod and Domar devised by dynamising Keynes.[32] Harrod and Domar were initially concerned, like Keynes, with the problem of full employment and went beyond Keynes only in extending his analysis to a growing economy. But their caricature of a dynamic economy in which the rate of capital formation is the only determinant of economic growth became enormously influential in the early years of postwar development economics. From this perspective, the most elementary fact about the less developed countries was that they were "capital hungry."[33] "A shortage of capital is almost by definition a characteristic of underdeveloped areas."[34]

One of the first purposes to which the Harrod-Domar approach was applied was to estimate the "capital requirements" of less developed countries. The United Nations group of experts, which reported in 1951 on this subject in *Measures for the Economic Development of Underdeveloped Countries*, concluded, on the basis of a little model devised by Singer,[35] that the capital required by underdeveloped areas each year to raise their national income per capita by 2 percent annually was about (1949) $US20 billion.[36] Before long, incremental capital/output ratios became a standard tool of development planners. "The first question in development planning is, 'How much total investment is needed to produce target increases in per capita income?' Answering this question requires determining the . . . incremental capital output ratio (ICOR)."[37]

The UN experts were interested in the capital requirements of underdeveloped areas chiefly because they had been asked to recommend measures requiring international action, and one of these clearly was the provision of external capital by rich to poor countries, through loans, aid, and private investment. Their estimate was that domestic saving in the underdeveloped areas could supply just over $US5 billion towards the total annual requirement of $US20 billion, leaving a deficit of about $US15·billion to be filled from abroad. While the UN experts and many others[38] were undoubtedly motivated by the needs of the poor countries, others had for some time been advocating large-scale capital exports from the rich to the poor countries for another reason, or had at least, like Sun Yat-sen a generation earlier,[39] been using it as a selling point for aid, and that was the contribution which such capital exports could make to the maintenance of full employment in the developed countries.

Some explicitly referred back to Sun Yat-sen. "The conjuncture of overcapacity in the industrial countries and industrial needs in the backward countries offered an opportunity after the last war. The great leader of the Chinese Revolution, Dr. Sun Yat-Sen, . . . offered the needs of China as a solution for the industrial problems of the West. . . . The practical suggestions . . . were not very convincing. Its fundamental thesis remains sound."[40] The Chinese delegate to an early session of the UN's Economic and Social Council (ECOSOC) was probably under the same influence when he said that the development of the underindustrialised countries is not only one of the most important economic questions in the world but "also gives us the clue to the solution of the problems of stability and full employment in the industrialized countries."[41] Others argued simply that "a vigorous development program for underdeveloped areas will yield markets both in the United States and Western Europe"[42] or referred to "the double object of raising standards of living in underdeveloped areas and furnishing new outlets for the productive capacity of existing industrial countries."[43] How strongly the Keynes-Hansen stagnation thesis dominated thinking in the early postwar years is illustrated by a remarkable outburst by the distinguished economist Oscar Lange, who represented Poland at the ECOSOC meeting just referred to. Protesting that the policy of restoration of the productive capacity of West Germany must inevitably fail, he argued that, "in the absence of an adequate demand from eastern Europe, the industrial products and export surplus of western Europe, and particularly Germany, will prove unmarketable. The countries of western Europe are industrially competitive rather than complementary. Where will they—and again, expecially, where will Germany—export their surplus? To Latin America, in competition with the United States? To the British Commonwealth, in competition with the United Kingdom? Or to the Middle East?"[44] In the following years, as fears of a postwar depression and stagnation receded, this argument also lost favour. But for a time it almost certainly reinforced the emphasis on capital formation as the key to economic development.

Finally, some weight must be given to the tendency in the early years to think of economic development as virtually synonymous with industrialisation; indeed, as we noted before, it was only towards the end of World War II that the term "economic development" replaced "industrialisation" in general usage. The reasons are fairly obvious. Industrialisation had been the most conspicuous feature of capitalist economic development in the now developed or industrialised countries and had more recently been the chief ingredient in Soviet development under Lenin and Stalin. As an objective, industrialisation implied urbanisation with its connotation of modern urban civilisation. The vulnerability of primary exporting countries during depression and war had, especially in Latin America, given an impetus to demands for industrialisation as a means of economic diversification. Whatever the motives, industrialisation required fixed capital—factories, plant and equipment; and if it also required technical knowledge, "an advance in technical knowledge may be of no economic relevance if there is no capital in which to incorporate it."[45]

The emphasis on capital formation, in turn, was embedded in a wider ideological setting which coloured almost all thinking about economic development in the early postwar years, in the Western literature as much as in the less developed countries themselves, and to which some reference must be made.

Economic development could not be left to market force. It had to be planned. To the nationalist leaders in India and other colonial territories this seemed an obvious inference from the legacy of underdevelopment which they associated with laissez-faire or imperialist colonial rule. To many of them, the Soviet example underlined the inference and pointed the way. Five-year plans became the order of the day, some of them, such as India's second plan, consciously inspired by the Soviet model. But in the West, too, following the debacle of the Great

Depression and the apparent successes of economic planning for war, economic liberalism was on the defensive. Under Keynesian-Fabian influence, governments assumed responsibility for full employment and social welfare and increasingly, as economic growth became the prime objective, planning for growth came to seem imperative.[46] In this intellectual climate it was an easy step from recognition of a problem to demand for government action, from acceptance of the urgency of economic development to the conclusion that economic development must be planned. Here, too, at least in the warm glow of the wartime alliance, the Soviet model was influential. "Only once in modern times has there been any attempt on the part of a great state to solve problems of such magnitude, namely, the Russian Revolution. . . . Collective planning can now be regarded as a key concept."[47]

Very soon Western economists concerned with economic development devised neat formulations of the need for government intervention. The intellectual foundations for most of this development–planning literature were laid by Rosenstein-Rodan in his 1943 article. In one sweep, following the clue provided by Allyn Young in his dynamic interpretation of Adam Smith's dictum that "the division of labour depends on the size of the market," he rested the case for "planned industrialisation" on a Pigovian divergence between the social and private marginal product arising from "external economies" on the side of demand and argued for a "big push" aimed at internalising these external economies through "balanced growth," i.e., investment on a broad front of industries, which would put the "agrarian excess population" to work through a massive inflow of foreign capital.[48] In the years around 1950, Singer, Nurkse, Myrdal, and others developed and spelled out these ideas.

Singer, in a short article, brought together and expressed in vivid language almost all the themes of what was to be the dominant school of thought on economic development in the next decade. There were epigrams about the "vicious circle" of underdevelopment. "An underdeveloped country is poor . . . because it is poor." "One thing leads to another, but nothing leads to nothing."[49] The way to break out of this

vicious circle was a big push aimed at "multiple development."[50] "What is needed is a big initial effort to carry through
the barren period due to increasing returns and long gestation
periods."[51] Singer also stressed the importance of external
economies but, in contrast to Rosenstein-Rodan, "external
economies in economic production, especially in the fields of
transport and power," rather than on the side of demand.[52]
Singer's idea that the vicious circle can become a "virtuous"
circle and that "economic development is a cumulative process of this kind"[53] was taken up by Myrdal, who expounded
the "hypothesis of circular cumulative causation" as "the
principle upon which an underdeveloped country can hope to
'lift itself by the shoe strings,' if only it can manage to accomplish what Professor W. W. Rostow calls the 'take-off into self-
sustained growth'."[54] Nurkse, for his part, spelled out Rosenstein-Rodan's idea of "balanced growth" and developed his
notion of "agrarian excess population" into "the saving potential concealed in rural unemployment."[55]

It would be quite wrong to suggest that these ideas, of what
might be called the orthodoxy of the first phase of postwar
thinking about economic development, were universally accepted, even among the rapidly growing development profession, let alone by practical men, administrators, or
revolutionaries. The authors who put the ideas forward themselves qualified them, and others, even among those who
viewed economic development (primarily) as economic
growth, questioned them. Thus Singer would say that it is
"true, although only partially true, that underdeveloped
countries are poor because of a lack of capital,"[56] a qualification which Condliffe had made more emphatically some years
earlier—"capital is not the sole or even the main need of underdeveloped countries, . . . their primary need is skilled administrators and technicians"[57]—and which was repeated
again and again.[58] The whole Harrod-Domar approach soon
ran into damaging criticism.[59] Buchanan and others questioned the usefulness of estimates of "capital requirements,"[60]
Viner and others the overemphasis on industrialisation.[61] The
doctrine of "balanced growth" was soon criticised on several
grounds, by Fleming because it neglected complementary in-

puts in inelastic supply in underdeveloped countries,[62] by Hla Myint because it neglected international trade,[63] and by Hirschman because it neglected the importance of "strategic imbalances" needed to induce investment in a dynamic economy.[64]

Indeed, so quickly did the literature on economic development proliferate that there are few points of any substance about economic development which cannot be found, persuasively argued, in books, articles, or reports written in the first ten years after the end of World War II. Nonetheless, there can be little doubt that, during those years and at least until the end of the 1950s, the themes discussed in this section, capital formation and the associated concepts of planned industrialisation, big push, and balanced growth, dominated the discussion. It was around 1960 that the emphasis began perceptibly to change.

Human Capital

In 1959, the first edition of one of the best-known textbooks of development economics still insisted that "capital accumulation is the very core of economic development."[65] Two years later, H. W. Singer told a conference in Addis Ababa that there had been "a shift in our whole thinking about the problem of growth and development"—from physical to human capital. "The fundamental problem is no longer considered to be the creation of wealth, but rather the *capacity* to create wealth," and this capacity resides in the people of a country. "It consists of *brain power*."[66]

The shift of thinking to human capital, which occurred in just two or three years around 1960, had its origins in the then current preoccupation with economic growth and its causes in developed countries. But it was quickly taken up by those who were writing about economic development. One result was to revive the somewhat dormant interest in technical assistance, as contrasted with capital aid, to developing countries; another was to introduce new themes—investment in education, manpower planning, the "brain drain"—into the development literature.

The Residual Factor

In the first modern survey of what economists have to say about economic growth, Abramovitz wrote in 1951 that "it is probably safe to say that only the discovery and exploitation of new knowledge rivals capital formation as a cause of economic progress." But about the relative magnitude of the contribution to growth of advances in knowledge he was agnostic. "While it is clear enough in a general way that technical improvement leads to increases in output, and while we may be confident that, directly and indirectly, a very large share, if not the bulk, of the increase in output is to be attributed to advances in knowledge, measurement of the relation between changes in the stock of knowledge and the pace of economic growth has so far proved impossible."[67]

In the next few years, he and others, including Fabricant, Solow, Kendrick, and Denison, tackled this problem.[68] A succession of empirical studies of the aggregate production function, first for the United States and then also for other industrial countries, all agreed on one conclusion: the proportion of the increase in GNP that could be attributed to measurable inputs of capital and labour was much smaller than had been expected. If, as these studies suggested, the contribution of inputs of capital and labour explained only 10-20 percent of secular growth of total output,[69] the explanation of economic growth, and of differences in the rate of economic growth among different countries, had to be sought in the "residual factor"[70] which tended to be equated with technical progress or, more generally, advances in knowledge, including those resulting from education.

Subsequent discussion of the problem suggested that there were no simple answers. "The critics have argued that what is called technical progress may not be technical progress at all, let alone advances in knowledge, but the result of (a) substitution of capital for labour, (b) economies of scale, (c) learning by experience, (d) increased education, (e) resource shifts, and (f) organisational improvements, plus (or minus) any errors in the measurement of the variables."[71] Indeed, as the editor of a symposium on the subject wistfully asked: "Is the 'residual factor' a measure of the contribution of knowledge or is it simply a measure of our ignorance of the causes of economic growth?"[72] The immediate effect of this debate, however, was to focus interest on human capital as a factor in economic growth.

The man who, almost single-handedly, introduced this concept into economics was T. W. Schultz. He has explained how this happened. "My own interest in this field took shape during 1956–57. I had been puzzled by the fact that the concepts I was using to measure capital and labour were close to being empty in explaining the increase in production that occurred over time. . . . I began to see that the productive essences of what I was identifying as capital and labor were not constant but were being improved over time and that these improvements were being left out in what I was measuring as capital and labor. It became clear to me also that in the United States many people were investing heavily in themselves as human agents, that these investments in man are having a pervasive influence upon economic growth and that the key investment in human capital is education."[73] In the early 1960s, Schultz, Becker, and others developed the concept of investment in human capital and its implications.[74] One effect, reinforced by temporary alarums in Western countries related to rising costs of education and an apparent shortage of certain kinds of skill, was the creation of a virtually new branch of the discipline, economics of education.[75] It is hardly surprising that these ideas quickly spilled over from thinking about economic growth in the industrial countries to thinking about economic development in the Third World.

Technical Assistance

Shortage of skills, as well as of capital, as an obstacle to economic development had, of course, been a theme in the development literature from its beginnings. The United Nations experts of 1951 were not saying anything very new when they began their chapter on technology by pointing out that "one of the most striking features of underdeveloped countries is their low level of technology. . . . As a result of the remarkable progress in science during the past two hundred years, the gap in technology between the developed and the underdeveloped countries has grown wider and wider."[76] The experts shared the then widely current optimism that this very gap held out a promise: "If the obstacles to the absorption of new technology are overcome, the existence of highly productive methods and processes, which do not have to be discovered anew, but are available for transmission and appropriation, lays open wide opportunities for the underdeveloped countries to profit from experience later gained. . . . They may be able to achieve a rapid advance."[77] But they also warned that absorption of new technology is a difficult and costly process, that it needs well-developed administration, experts and technicians, literacy and educational institutions.[78] It was the idea that the more developed countries could help remedy the shortage of skills of the less developed that had provided the rationale for the early postwar enthusiasm for technical assistance.

The impetus for this assistance had come suddenly and almost fortuitously with President Truman's "Point Four." Some provision of experts and training facilities had for some time played a part in British, French, and other colonial policies and had been initiated by the United States in January 1940 when the Inter-American Development Commission was established to promote "commercial, cultural, educational, and scientific aspects of Hemisphere defense relations."[79] One of the first resolutions of the UN General Assembly relating to underdeveloped countries had noted that "some were in need of expert advice on methods of meeting the requirements connected with economic development"[80] and much of the work of the new specialised agencies of the United Nations, UNRRA, UNICEF, and later the FAO, had consisted of technical assistance in various forms. But this had been on a modest scale. Large-scale technical assistance, bilateral and multilateral, began when President Truman proclaimed, as Point Four in his inaugural address of 20 January 1949, "a bold new program for making the benefits of our scientific advances and industrial progress available for the improvement and growth of underdeveloped areas."[81]

The origins of Point Four, as one of the administrators of the program later conceded, are "murky."[82] In his memoirs, President Truman explained them very simply. "The Point Four program was a practical expression of our attitude toward the countries threatened by Communist domination."[83] But while the Cold War was an important motive for a more vigorous US program of development assistance, there were other reasons for the particular emphasis on technical assistance. Partly for Cold War reasons, the United States was according priority to postwar reconstruction in Europe. The Marshall Plan was pre-empting resources for capital aid. Washington was under pressure, especially from Latin America, for more generous assistance. Technical assistance was relatively cheap. "There are many aspects of development in which much can be accomplished through technical aid requiring relatively small expenditures for supplies and equipment."[84] As Truman explained: "The material resources which we can afford to use for the assistance of other people are limited. But our imponderable resources in technical knowledge are constantly growing and are inexhaustible."[85] But Truman also reflected a widely shared conviction that "greater production is the key to prosperity and peace. And the key to greater production is a wider and more vigorous application of modern scientific and technical knowledge.[86] Perhaps because of this faith in the power of science and technology, Point Four marked, to a degree that is not easily remembered, the peak of optimism about what development assistance could do. "Prospect of an expanded program of technical assistance fired the imagination and evoked the enthusiasm not only of government officials but of peoples as well."[87]

Point Four had not only launched a new US program for technical assistance to developing countries but had also within a few months induced the United Nations to coordinate and widen its own operations and those of the specialised agencies in an Expanded Program of Technical Assistance[88] and stimulated bilateral programs such as the Colombo Plan of the British Commonwealth countries, which had a large technical assistance component.[89] These programs continued and indeed expanded during the 1950s but the early enthusiasm quickly waned; technical assistance was increasingly over-shadowed by capital aid. One reason was the priority accorded to capital formation as a source of growth. "With developers preoccupied by capital flow problems, technical assistance suf-fered more from neglect . . . than from outright opposi-tion."[90] But it also became increasingly evident that the developing countries generally preferred money to advice and that technical assistance was much more difficult than had initially been realised. "Everywhere the adoption of new methods encountered difficulties rooted in local culture and tradition."[91] "As it turned out, the task was much more com-plicated. The teaching of technology, by itself, is the easiest part. What is infinitely more difficult is identifying what knowledge is relevant, and fitting its use into existing systems of human effort."[92] By the end of the decade, it became fash-ionable to address issues such as "Why Visiting Economists Fail."[93] The conclusion seemed inescapable that "the opti-mism which prevailed when President Truman devised point 4 was mistaken. It is not enough to send highly skilled people to developing countries as experts and hope for quick results, if these experts are bringing techniques which have only proved to be economically effective in economically advanced countries. Technical assistance is a long-term task."[94]

It was at this juncture that the new ideas about human capital and education as investment in man revived interest in technical assistance, but with a new orientation. Singer was quick to point the moral. "The educational deficiencies of un-derdeveloped countries can, in the short run, be dealt with by measures [such as] . . . the employment of foreign experts and technicians. . . . [But transfer of existing technology by means of] technical assistance . . . is not the fundamental so-lution." What is needed is a different kind of technical as-sistance, "to assist underdeveloped countries in making their own type of investment in human capital and in research and development."[95] Soon this distinction was made more ex-plicit. "The function of technical assistance and other forms of human resources is twofold. It can help fill gaps between the skill requirements implicit in development programmes and the domestic stock of skills. But it is also needed to strengthen and supplement a country's capacity to produce new skills via its education system."[96]

During the early 1960s, a spate of conferences, books, and reports developed this reorientation of technical assistance.[97] The emphasis in training shifted from scholarships to Western universities, with the attendant dangers of alienation, to "institution-building" in the developing countries themselves.[98] In line with the reformulation of the purpose of development assistance that inspired the Kennedy program "aid to end aid,"[99] technical assistance, especially in the field of education and training, came to be presented as a matter of "helping people to help themselves."[100]

How much difference all this made to the character and effectiveness of the whole technical assistance effort is not easy to judge. Technical assistance has continued to be of both kinds, short-term and long-term, experts and training. Institution building as a form of technical assistance has proved to be so much more expensive and difficult, if in the long run more rewarding, that it has supplemented rather than replaced the two older kinds, supply of experts and overseas training facilities. "The complexity of the undertaking"[101] has come to be more fully recognised, with enough successes or passable results mixed in with failures and disappointments to ensure that the whole process, buttressed by vested interests in donor and recipient bureaucracies, continues unabated.

Manpower Planning

The suddenly heightened interest around 1960 in human capital as a factor in economic growth and development happened to coincide with the peak of enthusiasm for economic planning, "indicative planning" on the French model in Western countries and five-year plans influenced in varying degree by the Soviet example in developing countries.[102] The result was a vogue for manpower planning.

Centralised planning in the Soviet Union depended on "material balancing," matching supply and demand of physical quantities of inputs and outputs. Matching future supply and demand of categories of labour with different skills fitted naturally into this pattern, and Soviet planners had unquestionably been successful in vastly increasing the country's supply of scientific and technical manpower. Inspired by the Soviet example, the chief authors of the second and third five-year plans in India, Mahalanobis and Pitambar Pant, launched ambitious programs of manpower planning for India, including "special studies of the requirements for engineers, agricultural specialists, chemists, physicists, geologists, geophysicists, doctors, etc. in India."[103] In the early 1960s, the idea was taken up by international organisations and in many developing countries.[104] Optimists entertained "the notion that it is possible to ascertain the optimum amount of education for achieving specified growth targets."[105] Forecasting of manpower requirements, in turn, was viewed as the starting point for education planning. "In making projections of the needs for skilled manpower of all sorts, it has been possible to calculate back into the education system the number of educated people required to produce the necessary skills."[106]

Within a few years, some of the more extreme pretensions of the manpower planners came under critical scrutiny. Economists questioned their engineering approach, evincing "a dual scepticism, first of long-period forecasts . . . and, secondly, of a notion that an economic concept of 'shortage' can manifest itself without the classic economic indications, of which a rising price is the surest."[107] "There is a tendency to talk of the 'needs' for development as if they were quite independent of the actual structure of job opportunities in the economy. . . . Cumulative errors in the projections of a whole range of manpower needs can ultimately add up to an alarming misallocation of scarce resources."[108] The importance attached to education could be overdone. "To attribute all improvements in productivity to education would therefore be more than a little naive."[109]

Part of the difficulty in developing countries is that "the education system produces the wrong kinds of education."[110] But there was no universal consensus about the right kinds. The predominant view was that the emphasis had to be on the "formation of scientists and engineers."[111] Others, seeing the basic causes of underdevelopment in the attitudes and motivations of traditional cultures, took a different view. "Logically, one might perhaps expect a great upsurge of a liberal education policy encouraging individualism, enterprise and innovations to break down the rigidities both of the traditional and of the colonial systems."[112] By the end of the 1960s, the potentialities of manpower and education planning had come to be seen in more sober perspective. "Forecasting is necessary and must be done."[113] But unless the demand for each kind of skill is wholly under centralised control, as in a socialist command economy, even imperfect market signals may be a better guide to supply than long-term forecasts by planners.

Brain Drain

Another by-product of the emphasis on the importance and shortage of skills was concern about "brain drain." The first rumblings were heard around 1960 when Nehru called attention to the number of Indian scientists who had settled abroad and when the Shah of Iran appealed to Iranian students to return from abroad.[114] In 1961, Brinley Thomas, in the context of a broader study of international factor movements and economic growth, referred to the "two-way traffic of skilled personnel between the poorest and the richest countries. On the one hand, we find a 'perverse' emigration of trained people from the countries in the lowest income bracket to the advanced countries; on the other hand, there is the reverse movement of experts financed out of public funds." He warned that "under a regime of *laisser faire laisser passer* the transfer of skilled personnel from poor to rich countries could be on such a scale that the former could never begin the process of economic growth" and called for "measures . . . to protect and increase [their] supplies of skills."[115]

In the following years, particularly after relaxation of US immigration restrictions in 1962, which helped to swell the flow of engineers, doctors, and other professionals to the United States,[116] the subject was widely debated, not least in developed countries which were losing trained people to the United States—the phrase "brain drain" was coined in Britain[117]—but the debate helped to put the problem in better perspective and thus fairly quickly ran its course.

That the brain drain was harming the countries of emigration, if only through loss of taxation costs of educational investment, was admitted even by the most sternly neoclassical "internationalists" in the debate.[118] They tended to suggest, not very helpfully, that less developed countries (LDCs) should stem the outflow by paying their doctors higher salaries and impose an obligation on those who nonetheless emigrated (or on their foreign employers) to repay to the home country the cost of their education.[119] On the other side were the "nationalists," who were not content to view the problem in terms of a "world social welfare function" and insisted on the right to view it from the point of view of the national interests of the "brain-losing" countries.[120] They were supported by some of those involved in formulating and administering foreign aid policies who saw a conflict "between our efforts to train people in the less developed countries and our drain of foreign specialists to fill important jobs here in the United States."[121] But even these were, generally, not prepared to suggest that the outflow should be stopped by iron or bamboo curtains and had little more to offer by way of remedies than advice to the LDCs to "deal with the problem by persuasion, appeals to a sense of patriotic responsibility, and making the necessary adjustments in their social and economic structure."[122]

This last piece of advice presumably referred to the widely held view that outflow from some of the LDCs largely reflected domestic imbalance between supply and demand for skilled manpower, or an excess supply of graduates relative to effective demand at the levels of income expected by graduates whose primary objective was "the 'middle class' standard of living associated with the educated elite in the past."[123] Such imbalance seemed unlikely to persist indefinitely under the pressure of market forces. Similarly, the belief that "the United States as a mature but still growing nation has an apparently unlimited demand for" LDC doctors and engineers[124] which inspired some of the more extreme fears about the magnitude of the brain-drain problem proved unrealistic. As excess demand for many kinds of highly skilled manpower gave way to excess supply after years of rapid university expansion and with the slowdown of economic growth, the pull effect diminished. By the end of the 1960s, there was fairly general agreement with Myint's conclusion that "whatever our views on the welfare aspects of the brain drain, its effect on the retardation of the economic development of the underdeveloped countries is less alarming than it appears at first sight."[125]

Conclusion

Those who in the 1960s insisted on the importance of education for economic development interpreted the objective of economic development in terms not significantly different from those who in the previous decade had put the chief emphasis on physical capital formation. What they were concerned with was, in the words of a United Nations report, "the organization of education and training of the whole of the people as primary factors in the *economic growth* of the less developed countries."[126] They did not in any direct way challenge the prevailing orthodoxy which virtually equated economic development with growth of per capita income.

Indeed, it is arguable that they did not even challenge the primacy of capital formation among the means to economic development. The central contribution of the Chicago economists, Schultz and Becker, was to identify education as a factor in economic growth precisely *because* it is a form of capital formation. As the argument was put by R. B. Goode, perhaps even a little before Schultz, "it is generally agreed that capital formation is one of the principal requisites of economic progress. . . . Although Adam Smith included in a country's stock of fixed capital 'the acquired and useful abilities of all the inhabitants,' most economists have given little attention to human capital." The acquisition of human, as much as of physical, capital involves an economic cost and promise of future return. He therefore proposed to widen the definition of capital formation: "Investment or capital formation is taken to consist of the devotion of resources to making additions to the stock of physical and human capital."[127]

Once this step was taken, it followed naturally that education could be thought of as "investment in man" and that it should be possible to estimate the "economic value of education" interpreted as the rate of return on investment in man.[128] H. G. Johnson merely dotted the i's and crossed the t's when he proposed the idea of thinking of "development as a generalised process of capital accumulation,"[129] where capital is defined as including anything that yields a stream of income over time, and income as the product of capital.[130] Johnson may or may not have been right in claiming that such a generalised concept would help restore some balance after a period of "exaggerated concentration" on human capital, with the prospect of "a rehabilitation of investment in material capital as a potent source of economic growth."[131] What matters in our context is that the shift of emphasis from physical to human capital did not, in itself, denote a change in the meaning given to the development objective. But this was a case—and we shall encounter more than one—where a change of emphasis about the means brought with it subtle changes in the way people thought about the ends.

Whereas expenditure on capital goods is investment pure and simple, expenditure on education is part investment, part consumption. Thus, though development economists were out "to suggest that some of the outlays for education could be considered as investment rather than simply current consumption or 'social' expenditures,"[132] the effect was to some extent the reverse. They came "to stress the general importance of education"[133] and it was hardly possible to think about education merely as investment aimed at economic growth. When Schultz wrote about the economic value of education, he thought it necessary to apologise for what must look "as an intrusion which can only debase the cultural purposes of education."[134] And when Harbison and Myers expounded the principles of manpower planning, they began by insisting that "it is incorrect to assume that the central purpose of human resource development is to maximize man's contribution to the creation of productive goods and services"[135] "As economists," they still thought, "we are first of all interested in economic growth." But their interest in education and manpower planning made them acutely conscious of the inadequacy of so narrow an interpretation of the development objective. "We are convinced that the world-wide aspiration for development is much more than a desire for economic progress. It is a quest as well for status, prestige, recognition, and social and political modernization."[136]

In these ways, the new emphasis on human capital, though explicitly wholly concerned with the promotion of economic development in the sense of economic growth, pointed towards the broader interpretations that were beginning to enter the development literature. But before we turn to these, we must deal with one more strand in thinking about development which was still firmly in the economic growth school.

Trade as the Engine of Growth

In December 1961, the United Nations General Assembly passed Resolution 1707, "International Trade as the Primary Instrument for Economic Development."[137] It was an event that few would have predicted ten years earlier and that still causes surprise in retrospect. How, after a decade and more during which capital formation, physical and human, had occupied the centre of the development stage, did trade come to be elevated to that position?

Import Substitution

Controversy about the future of international trade and commercial policy had been part of the discussion of postwar plans even before the end of World War II and the controversy continued into the postwar years. There was argument for and against the view expressed in the late 1930s by D. H. Robertson that, for various reasons, international trade was unlikely in the twentieth century to play the role of "an engine of growth," which it played in the nineteenth.[138] Official US policy spokesmen, supported by economists such as Jacob Viner, pleaded and campaigned for a liberal trading system, removal of trade barriers, and the principle of nondiscrimination.[139] In Britain, official policy was more ambivalent, and there were those who drew the lesson from the interwar years that henceforth "there will have to be direct planning of international economic intercourse . . . there is much to be said for superseding the free play of market forces."[140] The dispute was partly a revival of the nineteenth-century argument about free trade and protection. Even more so, it was part of the wider ideological debate between advocates of a market economy and of planning or, more crudely, of capitalism and socialism.

During the first postwar decade, the literature on the economic development of less developed countries, insofar as it concerned itself with international trade and commercial policy, was dominated by critics of free trade. Ragnar Nurkse applied D. H. Robertson's trade pessimism to developing countries, arguing that "the tremendous expansion of Western Europe's and especially Great Britain's demand for foodstuffs and raw materials" which had provided "the basic inducement that caused them [especially the United States, Canada, Argentina, and Australia] to develop" could not be expected to function as the engine of growth for the still underdeveloped countries of the Third World. He therefore advocated balanced growth.[141] A school arose, represented most prominently by Raul Prebisch and Gunnar Myrdal, each an executive secretary of a United Nations economic commission (Prebisch for the Latin American and Myrdal for the European), who rejected the classical theory of international trade as inapplicable to less developed countries and argued that, far from acting as an engine of economic growth, international trade had been responsible for hindering development. In a programmatic study of "Growth, Disequilibrium, and Disparities: Interpretation of the Process of Economic Development" (1949), which was to become extremely influential, Prebisch argued that the growth of the West "had left untouched the vast peripheral area with its enormous capacity for assimilating technical progress so as to raise the very inade-

quate standard of living of the great masses of its population."
A major reason was that, because of inelastic world demand
for primary products and a combination of monopolistic pric-
ing of manufactures with competitive markets for primary
commodities, "the periphery tends to transfer a part of the
benefits accruing from its technical progress to the centres
while these latter retain their own benefits for themselves."[142]
This explained the secular decline in the terms of trade for
primary products between the 1860s and 1930s which a United
Nations study had recently documented. The Prebisch-Singer
thesis,[143] about the declining terms of trade for primary products, despite seemingly conclusive refutations of both the empirical evidence and the theoretical explanation by a
succession of economists, became, and has remained, a centrepiece of Third World ideology.[144]

Myrdal developed a more systematic theory of international
trade as a mechanism of international inequality. "Contrary to
what the equilibrium theory of international trade would seem
to suggest, the play of market forces does not work towards
equality in the remuneration to factors of production and, consequently, in incomes."[145] On the contrary, international
trade strengthens the industrial countries while the underdeveloped countries find their traditional industry ruined by
cheap imports, their skills impoverished. International trade
has, it is true, stimulated the production of primary products,
but these face inelastic demand and excessive price fluctua-
tions and tend to be confined to plantations and mining enclaves, which do little to promote general economic
development. "Under these circumstances the forces in the
markets will in a cumulative way tend to cause ever greater
international inequalities between countries as to their level of
economic development and average national income *per capita*."[146] Nurkse summed up this view in his Wicksell lectures:
"In a world in which (outside the Soviet area) over nine-tenths
of the manufacturing and over four-fifths of the total productive activity are concentrated in the advanced industrial countries, the ideas of symmetry, reciprocity and mutual
dependence which are associated with the traditional theory

of international trade are of rather questionable relevance to trade relations between the centre and the periphery."[147]

The chief policy inference for the underdeveloped countries drawn from this analysis was an urgent need for rapid industrialisation based on import substitution. Prebisch, in the 1949 ECLA study, stopped short of actually advocating such a policy, but the whole argument pointed towards it. "There is, in fact, a dynamic element in industry which is not found to a comparable extent in primary production." "The attempt to raise income in the Latin American countries by means of exports may run into serious difficulties caused by competition from other countries" and technical progress in agriculture, while necessary to raise rural incomes, inevitably creates a surplus of labour.[148] "Since there is no other way of absorbing the gainfully employed population and increasing its productivity, the activities which can be developed by protective tariffs do, within certain limits, give rise to an increase in real income."[149] Myrdal, while pointing out that wartime interruptions of supply and postwar balance of payments problems had led many LDCs to adopt import restrictions, argued strongly that LDCs "have quite a number of other sound reasons, based on their peculiar situation, for using these restrictions for protective purposes."[150] In line with the argument developed by Rosenstein-Rodan and Nurkse that a major obstacle to economic development is a Keynesian-type insufficiency of effective demand because the inducement to invest is limited by the size of the market,[151] Myrdal argued that "import restrictions afford a means . . . of creating at once the necessary demand for a particular domestic industry."[152]

A whole new literature of LDC protectionism grew up around new infant industry and "infant economy" arguments which found ammunition even in the writings of liberal economists, such as Lewis's case for compensating manufacturing industry for the high cost of labour set by average income in agriculture, and Hirschman's, based on the historical experience of the industrial countries, for infant industry protection until a "threshold" is reached.[153] The Soviet model of autarkic industrial development was influential, especially in India through the role of Mahalanobis, physicist turned planner, who *"implicitly* assumed a closed economy or a situation of stagnant export earnings through inelasticity of export demand."[154] Nurkse's balanced-growth model could be interpreted as having similar implications since, as a critic later pointed out, "there can be no specialisation for the home market."[155]

The new protectionism for LDCs was not without its critics. Western economists submitted the new arguments to scrutiny.[156] At the official level, the United States had failed in its early postwar efforts to establish an international trade organisation to monitor a liberal "charter" but had salvaged that part dealing with liberalisation of tariffs in the General Agreement on Tariffs and Trade. The GATT, through successive rounds of tariff negotiations, did much to liberalise trade in manufactures among industrial countries. Its efforts, and those of the Organisation for European Economic Cooperation (OEEC) (later the Organisation for Economic Cooperation and Development, OECD) which encouraged the removal of import restrictions and the liberalisation of trade within the two new regional groupings, the European Economic Community (EEC) and the European Free Trade Area (EFTA), made a substantial contribution to accelerating economic growth in the industrial countries during the 1950s and 1960s, but this liberalisation did not extend to trade in agricultural and other primary products. It was not seen as giving any direct help to developing countries—indeed many of their exports confronted new barriers erected by the EEC's Common Agricultural Policy—and did nothing to discourage their generally inward-looking policies.

The emergence during the 1950s of the notion that international trade might play a more positive role in economic development than the first generation of postwar development economists had assumed was due not to these Western protagonists of liberal trade policies. It derived from three other influences: concern about the "foreign exchange gap" of developing countries; growing disenchantment with the import-substitution strategy in Latin America and elsewhere; and Soviet efforts to neutralise the role of GATT, reinforced by the emerging political muscle of the Third World. It was the partly fortuitous confluence of these three that led to the UN Assembly resolution of 1961 and ultimately to the first United Nations Conference on Trade and Development (UNCTAD I) of 1964.

Internationalisation of Protection

In 1957, the GATT appointed a group of economists under the chairmanship of Professor Haberler to report on "certain trends in international trade, in particular the failure of the trade of less developed countries to develop as rapidly as that of industrialised countries, excessive short-term flunctuations in prices of primary products, and widespread resort to agricultural protectionism."[157] These terms of reference reflected the special interests of Australia (which had taken the initiative for the appointment of the group) and a concern which had become increasingly prominent in discussion of the problems of developing countries in the preceding years, their "foreign exchange gap."

After the earlier phase when estimates of the capital requirements of LDCs had revealed major "saving gaps," economists were now making estimates of LDC import requirements, usually based on assumed target rates of economic growth together with fixed import coefficients. Uniformly, they revealed the prospect of "foreign exchange gaps" left by adverse prospects for LDC exports and inadequate aid by developed countries.[158] Of the two gaps, the foreign exchange gap appeared as the more serious constraint on economic development, as the LDCs with few exceptions struggled to meet chronic balance of payments difficulties through import and foreign exchange controls. In the theoretical literature this gave rise to "two gap analysis" (and debate about its analytical soundness); in practical policy discussion it led to the slogans "trade not aid" or "trade and aid."[159]

The Haberler Report picked up this theme. Its criticisms of the tariff and other barriers erected by developed countries, which it described as an important factor contributing to the foreign exchange difficulties of LDCs, led to the appointment by GATT of a standing committee—the famous Committee III—with the task of encouraging policies to help their exports. In passing, the report also commented adversely on LDC policies of import-substitution which "had almost certainly been to the disadvantage of the underdeveloped countries themselves."[160] But its recommendations were entirely addressed to exports of primary (and semiprocessed) commodities. Very soon, however, attention began to be directed to the need for freer access to developed-country markets for LDC manufactures. Wyndham-White, director-general of GATT, in June 1960, sounded a note that would become much more prominent two decades later: "It is difficult . . . to escape the conclusion that one of the contributions which the older industrialized countries will have to make will be to surrender some sectors of light manufacturing to new industries in the developing countries, finding their compensation in the more specialized and dynamic forms of industrial production on which their economic growth in any case depends."[161] A few months later, the UN Economic Commission for Europe published a study of "Europe and the Trade Needs of the Less Developed Countries," in which it argued that, since aid and exports of primary products would meet only two-thirds of the import requirements of the Third World in 1980, "this would leave the remaining one-third, i.e., at least $15 billion, to be filled by exports of manufactures" and on infant-industry grounds proposed the first scheme for a generalised system of preferences (GSP) for LDC manufactures, very much on the lines of the scheme later adopted by the EEC.[162]

Meanwhile, Prebisch himself had begun to have second thoughts about the merits of the import substitution strategy. The UN *Economic Survey of Latin America for 1956* expressed disappointment that import substitution appeared to be failing in two of its major objectives, saving of foreign exchange and thus reduced dependence on world markets. "Unbalanced development may involve a rapid growth of certain essential imports, so that, in the final analysis, the economy is as much as ever at the mercy of events overseas—or even more so. . . . This leaves an increase in the volume of exports as the only reliable source for the financing of the expanding volume of

imports."[163] While this suggested the need to pay more attention to exports, it did not at first induce any rethinking of
industrial development strategy. "This leads to the rather paradoxical conclusion that the only way of financing the imports
for growing secondary industries is to expand the volume of
exports of primary products."[164] But two years later, while
continuing to insist that import substitution was "the only
way to correct the effects on peripheral growth of disparities in
foreign trade elasticity,"[165] he began to advocate regional integration among LDCs—"preferential treatment is needed in-
side the area to promote specialisation in industrial products
and primary commodities"[166]—and to argue for nonreciprocal tariff cuts by developed countries on imports from
developing countries, as well as for measures to ensure more
equitable and stable prices for primary commodities.[167]

Thus, intellectually, the stage was set for the UN resolution
of December 1961 declaring international trade to be the primary instrument of economic development. But, politically,
its adoption as a plank of the ideological platform of the Third
World had different origins.

One front in the Cold War of the 1950s was that on which
the two superpowers manoeuvred for the sympathy of the
Third World. As GATT moved in 1956 to demonstrate its concern for the trade problems of the developing countries, the
Soviet Union countered by proposing the holding of a world
economic conference to discuss problems of trade and development;[168] with the support of other Soviet-bloc countries, it
repeated this proposal for some years. As long as the proposal
came from this source, it was not taken very seriously in the
West. During the second half of the decade, however, with the
sudden acceleration of decolonisation and the admission of
numerous new member countries, voting strength in the
United Nations General Assembly shifted,[169] and the bloc of
seventy-seven "nonaligned" countries, which had emerged
from the Bandung Conference of 1955, gradually took over the
initiative. At the Belgrade Conference in September 1961,
President Tito launched the idea of a World Conference on
Trade and Development. A few weeks later (7 December
1961), GATT responded with a declaration on the need for

rapid and sustained expansion of export earnings of less developed countries, including a pronouncement that "aid can be no substitute for trade" and a call for reduction of restrictions on access to DC markets for LDC products. A fortnight after this (19 December), the UN General Assembly endorsed President Kennedy's designation of the 1960s as the "UN Development Decade" and passed Resolution 1707, which gave approval in principle to the idea of a conference. In the following year, another nonaligned conference (Cairo, June 1962) gave more precise form to the demand for a conference on trade and development. The Western countries now abandoned their opposition. ECOSOC resolved to convene UNCTAD (now known as UNCTAD I), established a preparatory committee, appointed Prebisch secretary-general of UNCTAD, and invited him to prepare a report to outline the issues.[170]

The report which Prebisch submitted to the conference was entitled "Towards a New Trade Policy for Development." H. G. Johnson has said of it that it was "an unusually comprehensive, well-balanced and philosophically coherent analysis and set of recommendations for promoting the development of the less developed countries through changes in the trade policy of the developed countries."[171] Starting out from a historical survey of the nineteenth-century pattern of world trade and its breakdown in the Great Depression of the 1930s, Prebisch argued that the "Old Order" could no longer serve the needs of development, and that merely negative policies of removal of trade barriers had to be supplemented by positive policies to assist the trade of developing countries. A restatement of his familiar thesis about the terms of trade for primary products provided the basis for a program designed to raise and stabilise the prices of primary products by commodity agreements and to make good by compensatory finance losses of export earnings from worsening terms of trade. It was a program which, in Johnson's words, extended "to primary-producing less developed countries the types of protection that developed countries extend to their own primary producers, with the significant difference that the subsidies involved would go to the governments and not the individual producers of those countries."[172]

The main policy innovation of the Prebisch report was a new emphasis on the need for developing countries to export manufactures. The Great Depression had "compelled industrialization to turn inwards like a simple import substitution process—simple but costly. . . . The Second World War gave this form of inward-looking industrialization still further impetus." The policy had helped raise income but much less than "a rational policy of combining import substitution with industrial exports" would have done. The simple and relatively easy phase of import substitution was reaching its limits in most advanced industrialising LDCs. The relative smallness of their national markets added to other adverse factors. Excessive protectionism had "generally insulated national markets from external competition, weakening and even destroying the incentive necessary for improving the quality of output and lowering costs under the private-enterprise system. It had thus tended to stifle the initiative of enterprises as regards both the internal market and exports."[173]

Whereas a few years earlier Prebisch had questioned the import substitution strategy merely because of its failure to yield significant saving of foreign exchange, he now conceded much of the classical case against it, chiefly that it deprives countries of the dynamic benefit of international trade, which Haberler had recently restated in his influential Cairo lectures.[174] But the inference Prebisch drew was not the desirability of general liberalisation of trade, by developing as by developed countries, but a case, on infant industry or "infant economy" grounds, for nonreciprocal concessions by developed countries. The GSP scheme for LDC exports of manufactures which he proposed to the conference followed fairly closely that outlined in the ECE study of 1960.

As Johnson pointed out, the program which Prebisch presented to UNCTAD and which has remained the core of the Third World's demand for a New International Economic Order was based on "a philosophy of international economic policy that might be described as the internationalization of protectionism for less developed countries."[175] To this extent, it constituted a step, though as yet only a small step, towards an outward-looking development strategy.

Outward-Looking Policies

Meanwhile, and increasingly during the 1960s, while a frustrating and often acrimonious North-South dialogue[176] arose from UNCTAD I, with the South pushing for the Prebisch program and the North for multilateral tariff negotiations coupled with grudging acceptance of the principle of LDC preferences, the case for outward-looking industrial development strategy was carried much further than Prebisch had taken it. The most influential contribution to this case was made by an ambitious study of the industrialisation experience of a number of developing countries which was initiated at the OECD Development Centre by I. M. D. Little (whose interest in these problems had been stimulated by a period working in the Planning Commission in New Delhi) and which culminated in the Little-Scitovsky-Scott report *Industry and Trade in Some Developing Countries.*[177] Other contributions were made by a team at the World Bank associated with Bela Balassa;[178] by the London-based Trade Policy Research Centre, which initially tried to promote the idea of an Atlantic Community as an alternative to British entry into the Common Market but later concentrated on propagating the case for freer trade;[179] and by a Tokyo-centred group which in conferences and papers on Pacific trade and development lent its weight to the case while injecting some ideas with a Japanese flavour into the discussion.[180]

In part, the case for more outward-looking policies drew on mounting evidence in industrialising LDCs of the adverse effects of the import substitution strategy to which Prebisch had already pointed in his report. One of the first studies outside Latin America was one by John Power of the Pakistan case.[181] Power noted that the saving rate had failed to rise as had been hoped and suggested that "the character of the industrialization itself, with its emphasis on import substitution—especially the replacement of imported consumption goods—

had something to do with it."[182] Import licensing, initially to conserve foreign exchange, gave greater encouragement to domestic production of consumption goods than of capital goods, and of inessential than of essential consumption goods. In a necessarily small home market, it could not take advantage of economies of scale, and, in the absence of backward linkages or opening of export markets, the momentum of industrial development based on import replacement could not easily be maintained. "There is no natural, spontaneous evolution from the kind of 'hot-house' industrial growth induced by shutting out imports to . . . self-sustaining growth."[183]

The Little-Scitovsky-Scott report, drawing on the experience of seven countries, strongly reinforced and extended this negative case. "The studies on the seven countries indicate that these countries have now reached the stage where policies that are followed to promote import-substitution are proving harmful for the economic development of these countries. Industrialization sheltered by high levels of protection had led to the creation of high-cost enterprises; these enterprises are producing expensive products, many of which are for use by a restricted middle class, and so production is rapidly coming up against the limits of the home market. . . . With high industrial prices, maintained behind high tariffs, industrialization has been carried out at a high cost to agriculture. . . . Ponderous administrative control has held up decisions and has led to excessive stocks and the creation of a multitude of firms operating below capacity. . . . The most serious result of these policies, however, is that the nascent industries have come to depend for their profits on government decisions, and so have formed the habit of devoting their efforts to obtaining privileges by pressure on the government rather than by cutting their costs."[184]

To the negative experience of import substitution in some industrialising countries was added the encouraging experience of an increasing number of small countries, chiefly but not exclusively in East and Southeast Asia, which appeared to be successful in following the earlier example of Japan by pursuing an export-oriented strategy based on export of labour-intensive manufactures. The first "showcase example of industrialization for export," noted in the literature as early as 1959, was that of Puerto Rico, but this could be regarded as a special case because of its preferential access to the US market.[185] To some extent, this applied also to the second success story of export-led growth, that of Hong Kong, to which Myint drew attention in 1969, since Hong Kong enjoyed useful preference in the United Kingdom.[186]

But by 1967 the list of countries "where the growth of manufactures has been at least somewhat export-oriented" had lengthened to include Taiwan, South Korea, Israel, Mexico, and Pakistan.[187] Several of these were achieving very high rates of growth of exports of manufactures in the face of DC protectionism and without the benefit of preferential treatment. A study published in that year claimed that "contemporary experience of LDCs in the realm of trade policy has shifted a considerable body of influential opinion . . . towards what might be called an outward-looking strategy of trying to export manufactures early in the process of industrial development." It listed, as the main benefits of such a strategy, increasing returns in production for a larger market and the value of competition: "Export promotion goes hand in hand with efforts to conquer and defend the home market, but a degree of foreign competition is tolerated at home to toughen the competitive fibre of local industries."[188]

When the Asian Development Bank two years later commissioned the study *Southeast Asia's Economy in the 1970s*, the author of the chapter on the manufacturing sector, Helen Hughes, stated the new doctrine very firmly: "The further pursuit of import-substituting, inward-oriented industrialization strategies will lead to more high costs and balance of payments difficulties. In the Philippines, industrial growth had already slowed down in the 1960s, and in Malaysia and Thailand . . . industrial growth is in danger of slowing down in the 1970s, because the relatively easy import-substitution possibilities have been exhausted. An alternative, outward-looking industrialization strategy, already adopted with remarkable success in Singapore, entails a difficult and painful adjustment of policies."[189]

The same volume contained a (primarily) Japanese contribution which supported this general approach—"there is a need to search for new engines of economic growth in the international economy, and to push the development of export-oriented industrial activity appropriate to the economic circumstances, resource endowment, and demand structure of particular developing countries"[190]—but with nuances that reflected Japanese experience and viewpoints. Among these were an emphasis on "horizontal" trade, i.e., exchange of manufactures for manufactures, and on a "new international division of labour" based on the (Heckscher-Ohlin) comparative advantage of developing countries with their cheap and abundant labour and developed countries with their superiority in capital and technology. But since the guiding principle must be "dynamic" comparative advantage which will not be attained through the free market, there was emphasis also on "agreed specialisation"[191] including planned "structural adjustment"[192] in the advanced countries, such as was being undertaken in Japan, and on "planned transfer of manufacturing activity from developed to less developed producers."[193]

Hla Myint, in his overall report in the same volume, endorsed the general recommendation that "the Southeast Asian countries should move away from import-substitution policies towards a radically different approach to industrialization," but gave no support to "agreed specialisation" and was a good deal more cautious about the kinds of export on which LDCs should concentrate. These should not be just labour-intensive—such exports were "likely to face stiff competition." Prospects were best in lines which could make use of specific skills and aptitudes of labour; most promising for resource-rich countries would be a shift from raw to processed materials for which he coined the term "export substitution."[194]

During the 1970s, as growth in the industrialised countries slowed down, trade pessimism revived. Arthur Lewis, in his 1979 Nobel lecture, claimed that "for the past hundred years the rate of growth of output in the developing countries has depended on the rate of growth of output in the developed world. When the developed grow fast, the developing grow fast, and when the developed slow down, the developing slow down." The link between DC and LDC growth has been DC demand for "LDC primary commodities, a link in terms of physical volume, not much affected by prices." As for LDC exports of manufactures, the DCs are "willing to let in manufactured exports only when they are prosperous." Thus, if DC growth cannot be expected henceforth to exceed on average 4 percent a year, LDCs cannot rely on DC markets to achieve the 6 percent growth rate they need (to narrow the gap in per capita incomes, given their higher rate of population growth). They will need increasingly to trade with one another and/or promote further import substitution.[195]

Lewis's thesis did not carry universal conviction. A decade earlier Kravis had pointed out that even in the nineteenth century high rates of economic development had not been closely correlated with export expansion; trade had served as the "handmaiden," rather than as the engine, of growth. "Growth where it occurred was mainly the consequence of favourable internal factors, and external demand represented an additional stimulus which varied in importance from country to country and period to period."[196] As empirical evidence for the 1970s became available, it cast considerable doubt on Lewis's assumption that LDC growth depended on DC demand for primary products. The commodity composition of LDC exports had shifted markedly from primary products to manufactures—though at very different rates, with most countries of Africa remaining dependent on exports of cash crops—and the annual rate of growth of manufactured exports was as high in the 1970s as in the 1960s despite a fall by half in DC real-growth rates.[197] Contrary to Lewis's expectations and widespread fears, DC protectionism had not prevented those developing countries with open economies from significantly increasing their share of the world market.[198] It appeared that LDC export growth depended "less on growth of the market than on the capacity of LDCs to supply manufactured exports at competitive prices,"[199] and this capacity clearly varied greatly among Third World countries.

Of course, it remained arguable that for the majority of LDCs, especially in Africa, Lewis's pessimistic conclusion held

good, and that success in export-oriented industrial development would become more difficult as the number of countries
attempting it increased. In fact, while the case for export-oriented industrial development won more adherents during the
1970s, both in theory and in practice, it remained a minority
view in the Third World, politically wholly overshadowed by
the UNCTAD ideology with its demand for a new international economic order and in the development literature also
by the shift of emphasis from economic growth to social objectives. Even its more enthusiastic exponents, both among academics and practitioners, put it forward with qualifications.
Most of them conceded that it was more conclusive for small
than for large countries,[200] and that import substitution remains "inevitable and legitimate at the outset in most countries."[201] In its more sophisticated version, therefore, the case
is not against import substitution as such, but against the notion that, as Myrdal put it in the early 1950s, while manufacturing for exports will become desirable at a later stage of
industrial development of underdeveloped countries, "for a
long time they have had their hands full in trying to meet the
demands of their domestic market."[202] The new view is that
"unfortunately, this two-stage theory of development is impractical. It is just too difficult, and at best an extremely slow
process, to get away from the first stage *unless* the growth of
grossly inefficient industries has been ruthlessly suppressed
from the beginning and the second stage has been explicitly
kept in view and made an essential ingredient of the economic
policies in the first stage."[203] And even the proponents of this
austere prescription would presumably admit that it is never
too late for a sinner to repent and for a country that began with
import substitution pure and simple to change to a more export-oriented policy as soon and as best it can.

4

Social Objectives (1965–1975)

Towards the end of the 1960s, there was a more far-reaching change in the climate of opinion, and this time more clearly about the objectives of development, about ends rather than means.

There had been straws in the wind. In 1965, H. W. Singer published an article with the then surprising title "Social Development: Key Growth Sector." In it he pleaded for more attention to the social aspects of development—health, education, nutrition. "The problem of the underdeveloped countries is not just growth, but development. Development is growth plus change; change, in turn, is social and cultural as well as economic, and qualitative as well as quantitative. . . . The key concept must be the improved quality of people's life."[1] The same theme, indeed, some of the same formulations, had appeared a few years earlier in a United Nations document (in the drafting of which Singer, then still senior economist in the UN Secretariat in New York, almost certainly had a major part), *The UN Development Decade: Proposals for Action*.[2]

Social Development

The concept of "social development" was even then not new. Indeed, it went back to the earliest days of the United Nations.[3] The two supreme organs of the United Nations were from the beginning the Security Council and the Economic and Social Council (ECOSOC). In 1949, the General Assembly invited ECOSOC to initiate a survey of the "world social and cultural situation," intended as a counterpart to the regular survey of the world economic situation (later the annual *World Economic Survey*). A small team in the Secretariat, the embryo of the later Social Division of the Department of Economic and Social Affairs, produced a *Preliminary Report on the World Social Situation* in 1952 and in 1955 the *International Survey of Programmes of Social Development.* The second *Report on the World Social Situation,* which appeared in 1957, was said to demonstrate "the need for a much closer integration of economic and social objectives than has yet been achieved in most societies."[4] It also referred to work that had begun in the Social Division on indicators of social development, with the object of replacing the inadequate measure of per capita income by "analysis of various 'components' representing internationally accepted values (health, nutrition, education, housing, employment, personal income) and by the use of various statistical indicators for these components."[5]

To strengthen this work, Tinbergen persuaded the Dutch government to finance a separate institution. The United Nations Research Institute for Social Development (UNRISD) was established in Geneva in 1963, with H. W. Singer and I. F. de Jong as initial co-directors, "to conduct research into problems and policies of social development and relationships among various types of social development during different phases of economic growth."[6] In the 1970s UNRISD came to be associated with quite radical approaches to development. But in its early years, it was true of UNRISD, as of most others until the late 1960s, that "issues of social development were generally considered secondary to those of economic growth."[7] The emphasis was at most on "balanced economic and social development."[8] The UN reports on the "world social situation" maintained a tone of qualified optimism; the statistics suggested that the social situation was continually "improving."[9] Singer himself, in an article written in 1968, his last year with the United Nations, deprecated "the current fashion of talking about a 'decade of frustration' [as] . . . somewhat exaggerated." If anything, he seemed to suggest, statistics of GDP growth understated the improvements that had occurred. "When we substitute other more indirect indicators, such as improvement in the literacy rate, increases in the stock of educational capital within the population, or health indicators such as the incidence of certain diseases, the picture of the 1960s is by no means of slower progress than in the 1950s; rather the contrary."[10] In any case, he and others interested in social development in that period did not see a conflict or trade-off between economic and social objectives. As Singer put it in his 1965 article, "improvements in people's level of life can be achieved both directly ('social development') and indirectly via income and economic resources ('economic development')."[11] "Better health, better education, better nutrition" are themselves "the keys to growth."[12]

This earnest and sober concern with social development quite suddenly gave way in 1969 to vigorous denunciation of the growth-oriented development economics of the previous twenty-five years. The first dramatic statement of this new view was by Dudley Seers, of the Institute of Development Studies at Sussex University, in his presidential address to the Eleventh World Congress of the Society for International Development (SID) in New Delhi in November 1969, which was published under the title "The Meaning of Development."

"We have misconceived the nature of the main challenge of the second half of the twentieth century" by making a 5 percent growth rate of GNP the target for the First Development Decade. It was "very slipshod of us to confuse development with economic development and economic development with economic growth." It was naive to assume that "increases in national income, if they are faster than population growth, sooner or later lead to the solution of social and political problems." "It looks as if economic growth may not merely fail to solve social and political difficulties; certain types of growth can actually cause them." "The questions to be asked about a country's development are therefore: What has been happening to poverty? What has been happening to unemployment? What has been happening to inequality? If one or two of these central problems has been growing worse, especially if all three have, it would be strange to call the result 'development' even if per capita income has doubled."[13]

Two years later, the Pakistani economist Mahbub ul Haq, then with the World Bank, gave the same ideas an even sharper formulation in his address to the Twelfth SID Congress at Ottawa. "A high growth rate has been, and is, no guarantee against worsening poverty and political explosions. Where did the development process go astray? We conceived our task not as the eradication of poverty but as the pursuit of certain levels of average income. . . . The basic problem of development should be redefined as a selective attack on the worst forms of poverty. . . . Development goals must be defined in terms of reduction and eventual elimination of malnutrition, disease, illiteracy, squalor, unemployment and inequalities. . . . We were taught to take care of our GNP as this will take care of poverty. Let us reverse this and take care of poverty as this will take care of GNP. In other words, let us worry about the *content* of GNP even more than its rate of increase."[14]

For some years during the early 1970s, this became the dominant theme in the development literature, to the point where some of the protagonists felt able to speak of the "current consensus."[15] In quick succession, employment, equality, poverty eradication, and basic needs fulfilment became the goals of new "development strategies." The rest of this chapter is devoted to an account of this phase in development thinking.

Employment

In September 1970, David Morse, long-time director-general of the International Labour Office (ILO), in a speech which became famous because it gave the world—or at least the profession—the slogan "dethronement of GNP," told a Cambridge conference "to make employment a major goal and criterion of development."[16] "Unacceptably high rates of unemployment and underemployment," he argued, "have not only prevailed over the past decade but have in fact often increased, even in developing countries which have claimed reasonable rates of economic growth."[17]

The ILO, the oldest of the specialised agencies of the United Nations, had always regarded problems of unemployment and employment as one of its major responsibilities. In the interwar years, unemployment in the advanced industrial countries had been the dominant concern. In the postwar years, with the developed countries enjoying full employment, attention shifted to problems of unemployment and underemployment in the Third World. As early as 1961, almost ten years before the Cambridge conference, the ILO published the report *Employment Objectives in Economic Development*, in which an expert group, while emphasising that the employment problems of developing countries could not be solved without rapid economic growth, also argued that even rapid growth might not provide enough jobs and suggested that "employment objectives should be given weight in the choice of alternative patterns of economic development."[18]

Toward the end of the decade, this idea of an "employment-oriented approach to development" inspired something of a crusade. In 1969 the ILO, in close association with the Sussex Institute, of which Dudley Seers was director and which had meanwhile been joined by Singer as well as Richard Jolly, launched a "World Employment Programme."[19] The ILO and the OECD undertook studies of the available statistical evidence on unemployment in developing countries[20] and the ILO organised a series of employment missions to selected countries to assist their governments in drawing up comprehensive employment policies. The first two of these missions, to Colombia and Sri Lanka, were led by Dudley Seers, the third, to Kenya, jointly by Singer and Jolly.

The central theme of the Colombia report, published in 1970 under the title *Towards Full Employment*, was "the limited significance of economic growth."[21] In Colombia, "the poorest sections of the population have gained little, if anything, from the growth of some 5 per cent per year (in real terms) of the economy since the mid-1950s," and growing unemployment is at the heart of this problem.[22] The mission therefore made it its task to produce "a development strategy in which reduction of unemployment is given the highest priority."[23] But "unemployment," in this context, was given a very wide meaning, to cover not only those without work but also those for whom employment provided by the economy is inadequate in the sense that "they have jobs but want to work longer hours or more intensively" or that they "lack a source of income both reliable and adequate."[24]

Both the Colombia and the Sri Lanka missions confirmed

what other studies had already brought to light, and what should have been obvious, that in developing countries, where the state does not provide income support for the unemployed, open unemployment is very largely confined to young, urban, relatively educated, middle-class people who can afford to wait for better jobs than are readily available. Nor, it appeared, could the problem be adequately described in terms of "underemployment," although there were no doubt large numbers especially in rural areas of developing countries who found work only intermittently or who were "technically at work but virtually idle."[25] In fact, it became increasingly evident that, as the rapporteur of the Cambridge conference put it, "it was impossible to make progress so long as unemployment was taken as the starting point. . . . The problem had been misstated, and it was not really an employment problem at all."[26]

"The findings of the three employment missions (as distinct from their original terms of reference) . . . ," Singer later conceded, "pretty quickly made it clear that the *unemployment* concept . . . was quite unsuited to the developing countries." "Disguised unemployment" or "underemployment" were equally inappropriate terms. "These people often worked extremely hard and extremely long hours and it seemed absurd to describe them as underemployed."[27] It was the Kenya mission, led by Singer and Jolly, which drew the logical conclusion.[28] It put the emphasis overwhelmingly on "the working poor [who] work long hours for low incomes"; for this, as the report noted at the outset, "is the most pervading and basic issue."[29]

If the problem was the low productivity of the working poor, rather than unemployment or underemployment, the argument seemed to have come full circle. The task of development policy was, it seemed, not so much to find jobs as to increase the productivity of people in work or, in the words used in the Kenya report and frequently in subsequent discussion, to create "more *productive* employment opportunities." As an early commentator on the Kenya report pointed out, "one would have expected the mission to acknowledge that poverty is the ubiquitous condition which is altered by growth."[30] All three missions, in fact, despite their "employment orientation," included ambitious economic growth targets in their policy recommendations. The Colombia report, for all its "dethronement of GNP," demanded an average growth rate of 8 percent for the 1970s, significantly higher than the 5.5 percent rate the country had achieved in the 1960s,[31] and the Kenya report stressed "our emphasis on continued growth and expanded production in every sector."[32] But growth of total or per capita income was now only part of the answer and apparently not by any means the most important part. The focus shifted to its composition and distribution.

The shift began with the Colombia report. For although its authors still saw the problem primarily in terms of unemployment, they "came to the conclusion that it would be impossible to achieve a high level of employment in Colombia without changing the distribution of income."[33] The reasons they gave were, first, that the rich tend to spend their income on goods with a high import content and, second, that production of the goods purchased by the poor tends to be more labour intensive than production of those demanded by the rich.[34] Thus one part of an employment-oriented development strategy must be a change in the pattern of demand through a redistribution of income from rich to poor. "Income distribution lies at the heart of the employment problem."[35]

A year later, in the Kenya report, significantly entitled *Employment, Incomes and Equality*, the central problem was seen as inequality itself, "imbalance of opportunities." "If the problem is primarily lack of jobs, the solution must be the provision of more jobs. But if the problem is primarily an imbalance of opportunities, the solution must be to put right the imbalances. . . . Hence our emphasis on putting right the imbalances, on equity in place of gross inequality, in earnings, education, and land holdings, among regions, districts and individuals, and in other respects."[36]

Another novel, and for some time influential, theme of the report was its condemnation of the usual practice of LDC governments of favouring the modern over the traditional or, as it preferred to state it, the "informal" sector of craftsmen, petty traders, and purveyors of other services, and of hampering this sector by harassment and restrictions. The report stressed that, although the informal sector "is often regarded as unproductive and stagnant, we see it as providing a wide range of low-cost, labour-intensive, competitive goods and services."[37]

Thus, from about 1972, employment gave way to equity as the favoured orientation of development strategy. Before we turn to look at this more closely, one implication of employment orientation deserves brief discussion. This was the belief that the employment problem in developing countries demanded the use of labour-intensive technologies in industry and agriculture. In the words of the Colombia report, "levels of employment can be raised not only by improving the pattern of demand but also by producing things in more labour-intensive ways."[38] The view came to be widely supported that the employment problems of the Third World were aggravated by importation and encouragement of inappropriate technology, as well as by the "demonstration effect" of Western consumerism. "Since most new techniques are invented in the developed countries where unskilled labour is relatively expensive . . . they tend not to be well suited for developing countries where labour is cheap."[39] Moreover, "in general there have been both deliberate attempts to foster a capital intensive heavy industry base and the use of a range of policy instruments which tended to favour, not necessarily by design, capital intensive production."[40]

One possible inference from employment orientation was, therefore, that developing countries would do well to follow an outward rather than an inward looking industrialisation strategy, since "the main reason for development having proceeded along capital-intensive lines [appeared to lie] in the import-substitution policies adopted,"[41] while countries such as Hong Kong and Taiwan, which had followed an outward-looking policy had secured "a product mix and production techniques appropriate to actual factor proportions."[42] The author of a survey of "new thinking" about development published in 1972, therefore, linked the new concern about unemployment with the Little-Scitovsky-Scott advocacy of outward-looking industrialisation and inferred the desirability of LDCs making "use of market forces instead of tilting ineffectively and disastrously against them"[43] quite unlike most of the ILO-Sussex group who tended to agree with Mahbub ul Haq in his scepticism about "this faith in price adjustments."[44]

A second policy implication could be a less welcoming attitude by developing countries towards multinational corporations, since "the encouragement of foreign investment, under these conditions, has tended to lead to capital intensiveness in an acute form."[45] A third implication drawn by some was that it was desirable to develop "intermediate technology," between the capital-intensive technology of the West and the traditional handicraft technology of less developed countries. The best known proponent of this latter approach was E. F. Schumacher, who founded the London-based Intermediate Technology Development Group and, in his widely acclaimed book *Small Is Beautiful*, made intermediate technology part of a broad onslaught on Western industrial society.[46]

In these various ways, the proponents of an employment-oriented development strategy found common ground, on the one hand, with liberal advocates of outward-looking policies and, on the other, with radical critics of Western capitalism and even of Western style modernisation in any form.

Inequality and/or Poverty

The Kenya report was hardly published when the ILO-Sussex alliance received powerful support from what a few years earlier would have been considered an unlikely quarter—the World Bank. Robert S. McNamara, president of the bank since 1968, devoted most of his September 1972 annual address to the board of governors to the theme "Social Equity and Economic Growth." In words recalling Dudley Seer's 1969 presidential address, he questioned whether achievement of the 6 percent growth target recently adopted by the United Nations for its Second Development Decade would guarantee a significant advance in the quality of life for the majority of the two billion people of the less developed countries. Increases in national income would not benefit the poor if they did not reach the poor. "They have not reached the poor to any significant degree in most developing countries in the past. . . . The problems of poverty are deeply rooted in the institutional framework, particularly in the distribution of economic and political power within the system."[47] A year later, in Nairobi, he returned to the same theme. "Growth is not equitably reaching the poor. . . . Rapid growth has been accompanied by greater maldistribution of income in many developing countries." Absolute equality is chimerical, but "absolute human degradation when it reaches the proportions of 30 to 40 per cent of an entire citizenry—cannot be ignored, cannot be suppressed, and cannot be tolerated for too long a time by any government hoping to preserve civil order."[48]

McNamara, former president of the Ford Motor Company and then U.S. secretary of defense through most of the Vietnam War years, had from the beginning of his term as president of the bank, and even before,[49] been outspoken on the problems of the Third World, but initially his concern, as that of most others in the 1960s, had been mainly with the gap between the rich and poor *nations*. One of his first acts as president of the World Bank had been to carry out a proposal by his predecessor for the appointment of a high-level commission to report on this problem and on what the rich countries could do to alleviate it. When the Pearson Commission's report was discussed at a special international conference at Columbia University in February 1970,[50] McNamara's address still concentrated on the problem of aid, though significantly—as domestic social problems were increasingly competing for attention and resources—he spoke of the United States "twin responsibilities . . . to assist in alleviating underdevelopment at home and abroad."[51] But from 1971 onwards, in a succession of public statements and in the operational programs of the bank, he insistently called attention to the gap between rich and poor *within* developing countries.[52]

At first the stress was on inequality. In his 1971 speech to the board of governors he declared that, though growth in the Third World had reached 5 percent in the 1960s, "the distribution of this GNP increase has been so unequal—as between countries, regions and socio-economic groups—that it has finally created a reaction against growth as the primary development objective, and a demand for greater attention to employment and income distribution."[53] Addressing UNCTAD III in Santiago a few months later, he quoted estimates for Brazil, Mexico, and India as "not untypical" examples to illustrate "the severe maldistribution of income and wealth which exists within the developing countries" and urged action "to reduce the crushing disparities of opportunity."[54]

In the next two years, the emphasis shifted further, from inequality to poverty. In September 1972, McNamara suggested "the first step should be to establish specific targets, within the development plans of individual countries, for income growth among the poorest 40 per cent of the population."[55] A year later, in Nairobi, he urged that a major part of the development effort be directed at the bottom 40 percent, with the object of eradicating absolute poverty by the end of this century.[56] A year later again, in September 1974, he announced that Bank programs "will put primary emphasis not on the redistribution of income and wealth—as justified as that may be in many of our member countries—but rather on increasing the productivity of the poor, thereby providing for a more equitable sharing of the benefits of growth."[57]

The shift of emphasis from inequality to poverty in McNamara's thinking paralleled, and probably encouraged, a similar shift in the general development debate. The early demands for the"dethronement of GNP" had quite radical overtones. Dudley Seers in his 1969 address, after stating flatly that "the need is not, as is generally imagined, to accelerate economic growth—which could even be dangerous—but to change the nature of the development process," canvassed various approaches—"China and Cuba are trying"—and warned of the political difficulties of any drastic measures for the redistribution of wealth. "Those with high incomes . . . will inevitably try to find ways of maintaining privilege, resorting . . . to political violence rather than give it up."[58] Clearly, preoccupation with "Who gets the benefits?"[59] has radical implications to which only a minority among the Western development profession were ready to subscribe. It was also easier to agree on reduction of absolute than of relative poverty as a policy objective. For a situation where all sections benefit from growth, even though the rich benefit more than the poor, is not so obviously undesirable. Hence, after initially "proclaiming the necessity to sacrifice growth in order to achieve better distribution," the Sussex-ILO-Bank school and its sympathisers, on the principle that "it is only through an increase in GNP that there will be anything significant to distribute,"[60] began to advocate "redistribution with (or from) growth."

All agreed that "distribution cannot be left as a fortuitous by-product of growth but must be made a conscious and explicit element of policy."[61] The majority, however, came to favour what Singer in his later account called "incremental redistribution" because it implied "reducing poverty largely through creation of productive employment opportunities out of incremental income."[62] Rather than aim at redistribution of the existing stock of wealth—though land reform would still be needed in many developing countries—policy should seek to ensure that most of the growth in GNP would accrue to the bottom 40 percent. Such a policy would avoid the "inherent tendency [of] emphasis on GNP growth . . . to solidify and accentuate existing inequalities," yet "encounter much less political resistance" than outright redistribution.[63] This became the rationale of the "poverty-oriented strategy," with its aim of a guaranteed "minimum income" at or above some established "poverty line,"[64] which for some years dominated thinking in the McNamara-led World Bank. It was given an even more specific formulation when the ILO in 1975 launched its "basic needs" approach.

Basic Needs

The idea of a development program specifically directed at providing a minimum income for the poor had been in the air for some time. One of the first concrete proposals on these lines was published in 1962 by the Indian Planning Commission under the title "Perspective of Development, 1961–76."[65] It embodied ideas which its joint secretary, Pitambar Pant, had been developing in the preceding years. "The central concern of our planning has to be the removal of poverty as early as possible. . . . The minimum which can be guaranteed is limited by the size of the total product and the extent of redistribution which is feasible."[66] Arguing that, in a country as poor as India, poverty cannot be eliminated by redistribution, if only because "some degree of inequality of incomes . . . is an essential part of the structure of incentives in any growing economy," and that poverty reduction continues to depend on the most rapid possible growth of GNP, he suggested that it should be possible to plan for a guaranteed minimum income of Rp. 20 per month by 1975. This, he calculated, could be achieved by a 7 percent annual rate of growth of GNP and some redistribution: planning should aim at doubling per capita consumption of the bottom 20 percent, while that of the top 20 percent would increase by only 30 percent over the period.[67]

The Kenya report ten years later put forward a similar program. If half the projected 7 percent growth of GNP could be channelled to the bottom decile in the income distribution, while the income of those in the top decile was kept constant, then, allowing for population growth, the income of the poorest group could be doubled by 1985.[68] McNamara, similarly, demanded development plans aimed at income growth for the poorest 40 percent, such that their income would rise at least as fast as the national average in the next five years and significantly faster in the longer run.[69]

The idea of giving this minimum income approach the more pointed form of a "basic needs" strategy was the brainchild of Louis Emerij and others at the ILO, who in 1975 convened a World Employment Conference. "Basic needs" became the central theme of the conference document, published in 1976 under the title *Employment, Growth and Basic Needs,* and in just two or three years this theme was the subject of a very large literature.[70] Both Dudley Seers in 1969 and Mahbub ul Haq in 1971 had used the phrase "basic needs," though only in passing, when referring to the minimum bundle of goods and services that a minimum income must cover.[71] The phrase now became a slogan and a program.

The programmatic introduction to the conference document spelled out the concept. Starting out from the premise that "contrary to earlier expectations, the experience of the past two decades has shown that rapid growth of aggregate output does not by itself reduce poverty and inequality" and that "it is no longer acceptable in human terms or responsible in political terms to wait several generations for the benefits of development to trickle down until they finally reach the poorest groups," the document asked the conference to recommend "the adoption by each country of a basic-needs approach, aiming at the achievement of a certain minimum standard of living before the end of the century." For this purpose, "basic needs are defined as the minimum standard of living which a society should set for the poorest groups of its people." The standard should cover "the minimum requirements of a family for personal consumption: food, shelter, clothing," but also "access to essential services, such as safe drinking water, sanitation, transport, health and education" and an "adequately remunerated job for everyone willing to work." Finally, there should be "a healthy, humane and satisfying environment, and popular participation in the making of decisions that affect the lives and livelihood of the people and individual freedoms." To achieve these objectives, "some redirection or redistribution of investment over time, and a redistribution of the ownership or the utilisation of land" were essential. A prerequisite for overcoming political obstacles to such measures may be "the organisation of rural workers in trade unions and similar organisations." There was no reason to fear a necessary conflict between a basic-needs strategy and economic growth. "Such measures need not imply a slower growth of output. They place a greater emphasis on patterns of growth leading to a more equitable distribution of the gains from growth, and they may well lead to increasing growth rates as well."[72]

Little of substance was added to this in subsequent expositions. Some attempted to distinguish a basic-needs approach from the McNamara antipoverty approach on the ground that its target was the satisfaction of basic needs for the whole population, not merely the bottom 20 or 40 percent.[73] Not everyone agreed that there was no trade-off between basic needs and growth. A basic-needs approach, some thought, implied that "growth of output is pursued only to the extent that it is complementary to the reduction of economic and social inequalities."[74] A good deal was made of the notion that the first generation of the post-1945 development economists had expounded a theory of "trickle down" on which the basic needs approach was said to represent an intellectual advance. Since poverty in most developing countries was primarily a rural phenomenon, the basic-needs approach went hand in hand with emphasis on rural development,[75] and therefore also with decentralised administration and "community development rather than central planning."[76]

There was much discussion of the conceptual difficulties of defining basic needs, with a tendency to seek a way out by concentrating on "a core of basic needs."[77] But the temptation was great to widen the concept, both over time—"defining a standard of basic needs in absolute terms for a particular period of time but allowing for its subsequent revision upwards as national resources permit"[78]—and in scope. There were echoes of most of the issues debated in the domestic context in Western countries in the preceding years, the environment and nonrenewable resources,[79] participation, and discrimination. Singer thought it clearly right to emphasise "the social character of basic needs standards" but added a cautionary note. "There must be some question as to the extent to which it is useful to dilute this concept further by including participation, basic human rights, etc."[80]

There was also discussion of the implications of the basic-needs approach for aid, with suggestions that "a donor committed to the support of a poverty-oriented strategy of rural development" has a right to insist on appropriate performance criteria, on the one hand, and that "a basic needs approach has a promising potential for reanimating public support for development aid,"[81] on the other.

By the mid-1970s, when the basic-needs approach was conceived and popularised, the world scene had changed greatly from the days in the late 1960s, when social objectives first overshadowed economic growth in thinking about development. In the OECD countries, growth had slowed down, and stagflation, aggravated by the first oil shock, had displaced the

Vietnam War and the associated sociopolitical travails in public concern. The international economic repercussions which
severely affected many developing countries had, in turn,
made a New International Economic Order the priority issue
in the minds of most Third World spokesmen. Significantly,
by 1976, McNamara, while still referring to his many statements about the problem of absolute poverty during the preceding years, pointed out that international economic
developments now gave priority to "the problems of the
poorest countries" and the need to "recapture the momentum
of economic growth."[82] A year later, his annual address
focused on the North-South problem and on his decision to
invite Willy Brandt to head a commission on that subject.[83]

The basic-needs approach fell victim to these new preoc-
cupations. By the end of the decade, it came to be seen as a
passing phase in thinking about development, a phase which
had left an important mark on almost everyone concerned but
had certainly not achieved anything like a consensus. The
same fate befell another formulation of social objectives which
deserves a brief account before we look back on the social-
objectives chapter as a whole. This was the so-called "unified
approach" to development.

The same discontents which led Dudley Seers in 1969 to ask
questions about the meaning of development encouraged new
initiatives by D. V. McGranahan and others, who had, for
many years, first in the UN Social Affairs Department in New
York and then at UNRISD in Geneva, advocated social approaches to development and the design of development indicators better able than GNP per head to capture development
"as multi-dimensional, involving change in structure and capacity, as well as output."[84] One of these initiatives was a
meeting of experts on social policy and planning held in Stockholm in September 1969, with Gunnar Myrdal as chairman,
Benjamin Higgins as vice-chairman, and H. W. Singer as rapporteur.[85] The purpose of the meeting was "to clarify further
the role of social factors in development" and its chief result a
report which propounded the notion of a "more unified treatment" of "the development process as a complex whole."[86]

As Higgins explained in a later retrospective account, the

starting point of the unified approach was "a rejection of growth of national income as the sole objective of development planning. . . . It stressed the need to plan directly and simultaneously for all objectives of development with full cognizance of interactions and feedbacks among them."[87] "When 'development' comes to mean all elements of human life that contribute to human welfare, including nutrition, health, shelter, employment, the physical environment, the socio-cultural environment or quality of life, and such matters as participation in the decision-making process, a sense of human dignity, of belonging, etc., standard neoclassical and neo-Keynesian economics has only a limited contribution to make to development policy and planning."[88] The 1969 report was hardly less ambitious in its recommendation. "The dominance of economists among the social scientists and the earlier development and easier quantification of their concepts, has meant that certain nonmarket aspects—those unappropriately labelled 'social'—have been neglected in approaches to development."[89] "To achieve effective development planning, all planners should think in terms of all goals."[90]

ECOSOC and the General Assembly approved the experts' report and instructed the Secretariat to undertake further work on the unified approach. A research team at UNRISD, led by McGranahan, was entrusted with the task. It produced a preliminary report, a number of country studies, and yet another expert group which met, again in Stockholm, in November 1972, again including Myrdal and several other well-known names (Gamani Corea, Egbert de Vries, Ali Mazrui, Josef Pajestka, but not this time Singer) and with Higgins as rapporteur.[91] The report was not an unqualified success. As one who had been closely associated with the whole enterprise commented later, "each member of the team ended with his own 'unified approach.' "[92] As usually happens in such cases, "UA" continued for a while under its own momentum. ESCAP produced a Marxist version.[93] UNRISD, hampered by a shortage of funds, struggled to produce a final report in 1975. Meanwhile, "the 1970s saw, instead of progress toward consensus on a unified approach, a continual diversification of interpretations of development."[94] The unified approach, a complex notion, was soon superseded by the basic-needs approach, a simpler one. Basic needs, as a later director of UN-RISD noted—not, one suspects, without a trace of *Schadenfreude*—"rapidly achieved much wider acceptance in international circles, but its fall from favour after rejection by Third World governments has been equally rapid."[95]

Welfare or Modernisation

How does one account for the chapter in thinking about development which has been surveyed in the preceding pages, for what one is almost tempted to call the rise and fall of social objectives as the dominant theme in the development debate? The quick succession of formulations, from "social development" to "employment orientation," "equity," "poverty eradication," and finally "basic needs," invites Dore's sardonic reference to "the accelerating rate of slogan obsolescence."[96] No doubt, the "internal dynamics of the International Development Conference Community"[97] had something to do with it. But there can be no questioning the sincerity, indeed passionate conviction, with which Dudley Seers, Singer, McNamara, Mahbub ul Haq, and many others sought to arouse consciences about the terrible conditions in which hundreds of millions of human beings in the Third World were living and dying.

The explanation put forward by the dethroners of GNP themselves was quite straightforward. It was a case of learning from experience. The experience of the 1960s had demonstrated that even rapid economic growth does not necessarily alleviate unemployment, inequality, and poverty, and may even make them worse. "Unemployment rates and inequality," claimed Seers, had risen "by large steps" in the 1960s.[98] According to Morse, unemployment had increased "even in those developing countries which have achieved reasonable rates of economic growth"; growth has, "if anything, only increased the inequalities between the privileged few and the underprivileged masses."[99] Increases in national income, even at quite high rates, according to McNamara, "have not reached the poor to any significant extent in most developing countries";[100] Indeed, "rapid growth has been accompanied by greater maldistribution of income in many developing countries."[101] The authors of an influential statistical study of income distribution in developing countries, published in 1973, claimed that it carried "the frightening implication . . . that hundreds of millions of desperately poor people throughout the world have been hurt rather than helped by economic development."[102]

The trouble with this explanation was that the evidence on which it relied was quickly shown to be shaky or at best inconclusive. Case studies presented at the very 1970 Cambridge conference at which Morse proclaimed the dethronement of GNP had "one striking feature in common. They all seemed to show that unemployment, expressed as a percentage of the total labour force, might actually be declining."[103] In any case, as we have seen, the advocate of the employment-oriented approach quickly conceded that unemployment or even underemployment was not really the main problem; it was the poverty of the working poor. As regards trends in inequality and poverty, the data for the most part were, in the view of critics, inadequate to support firm or sweeping conclusions. But such evidence for pessimistic conclusions as was presented in the two most widely cited studies, those by Adelman and Morris and by Chenery et al., was soon subjected to devastating criticism. One reviewer concluded that the data showed neither any "significant decline in the absolute level of income, with rising per capita income, for the poorer income groups" nor any "marked relationship between income growth and changes in income shares."[104] Another concluded that "there is no evidence of large masses of people (like the lowest 60 per cent or 40 per cent or even 10 per cent) suffering from growth in any country. Even East Pakistan did better when undivided Pakistan was growing fast. Increased misery in Bangladesh has come from stagnation or decline, not growth."[105] Chenery himself conceded that "on the empirical side, the new conventional wisdom seems to be almost as misleading as the old. While in some growing economies the poor receive little or no benefit, in others the opposite is true: even the relative share of the poverty groups has increased in several notable cases."[106] At the end of the decade, a considered judgment on the still "scanty evidence" was that "where growth was very slow, in parts of South Asia and Africa, there may have been some worsening of the position of the poorest 20 to 40 per cent of the population, but this is far from proven. Where growth was rapid, all large sections of the population benefited, though some more than others."[107]

It is difficult to resist the conclusion that the dethronement of GNP among Western development economists around 1970 was less an ineluctable inference drawn from statistical evidence for the developing countries than a reflection of social crisis—alienation and rebelliousness among the young, doubts and tribulations among their elders—in the developed countries themselves. The "growing questioning of Western consumer-urban-industrial models" to which Jolly attributed the change in views about development[108] was far more obvious in the Western countries themselves than in the Third World, where it was confined in the main to Maoist or Islamic fundamentalists. As an astute Indian observer pointed out, the resurgence of interest in distributional problems among Western development economists had less to do with "development disasters" in Nigeria or Pakistan (for both of which nationalism provided as plausible an explanation as grievances about social injustice) than with the crisis of American politics and society of the mid-1960s—failure to solve traditional problems of poverty and race, questioning of the American dream that equality of opportunity through education could reduce inequalities of income and wealth, sharpening of domestic conflict over Vietnam—and the spread of this malaise from the United States to other Western countries.[109] It was no accident that in the first speech in which McNamara drew attention to poverty in the Third World he introduced the subject by referring to the poor *in the United States* and deploring the fact that, though statistically speaking their condition was improving, they were actually "growing poorer relative to the rich."[110] In an intellectual climate in which economic growth stood at an increasing discount in the West, assaulted by social critics, neo-Marxist radicals, environmentalists and Club-of-Rome prophets of doom,[111] it was an easy and natural step to "dethronement of GNP" also for the Third World.

Not unnaturally, there was a good deal of overlap in the Western literature on development between liberal (in the American sense) criticism of "neoclassical" growth-oriented development economics and the neo-Marxist and other radical criticism of imperialism, neocolonialism, and "dependency" which will be considered in the next chapter. When Seers spoke of "internal contradictions in the development process far more severe than those to which Marx drew attention"[112] and when Griffin declared, with reference to the green revolution that "technical change in agriculture is resulting in greater income inequality and a polarisation of social classes"[113] they might have been taken to belong to either camp.

The view that the shift towards social objectives of development derived mainly from Western anxieties is lent indirect support by the generally cool reception the shift had in the Third World itself. Obviously, there was concern among Third World intellectuals and politicians about their countries' vast problems of poverty—some of the earliest thorough statistical studies were by Indians about poverty in India.[114] So, as we have seen, was one of the first proposals for a guaranteed minimum income. But there was relatively little support either for ideological environmentalism—Pitambar Pant, in his paper for a preparatory meeting for the 1972 Stockholm conference said bluntly that in his country "the worst pollution is poverty"[115]—or for the successive new social "approaches" to development—employment-orientation, poverty-eradication, or basic needs.

Indian, Indonesian, Mexican, and Nigerian leaders were well aware of the need to create more productive employment opportunities, but they showed little enthusiasm for the labour-intensive industrialisation strategies recommended by Western advisers. The quip that "the clothing, footwear, canned mushroom or artificial wig pattern of the typical export success story is not every country's idea of a foundation for a modern industrial structure"[116] may have been a caricature, but it contained an important element of LDC thinking. As Jolly reported in his account of the 1976 World Employment

Conference, some LDC delegates made no secret of fear that "an unqualified emphasis on appropriate technology might forever relegate the Third World to inferior product status."[117] For similar reasons, LDC planners embraced with considerable reluctance the notion put forward and popularised by the ILO Kenya report that, both for equity and efficiency reasons, the informal or traditional sector of LDC economies should be strengthened rather than pushed aside.

Western advocacy of equity, poverty eradication, and basic-needs objectives fared little better. There was something inherently paradoxical in the Sussex-ILO-Bank admonitions to LDC governments and elites to pursue growth with redistribution. LDC administrators who attended the 1970 Cambridge conference, we are told, "did not see an appeal for a fundamental redistribution of resources as a sensible message to take back to their political masters."[118] As the Indian economist Srinivasan pointed out, major redistributions of wealth have in the past resulted only from war or foreign occupation or violent revolution. "These events are unlikely to be deliberately promoted by governments in power."[119] The Indonesian scholar Soedjatmoko, seeing "more and more donor countries jumping on the Basic Needs bandwagon," asked similarly pointed questions: "Are the donor nations prepared to accept the political consequences of such a deep intrusion on their part in the life of another people? History shows that only through foreign occupation after military defeat, or through the colonial relationship, could a foreign bureaucracy hope effectively to bring about, in such a short time, social changes which suit their own perceptions and values."[120] Performance criteria aimed at efficiency and growth had been resented; would performance criteria aimed at equity through rural development be more acceptable? "Would any developing country be prepared to accept foreign aid if it is combined with this kind of foreign presence in their rural areas?"[121]

When Soedjatmoko referred to the donors' "own perceptions and values" he touched on the most fundamental question. As a Western commentator put it, "there remain differences in values, in what different people may want for their country's future. Some may want faster progress towards modernity as they interpret it, which may include military and political power; others may lay stress on meeting basic needs. . . . Economists cannot tell people what they should want."[122] And if this assumed too readily that rulers and ruled, rich and poor, share common perceptions of "their country's future," Ronald Dore made much the same point when he asked "how far governments are receptive to egalitarian preaching anyway. What the Third World rulers actually do set as their objectives is a research topic too much neglected. I suspect that a major motive, over and above survival, is to increase national 'strength' and prestige, to raise the nation's position in the international pecking order and thereby their *own* position in the ranks of the world's rulers."[123]

Fundamentally, the reason why the basic-needs strategy was rejected by Third World spokesmen was that they considered it unlikely to promote, and possibly to impede, what to most of them were more important aspirations—modernisation at home and a New International Economic Order abroad. They tended to see "basic needs fulfillment as being at the expense of growth, at the expense, therefore, of the assertion of national strength they seek—a denial, in other words, of their quest for equality in the comity of nations"[124] and they were suspicious of Western motives in urging the strategy upon them. "Unfortunately, basic human needs as a strategy can appear as hypocrisy and bring rancor to relations between the Third World and the Western industrial powers . . . if it is taken as a substitute for the broad processes of modernisation which have brought wealth and power to the West."[125]

The quest for a New International Economic Order belongs to the next chapter. But the reference to modernisation makes this an appropriate place for comment on a contribution to the development debate which might have been expected to figure prominently in this chapter but has not yet been mentioned at all—Gunnar Myrdal's *Asian Drama.*[126]

Asian Drama was begun in Delhi in 1957 when Alva Myrdal had been appointed Swedish ambassador to India. It was published in three volumes eleven years later, in 1968. It was an encyclopedic work which, from an Indian vantage point, covered almost every conceivable aspect of development. It thus had a good deal to say about levels of living and inequality in underdeveloped countries. It acknowledged as "a major goal of planning for development in the region to raise the abysmally low levels of living for the mass of the people"[127] and that "in all the plans that spell out goals for development, the egalitarian ideology is prominent."[128] But the focus of the whole work was neither poverty nor inequality but what Myrdal called the "modernisation ideals" of India and other underdeveloped countries. As the "explicit value premises of the study," he explained, "among all the heterogeneous and conflicting valuations that exist in the countries of the region, we have deliberately selected the new ones directed toward 'modernisation.'"[129]

What Myrdal meant by "modernisation ideals" is perhaps best expressed in one of his footnotes, where he quotes from a speech by Nehru: "But we have to deal with age-old practices, ways of thought, ways of action. We have got to get out of many of these traditional ways of production, traditional ways of distribution and traditional ways of consumption. We have got to get out of all that into what might be called more modern ways of doing so. What is society in the so-called advanced countries like today? It is a scientific and technological society. It employs new techniques, whether it is in the farm or in the factory or in transport. The test of a country's advance is how far it is utilizing modern techniques. Modern technique is not a matter of just getting a tool and using it. Modern technique follows modern thinking. You can't get hold of a modern tool and have an ancient mind. It won't work."[130] Myrdal himself summed up what he conceived to be the main modernisation ideals as "national independence, national consolidation, rise of productivity, rise and redirection of consumption" and, perhaps, political democracy, though he stressed that "this ideal is not essential to a system comprising all the other modernization ideals."[131] Rising consumption and greater equality are there, but only as components of a much wider set of goals.

If there was one theme of *Asian Drama*, besides the emphasis on modernisation, which influenced thinking about development during the 1970s it was Myrdal's view of the countries of South Asia as "soft states" and his belief that "the success of planning for development requires a readiness to place obligations on people in all social strata to a much greater extent than is now done in any of the South Asian countries. It requires, in addition, rigorous enforcement of obligations, in which compulsion plays a strategic role."[132] It is arguable that Myrdal's outlook was closer to that of articulate public opinion in many Asian and other developing countries than was that of the Sussex-ILO-Bank proponents of social objectives. Certainly, development for social welfare was liable to be very different from development for modernisation.

5

Radical Counterpoint The Left

The preceding chapters have treated what might be called the *canto fermo* of thought—chiefly Western thought—about development as a policy objective for the Third World. What all these strands of thought have had in common is that their exponents broadly favoured "development," although the precise meaning given to this notion changed over time. Material progress in Adam Smith's sense formed an important component, but different authors and schools of thought attached different weight to it relative to other ends—justice, equality, freedom, national power. The ideas surveyed in the preceding chapters also had in common that, for the most part, they were, or became for a while, the conventional wisdom, at least among those who wrote about such matters.

In this chapter and the next we turn to the radical counterpoint on development, the views of those who were, one way or the other, at odds with the conventional wisdom. These radicals were not all necessarily against any kind of material progress. But they were either so preoccupied with the need to overthrow the existing inequitable social order, with revolution and redistribution, that they had little to say about the kind of development that would or should follow thereafter, or they were in varying degree sceptical about or opposed to Western-type modernisation for the less developed countries. The former version of radicalism might, for want of a more sensible terminology, be labelled Left, the latter Right. Among the former, various strands of neo-Marxism are obviously prominent. Among the latter, there is a spectrum from Western sceptics, such as Boeke and Frankel, to opponents of modernisation on religious grounds, such as Gandhi and the Ayatollah Khomeini. We begin with the Left.

From Marxism to Neo-Marxism: Paul Baran

Until World War II, Marxism had little to say about economic development in what we now call the Third World. To Marx and Lenin, as we saw in chapter 1, events in Asia and other "backward" parts of the world were of interest almost exclusively for their possible bearing on the prospects for revolution in Europe. When Marx thought about the future of these countries, he took it for granted that they would follow in the footsteps of the West, passing through capitalism to socialism. For Lenin, imperialism was important as the highest stage of *Western* capitalism—presaging its early end. For the few indigenous Marxists in the colonies, the objectives of ridding their people of capitalist exploitation and throwing off colonial oppression were still one and the same.

With the emergence of economic development as a major issue in world affairs in the postwar years, with the attainment of national independence by most of the former colonies, and with the victory of communism in China, the intellectual capital of classical European Marxism was obviously inadequate to the needs of a new generation of revolutionaries. The first to adapt Marxism to the new situation by presenting a Marxist view of the problems of the Third World was Paul Baran.

Baran was a Russian who had received his Marxist schooling in the Germany of the Weimar Republic. Ambivalent towards Soviet communism to the end of his life—he never wavered in his conviction that the Russian Revolution was the greatest victory for the side he was on, but confessed on returning from his last visit to Moscow in 1955 that "after a trip to the socialist countries only resuming life under capitalism could restore one's faith in socialism"—he found a niche and made his name as an American academic.[1] His first major contribution was an article, written in 1949 or 1950 but not published until 1952 in *The Manchester School*, with the telltale title "On the Political Economy of Backwardness."[2]

For the most part, Baran's analysis of the problems of the underdeveloped countries did not differ from that of the first generation of mainstream development economists, such as Rosenstein-Rodan, Nurkse and Singer. Like them, he deplored the fact that the "momentous expansion of productivity and welfare" yielded by nineteenth-century capitalism had been confined to Western Europe and a few countries of Western settlement and had left vast expanses and peoples of Eastern Europe, Latin America, Asia, and Africa "in the deep shadow of backwardness."[3] Like them, he saw the answer to the problem in economic growth. "The only way to provide for economic growth and to prevent a continuous deterioration in living standards is to assure a steady increase of total output (ahead of population growth)," and this required increased utilisation of underutilised resources, especially transfer of agricultural surplus labour to industrial pursuits, and economic planning to overcome the obstacles to private investment presented by lack of external economies.[4] Where he differed from the mainstream economists was in introducing into this analysis Marxist *political* economy.

"The crucial fact rendering the realization of a development programme illusory is the political and social structure of the governments in power."[5] The intrusion of capitalism into backward feudal societies did not produce capitalist development. "What resulted was an economic and political amalgam combining the worst features of both worlds—feudalism and capitalism—and blocked effectively all possibilities of economic growth."[6] The establishment of capitalist institutions was beyond the reach of the tiny middle class. The fledgling bourgeoisie in the underdeveloped countries sought nothing but accommodation with the existing order, through deals with feudal landlords or powerful foreign investors. In these circumstances, none of the policies proposed by mainstream development economists could achieve anything. The injection of planning into a society living in the twilight between capitalism and feudalism could but result in additional corruption.[7] Foreign aid was liable to do more harm than good.[8] What was needed—the McCarthyist atmosphere of the time made it inadvisable to advocate a socialist revolution openly— was "social collectivism." "The transition may be abrupt and painful."[9]

A year after the publication of the article, Baran gave a series of lectures at Oxford, which, in revised form, became *The Polit-*

ical Economy of Growth, first published by the *Monthly Review,* the Marxist journal established in 1949 and edited by Baran's friend Paul Sweezy.[10] The first book by a Marxist author to focus largely on the problems of underdevelopment,[11] it became enormously influential. Baran was happy to see "PEOGraphy" adopted as a distinct branch of Marxist theory.[12]

In the main, the book, like the earlier article, was a combination of current development economics with current communist doctrine. Baran had no doubts about the "absolute desirability of economic development," defined, synonymously with economic growth, as "an increase over time in per capita output of material goods."[13] Like Marx, he looked forward to "ever-increasing rational domination by man of the inexhaustible forces of nature,"[14] but he insisted on "the incompatibility of sustained economic growth with the capitalist system. . . . Socialist economic planning represents the only rational solution of the problem"[15] He still argued for industrialisation along Rosenstein-Rodan's lines, but now with much more emphasis on the Soviet model. "The military performance of the Soviet Union during the war and the rapid recovery of the war-ravaged economy provided the final proof of the strength and vitality of a socialist society." Guided by the same Soviet model, he saw no future in peasant agriculture; "mechanisation is the answer . . . modern machinery . . . under conditions of large-scale farming."[16]

There are, however, even in the first edition of the book, traces of a theme which was to become much more prominent in the radical left literature of the 1960s, traces which provide some justification for the view that Baran "can truly be called the founding father of neo-Marxism."[17] Like Marx, he still saw the problem of underdevelopment as a problem of backwardness. But unlike Marx, he no longer saw capitalism as a stage in the process of development. On the contrary, "the capitalist system, once a mighty engine of economic development, has turned into a no less formidable hurdle to human advancement."[18] The reason is that "economic development of underdeveloped countries is profoundly inimical to the dominant interests in the advanced capitalist countries."[19]

Drawing on Lenin's theory of imperialism, but with the spotlight now on the victims rather than the beneficiaries, he argued that "the backward world has always represented the indispensable hinterland of the highly developed capitalist West," as the source of raw materials, vast profits, and investment outlets.[20] Naturally, these dominant interests are bitterly opposed to the industrialisation of their "source countries."[21] Development aid by the West is a ruse, "expected to *lessen* popular pressure for industrialisation, to weaken the movement for economic and social progress."[22] Even the notion of neocolonialism (though not the word) made what may have been its first appearance: after attainment of independence, American imperialism imposes its control through "economic infiltration."[23] Japan achieved economic development *because*, lacking raw materials or a market for foreign manufactures, it "had no attractions to imperialism."[24] Something close to the essential thesis of neo-Marxism appeared in the statement that "the role of monopoly capitalism and imperialism in the advanced countries and economic and social backwardness in the underdeveloped countries are intimately related, represent merely different aspects of what is in reality a global problem."[25]

But Baran only hinted at the idea. Even the long foreword he wrote to a second edition of the book in 1962, under the impact of a decade of Maoism in China, of Khrushchev's condemnation of Stalinism, and of Castro's revolution in Cuba, did not develop this theme further. Neo-Marxism in this sense, though perhaps conceived at Stanford and subsequently nurtured at other American campuses, was of Latin American descent.

Neo-Marxism: Latin American Antecedents

In most of Asia and Africa, hope for a better future rested in the early postwar years on decolonisation, the attainment of national independence. In Latin America, any notion that it merely needed liberation from colonial domination for backwardness to give way to economic development was refuted by historical experience. Most of the countries of Latin America had been independent for at least a century, yet the great majority of their people remained in poverty. Indeed, by almost any yardstick, economic development in Latin America seemed in the last few decades to have fallen further behind Europe, North America, and Oceania. To radical intellectuals concerned with Latin America, neither Marx's conception of capitalism as a necessary first stage of development from feudalism nor even Baran's view of capitalism as an obstacle to emergence of these countries from underdevelopment sounded convincing. Neo-Marxism was a reformulation of Marxism to fit the Latin American case, and it drew on ideas developed in Latin America, chiefly by a group of economists around Prebisch at ECLA, the United Nations Economic Commission for Latin America, at Santiago in the 1950s. The two chief ingredients were what came to be known as the theories of *dependency* and *structuralism*.

Dependency

I noted in an earlier chapter Prebisch's "centre-periphery" interpretation of the world economy.[26] Few mainstream development economists would have disagreed, except perhaps in emphasis, with his statement that growth in the West "had left untouched the vast peripheral area" or with his complaint that the benefits of capitalist economic growth had been very unevenly shared between the developed "centre" and the underdeveloped "periphery," though most of them were sceptical about his theory of a secular decline in the terms of trade for primary products as a major cause. The first to translate this interpretation into a theory of "dependency" appears to have been the Brazilian economist Celso Furtado, in his historical study of *The Economic Growth of Brazil* (1957).[27] Here, and in subsequent elaboration, he defined the relationship between the centre and the periphery as one not merely of unequal sharing of the benefits of development but of dependence involving domination and economic exploitation. He saw as the chief mechanism of dependence what Nurkse and others had called the "demonstration" effect whereby the way of life of a small minority in the peripheral countries is modernised through transplantation of Western consumption patterns, while transnational corporations control access to modern technology. The result is "peripheral capitalism, a capitalism unable to generate innovations and dependent for transformation upon decisions from the outside. I call external dependence the structural situation in which such peripheral capitalism prevails in certain countries."[28]

The best known, and sharpest, formulation of the ECLA dependency theory was presented some years later by the Chilean economist Osvaldo Sunkel. Sunkel was not a conventional Marxist. In his earliest statement of the doctrine, he rejected both dependency and "the false option of socialist revolution" in favour of "authentically national development" which would "concentrate on basic productive sectors (steel, petrochemicals, etc.) . . . under multinational Latin American control."[29] But his disagreement was with "the classical Marxist approach," which had "restricted itself mainly to the role of international monopoly capitalism," neglecting its effects on the peripheral countries,[30] and his own view came close to this later neo-Marxist position.

The historical evolution of international capitalism, he argued, and "basic structural elements" of the system, have given rise to underdevelopment.[31] "It is postulated that underdevelopment is part and parcel of this historical process of global development of the international system, and therefore, that underdevelopment and development are simply the two faces of one single universal process. . . . The evolution of this global system of underdevelopment-development has, over a period of time, given rise to two great polarizations: First, a polarization of the world between countries, . . . the developed, industrialized, advanced 'central northern' ones . . . and the undeveloped, poor, dependent, and 'peripheral southern' ones. . . . Second, a polarization within countries, between advanced and modern groups, regions and activities, and backward, primitive, marginal and dependent groups, regions and activities."[32]

Dependency as the key problem of underdevelopment, at least in Latin America, was taken up and adumbrated by many others who were not Marxists or advocates of revolution. It served well to express both the frustration felt by Latin American intellectuals about the failure of capitalism in Latin America to match its achievements in Europe and North America and the resentment of the overwhelming power and presence of the United States. While Prebisch had focused chiefly on dependence through trade, especially the vulnerability of countries exporting primary products, the dependency theorists from Furtado and Sunkel on, after a decade of efforts to promote development by industrialisation based on import substitution, focused on the role of multinationals in production for the domestic market in the most advanced countries of Latin America—Brazil, Chile, Argentina, and Mexico.

Structuralism

In an economic sense structuralism has been described as a view of the world as inflexible. "In economic terms, the supply of most things is inelastic."[33]

In the nineteenth century and well into the twentieth, socialists and other critics of capitalism had condemned it chiefly on two grounds. First, that it was unjust and exploitative. Second, that it was unstable, prone to crises, and doomed to collapse. Rarely, if ever, had capitalism been criticised on the ground that it was inefficient, that its quintessential mechanism, of market forces operating through the price system, failed to work. This third line of criticism, which may be called the doctrine of market failure, was developed, chiefly in Britain, in the 1930s and 1940s.[34]

The classical and neoclassical thesis according to which market forces operating through the price mechanism can be expected to assure an optimum allocation of resources, statically and dynamically, was open to attack at three points. First, prices may give the wrong signals because they are distorted by monopoly or externalities. Second, labour and other factors may respond to price signals inadequately or even perversely. Third, although ready to respond appropriately to correct price signals, factors of production may be immobile, unable to move quickly if at all. It was this third leg of the "market failure" tripod that came to be called structuralism. Criticism of the working of the price system was initially directed at the first, the signalling, component. Major contributions were Pigou's systematic examination in *The Economics of Welfare* (1920) of external economies and diseconomies which give rise to divergences between private and social marginal net product; criticism of the assumption of perfect competition by Sraffa, Chamberlin, Joan Robinson, and others, which demonstrated that price signals are in practice likely to be distorted by imperfections, monopolistic or oligopolistc; and, most influential of all, Keynes's *General Theory*, which was also an attack on the signalling component since it rested fundamentally on a critique of the classical postulate of price flexibility in the capital and labour markets.[35] In the 1940s, Rosenstein-Rodan combined the Pigovian and Keynesian critique into an argument that economic development of less developed countries could not be left to market forces but had to be planned.

Criticism of the second aspect of the price system, the response component, remained subdued in relation to developed countries, although attacks on the model of economic man are as old as the model itself.[36] Such criticism played a key role in Western thought about economic development, in theories of economic dualism from Boeke onwards, the view that people in traditional societies do not respond to economic incentives, or respond perversely (backward-sloping supply curves).[37] But this line of criticism, of its nature, appealed to conservative sceptics about development rather than to socialist and other radical critics of capitalism.

Criticism of the third aspect, the mobility component, emerged in the 1930s and early 1940s as part of a more general and direct questioning of the efficacy of the price system. A series of studies by Oxford economists, later collected in a volume of *Oxford Studies in the Price Mechanism*, threw doubt on the interest-elasticity of investment, the efficacy of the exchange rate as an instrument of balance of payments adjustment, and on the mobility of labour.[38] An economic history of the interwar period, written under the influence of Rosenstein-Rodan, contains what may have been the first full exposition of what later came to be called structuralist doctrine. "Given the large maladjustments in the balances of payments and economic structure of different countries which the [first world] war had left behind, . . . their correction by means of adjustments in price/income levels had become impracticable or intolerable as a result of greatly increased rigidity in the cost and price structure of the advanced capitalist economies; . . . ultimately owing to the immobility of resources, market forces could not or—for good reasons—were not allowed to effect the necessary adjustments."[39]

A similar outlook inspired the work, during and after the war, of a group at the Oxford Institute of Statistics around the Polish economist Michal Kalecki, who from a Marxist starting point had in important respects anticipated Keynes's *General Theory*. At various times, the group included T. Balogh, E. F. Schumacher, and Dudley Seers and was in close contact with Rosenstein-Rodan, H. D. Henderson, and Kaldor (who after the war for a time joined Myrdal in Geneva, as director of the Research Division of the UN Economic Commission for Europe). All of these were prominent in the debate on planning and direct controls which took place as Britain emerged from the controlled war economy.[40]

They were also among the pioneers of development economics. Most, though not all,[41] of the first generation of development economists shared a broadly structuralist outlook, in the sense of scepticism about the efficacy of the price mechanism and a conviction that government planning and controls must make up for "market failure." Some, such as Rosenstein-Rodan and Scitovsky, emphasised the inadequacy of prices as a guide to investment decisions. Others, such as Myrdal and Singer, stressed what they believed to be the unacceptable social costs of the free play of market forces, especially its effects in aggravating inequality, nationally and internationally. All agreed that for various reasons all three components of the price mechanism work even less well in underdeveloped than in developed countries and that neoclassical economic theory was therefore largely inapplicable to

LDCs. Myrdal, in *Economic Theory and Underdeveloped Regions*, put this view in his usual *pour épater les bourgeois* manner: "In the less well integrated countries . . . where the state allows freer play to 'natural' forces and has, in fact, because of the general poverty so much less scope for policy interference— even short-term changes are continuously liable to start a development towards some sort of public disaster."[42]

In the late 1950s, structuralism in this broad sense gave rise to a specific structuralist theory of inflation in Latin America. The essence of this "structuralist," as against "monetarist," view of inflation was that "inflation is a natural accompaniment of growth; inflation cannot be curbed through monetary and fiscal means without provoking unemployment or stagnation of growth because of supply rigidities; the instability of export proceeds, generating a capacity-to-import bottleneck, as well as supply inelasticities inherent in the growth process, renders it impossible to curb inflation in the short run."[43]

The structuralist theory of inflation, like the dependency theory, was homemade in Latin America, chiefly by the ECLA group of economists assembled by Prebisch at Santiago. But, unlike the dependency theory, it owed a good deal to the structuralist economists in Britain, both through their influence on the general climate of opinion and through direct contact.

Chief credit for formulating the Latin American structuralist theory of inflation belongs to a Mexican economist and a Chilean one. Juan Noyola in 1956 published an article in which he argued that inflation is not a monetary phenomenon but the result of interaction between the two factors, "basic inflationary pressures" due to structural rigidities and the "propagating mechanism" of competing income claims.[44] In 1958 the Chilean economist Osvaldo Sunkel developed the idea. He stated the central proposition concisely: "Basic Inflationary Pressures. These are fundamentally governed by the structural limitations, rigidity or inflexibility of the economic system. In fact, the inelasticity of some productive sectors to adjust to changes in demand—or, in short, the lack of mobility of productive resources and the defective functioning of the price system—are chiefly responsible for structural inflationary disequilibrium."[45]

Both Noyola and Sunkel cited as their authority for the structuralist explanation an article by Kalecki published in Mexico in 1955 on the basis of lectures he had given there two years earlier. Sunkel developed his ideas while Kaldor and Chenery were visiting ECLA. The former was working on a paper on Chile's economic problems in which he further elaborated Kalecki's argument that inelastic supply of food had been a major factor causing inflation. Chenery expounded a general structuralist view in his advocacy of the use of input-output analysis and linear programming for investment planning in developing countries: "A central problem in development policy is the adequacy of free market forces in allocating investment resources. . . . Three kinds of defect in the free price mechanism . . . combine to produce a rigid market structure. . . . Serious structural disequilibrium in the use of labour, natural resources and foreign exchange" represents one of the situations requiring state intervention in investment decisions.[46] In the following years ECLA structuralist thinking received further reinforcement through visits to Santiago by Balogh and Seers.[47]

ECLA thinking about dependency and structuralism, though clearly antimarket and near-socialist in its implications, was still a long way from revolutionary Marxism and soon came under attack from more radical contemporaries. "In spite of their critical nature, ECLA economic theories and critiques were not based on analysis of social process, did not call attention to the imperialist relationship among countries, and did not take into account the asymmetric relations between classes."[48] Or, as another neo-Marxist put it more bluntly somewhat later, "the ECLA bureaucrats, however radical in the UN context, were divorced from the mass of the Latin American poor. Not surprisingly, ECLA managed to avoid the realities of the class struggle in Latin America and the role of the USA in that struggle."[49] The writer who did most to build a neo-Marxist edifice on ECLA foundations, through a "synthesis of ECLA structuralism and Marxism,"[50] was A. G. Frank.

Neo-Marxism: A. G. Frank

Andre Gunder Frank, like Paul Baran, came to the United States from Europe, but as a boy. He studied at the University of Chicago and like many others was caught up in the campus revolt of the mid-1960s, stirred by the events in Vietnam. After Khrushchev's denunciation of Stalin, and after Hungary and Czechoslovakia, the Soviet model had lost much of its appeal to young radicals. They were attracted by the image of Ho Chi Minh, by Mao's Great Cultural Revolution and, especially in the United States, by the nearby Cuban Revolution and the rhetoric of Fidel Castro. "Without Fidel Castro, Frank would have been impossible."[51]

In the very first sentence of the preface to his first major work, historical studies of development in Chile and Brazil, which were published in 1967 under the title *Capitalism and Underdevelopment in Latin America,* he stated his main thesis: "It is capitalism, world and national, which produced under-development in the past and which still generates under-development in the present."[52] Although he claimed to hold this view "with Paul Baran,"[53] it was really quite new. Baran had merely suggested an intimate relation between imperialism and underdevelopment. Frank, in striking contrast to Marx's view that capitalism was a necessary stage in lifting the underdeveloped world out of its backwardness and even to Baran's main view that capitalism constituted an obstacle to this process, maintained that underdevelopment was *caused by* capitalism.

In part, Frank's thesis rested on Lenin's theory of imperialism, with its implication that economic development in the metropolitan capitalist countries took place at the expense of the underdeveloped colonies, through expropriation of the latter's surplus. "The metropolis expropriates economic surplus from its satellites and appropriates it for its own economic development. The satellites remain underdeveloped for lack of access to their own surplus and as a consequence of the same polarization and exploitative contradictions which the metropolis introduces and maintains in the satellite's domestic economic structure. The combination of these contradictions, once firmly implanted, reinforces the process of development in the increasingly dominant metropolis and underdevelopment in the ever more dependent satellites until they are resolved through the abandonment of capitalism by one or both interdependent parts."[54]

But when Frank added that "economic development and underdevelopment are the opposite faces of the same coin"[55] he went much further than Lenin. It was, he claimed, only because of the intrusion of capitalism that the countries of South America experienced underdevelopment. "Because of capitalism, Chile's economy was already underdeveloping throughout the three centuries before independence."[56] Frank gave "underdevelopment" a transitive meaning: "I underdevelop you."[57] As another historian of Latin America with a similar outlook, Keith Griffin, explained: "Rostow's theory [of stages of economic growth, like Marx's] attributes a history to the developed countries but denies all history to the underdeveloped ones. . . . To classify these countries as 'traditional societies' begs the issue. . . . The history of the underdeveloped countries in the last five centuries is, in large part, the history of the consequences of European expansion. . . . The automatic functioning of the international economy which Europe dominated first created underdevelopment and then hindered efforts to escape from it."[58]

Griffin tried to generalise the idea to other parts of the Third World, citing a historian of Indonesia who claimed that the more observant of the Dutch merchants who came to the East Indies in the sixteenth century "had recognized that southern and eastern Asia were far ahead of western Europe in riches as well as in commercial ability" and were inferior only in military and navigational technology.[59] But the thesis that underdevelopment was caused by capitalism derived what plausibility it had from Latin American history and politics.

If there was something naively romantic about the notion that Aztec Mexico and Inca Peru before the arrival of the Spaniard were more "developed" than their twentieth-century successor societies, it was certainly true that, in the wake of the European expansion, "the indigenous societies were destroyed," frequently resulting in "a decline in the welfare of the subjugated people."[60] It was also true that, in contrast to most of Asia and Africa, where capitalist development remained peripheral to still predominantly precapitalist social and economic systems and where at least until World War II national independence movements united the politically articulate from all strata, "most of Latin America had been thoroughly incorporated into world capitalism. Hence it made no sense to speak of feudal, 'semi-feudal' or 'archaic' elements in Latin American society—elements which would give meaning to the idea of a 'bourgeois-democratic' revolution."[61] In Latin America the attainment of national independence had conspicuously failed to usher in a classless society or, with a few exceptions, a democratic polity. The local middle class had been inclined to take French culture rather than British or American business enterprise as its model. The national bourgeoisie which in Asia had been championed by Lenin as a potential ally against imperialism was dismissed by Frank, in the Latin American context, as a *Lumpenbourgeoisie*,[62] "incapable of carrying out the progressive role of the European bourgeoisie,"[63] subservient *comprador* members of an international coalition of owning classes.

The integration of Latin America into the international market economy had tended to exacerbate domestic inequalities and to strengthen trade and investment links which could easily be seen as involving dependence on the American colossus and its transnational corporations. In these conditions, the neo-Marxist interpretation fell on fertile ground—not least because "for half a century Latin American universities had been mass-producing an intellectual proletariat, larger than the opportunities for their employment in the law, journalism, literature, or other congenial professions."[64]

In the decade following the campus revolt, Frank's neo-Marxist doctrine came to dominate the radical literature in Western countries, widely taught and studied at Western universities and adumbrated in books, journals, magazines, and conference proceedings. It continued to be popular among Latin American intellectuals without giving rise to any major new ideas, but hardly evoked an echo in the rest of the Third World, in Africa, the Middle East, or south and east Asia.[65]

One of the few exceptions was the Senegalese, Samir Amin, who, in two books initially published in French in the early 1970s, applied the Latin American concepts of peripheral capitalism and dependence to West Africa and extended Prebisch's "terms of trade" thesis by drawing on the ideas of the sociologist Emmanuel (Greek but also francophone) on "unequal exchange."[66]

Whereas Prebisch had merely argued that the developing countries are adversely affected by a secular downward trend in the commodity terms of trade for primary products, Emmanuel put forward the proposition that all international trade between developed and developing countries constitutes "unequal exchange" (and is therefore presumably unjust) because it involves exchange at equal market values of goods embodying unequal amounts of current labour. As Amin recognised, "this inequality reflects the inequality in productivity."[67] But he failed to add the corollary that, given this inequality of labour productivity, the less developed countries can trade at all only because their wage levels tend to be proportionately lower.[68] Like most neo-Marxists, he saw the remedy not so much in development, which would gradually raise levels of labour productivity and real wages in the developing countries, but in "liberation of the periphery" through socialist revolution, for "complete socialism will necessarily be based on a modern economy with high productivity."[69]

An incidental but not unimportant by-product of the neo-Marxist definition of underdevelopment was that it provided much better intellectual support than the classical Marxist concept of backwardness for the consistent refusal of the Soviet Union to acknowledge any responsibility, whether through aid or trade, towards the countries of the Third World, on the ground that their economic problems were the consequence of Western colonialism (in which Russia of course had no part).

Neo-Marxism on "Development"

Compared to their strong and original views about *underdevelopment*, the neo-Marxists of the 1960s and 1970s had relatively little to say about development. There were at least two obvious reasons for this, both rooted in classical Marxism.

One was the preoccupation with distributive shares, implicit in the concept of economic surplus. In Marx's magnificent dynamics, economic surplus had played a key role as part of the mechanism of historical change, both as the substance of the class struggle and as the source of capital accumulation, and neo-Marxists continued to argue in the abstract that "control of this economic surplus determines the nature of the development process."[70] But in practice their overriding concern with what they saw as the exploitative, zero-sum-game character of capitalism, internationally and nationally, diverted their attention from analysis of economic development and from policies that might help promote it.

A second, related reason was that their prime objective was the revolutionary overthrow of the existing social order. When Baran put forward the seemingly paradoxical view that "development [is] inevitably a revolutionary and not an evolutionary process,"[71] he was echoing Marx's dialectical materialism. But the practical implication appeared to be that no development was possible until capitalist institutions were swept away and the expropriators expropriated; and if this was so, there was little point in worrying very much about the precise forms that postrevolutionary development might or should take.

For revolutionary activists, as for Lenin a generation earlier, the first task was to gain power. The question "What is to be done after the revolution?"[72] had to wait. The nearest Baran came to addressing the question in *The Political Economy of Growth* was in the final peroration in which he predicted a glorious future for the underdeveloped countries under socialism: "Drawing its energies from the immeasurable sources of free people, it will not only irrevocably conquer hunger, disease and obscurantism, but in the very process of its victorious advance will radically recreate man's intellectual and psychic structure."[73]

Of course, few of those who contributed to neo-Marxist thought were themselves revolutionary activists. The great majority were intellectuals, mostly academics and students, at American and other universities. During the 1970s, some of them borrowed suitable ideas from the mainstream debate on economic development which was discussed in the last chapter. "Small is beautiful" made little appeal, even as the Soviet model began to lose its glamour, and "intermediate technology" owed too much to neoclassical trade theory to be attractive. Most neo-Marxists also continued to follow the official Soviet line in deriding mainstream development economists' concern with population control—"screaming the horrors of overpopulation."[74] But the Club of Rome message could be adapted—"imperialism uses up resources so that by the end of the century irreplaceable fossil fuels and other mineral resources will largely be extinct"[75]—and some went so far as to demand deindustrialisation of the West: "Marxism is being asked in the twentieth century to preside over the deindustrialisation of part of the globe and the rural-based ecologically evolutionary development of the rest. Those who insist that such a process has nothing to do with Marxism merely ensure that what they choose to call Marxism will have nothing to do with what happens in the world."[76] But such ideas did not survive long among neo-Marxists any more than they did on all but the fringe of mainstream thinking about development.

There were also echoes of the distinction between "growth" and "development." But the strongest neo-Marxist statement on this issue, by Samir Amin, was mainly concerned to advocate a transition from "growth stimulated from abroad to internally generated and self-financing growth."[77] In the West African context, he thought, neocolonialism was continuing "the distortion toward export activities (extraversion) which . . . does not result from 'inadequacy of the home-market' but from the superior productivity of the center in all fields which compels the periphery to confine itself to the role of complementary supplier of products for the production of which it possesses a natural advantage: exotic agricultural produce and minerals."[78] There was already implicit in this a notion, which had a brief vogue a few years later, the notion that development requires the "breaking of links with the world economy."[79]

Once again, it was Dudley Seers, who, in an article published in 1977, sought to define "the new meaning of development."[80] In an analysis which owed a good deal to Latin-American neo-Marxist thinking, he cited radical critics who reject "redistribution with growth" as politically impractical: "Why should those with economic and political power give it away, as these policies require? . . . Social progress will be indefinitely prevented by a homogeneous ruling class until it is in due course overthrown in a revolution."[81] Instead of advocating revolution, Seers advocated breaking the "external links" to which he attributed many of the difficulties of domestic redistribution. Time was ripe, he declared, for another critical look at the meaning of development. "The element to add . . . is self-reliance."[82] On the economic side, this meant "reducing dependence on imported necessities, especially basic foods, petroleum and its products, capital equipment and expertise." Policies would be needed to change life-styles "using taxes, price policies, advertising and perhaps rationing." There was also a need to reduce "cultural dependencies on one or more of the great powers," e.g., by raising the proportion of higher degrees obtained at home.[83] The objective is not necessarily autarky. How far to go depends on each country's circumstances. The key to the new development strategy was "not to break all links, which would almost anywhere be socially damaging and politically unworkable, but to adopt a *selective* approach to external influences of all types."[84]

Most surprising at first sight, for someone so close to neo-Marxism, was Seers's "explicit endorsement of nationalism—which ceases to be an 'obstacle' to development and becomes instead part of the very essence of it."[85] But this, too, reflects Latin American ideology. Seers, in fact, at this stage of his thinking, stood somewhere between what have been called the two Latin American currents in the "alternative" approach—alternative that is, to the neoclassical approach of liberal mainstream development economics. One of these was represented by neo-Marxists, the other by the ECLA neo-corporatists—"neo" because, despite affinities, the Latin American variant differed from the European corporatism of the 1930s, which evolved into fascism.[86] "Corporatists 'deny the inevitability of class struggle.' It is not the capitalist class or the capitalist system that lies at the heart of underdevelopment in the periphery, but the way the international structure of that system has affected national development."[87] Clearly, there was in Latin America a spectrum from Peronist-type populism, which had much resemblance to the fascism of Mussolini or Franco, via ECLA "corporatism" to various strands of neo-Marxism, all united in their rejection of liberalism and neo-classical economics and in their conviction that the existing international order was to blame for the problems of underdevelopment.

Somewhere near the neo-Marxist end of this spectrum was another, also predominantly Latin American, strand of thought about development, often referred to as "liberation theology," mainly because, as its best-known exponent, Denis Goulet, explained, its ideas "made their greatest inroads in religious writings on development: papal encyclicals, documents issued by the World Council of Churches and the Pontifical Commission on Justice and Peace."[88] Priests, working among the poor in Catholic countries in Latin America or in the Philippines, often found themselves thinking on much the same lines as Marxist guerillas, and neo-Marxist ideas profoundly influenced official church pronouncements on development.

Goulet followed a Peruvian theologian, Gutierrez, in rejecting the term "development" in favour of "liberation." " 'Development,' although frequently used to describe various change processes, stresses the benefits said to result from these: material prosperity, higher production and expanded consumption, better housing and medical services, wider educational opportunities and employment mobility and so on." But " 'development' does not evoke asymmetrical power relations operative in the world or the inability of evolutionary change models to lead, in many countries, to the desired objectives." By contrast, " 'liberation' implies the suppression of elitism by a populace which assumes control over its own change processes." Liberationists stress ethical values. "Although all men must surely have enough goods in order to be more human, they say, development is simply a means to the human ascent."[89]

Another member of the same school, a former parish priest in Puerto Rico, Ivan Illich, went even further, denouncing the fraud perpetrated by UNESCO and others in arousing false expectations among the Latin American poor through the spread of primary education. "Underdevelopment as a state of mind occurs when mass needs are converted to the demand for new brands of packaged solutions which are forever beyond the reach of the majority. . . . The fraud perpetrated by the salesmen of schools is less obvious but much more fundamental than the self-satisfied salesmanship of the Coca-Cola or Ford representative, because the schoolman hooks his people on a much more demanding drug."[90]

Such extreme views probably commanded few followers. But the liberationists shared with more conventional neo-Marxists, and indeed with radical left writers on development who in the late 1960s and 1970s filled thousands of pages of books and booklets, the belief that there was, somewhere, a better path to development than that advocated by mainstream development economists, promoted by international agencies, or followed by most LDC governments. Goulet expressed this consensus when he said that "revolutionary Latin Americans resist this kind of development. They look instead to China, Cuba and Tanzania as examples of success."[91] Sometimes Vietnam was added to this list. But it was "China's path of development" that evoked most interest and enthusiasm.

Mao and Maoism

When Mao Tse-tung led communism to victory in China in 1949, his objectives were not, initially, very different from those of Lenin and Stalin in Russia. China, it is true, conformed even less than Russia to Marx's conception of a society attaining socialism after passing through a stage of industrial capitalism. Even more than Lenin's, Mao's was a "Communist-led revolution based on nationalism and agrarian discontent."[92] For some years before 1949, Mao, cautioned by Lenin's experience, had planned "to lead China in the direction of socialism, though capitalism will still be enabled to grow to an appropriate extent for a fairly long period."[93] After the seizure of power in 1949, landowners were expropriated and urban private enterprise was gradually nationalised, but, as the American radical economist J. G. Gurley has pointed out, Mao did not wait for the socialist revolution to be completed before "embarking on an enormous industrialisation effort. . . . Aside from its important military implications, heavy industry would be required if agriculture . . . was to be transformed into a modern sector, . . . with the infusion of modern inputs, such as electric power, machinery and tractors,"[94] and supported by massive Soviet assistance in the form of experts and capital equipment. Throughout the 1950s, there was little in Mao's thinking to differentiate it from orthodox Marxist-Leninism. As late as 1958, he would say, wholly in the spirit of Marx, that "the more [men] increase their power in the combat with nature, the more they freely command as by magic the latent productive forces, making them appear everywhere and develop rapidly";[95] and his sudden decision in that year to embark on the Great Leap Forward appears to have been motivated by the belief that "China would perhaps not need so much time as hitherto to catch up with the most advanced industrial countries."[96]

All this, however, is not what the world has come to associate with Maoism. Mao's "passionate desire to transform man, with its curious mixture of humanitarian and totalitarian motives,"[97] came to the fore in the early 1960s, when, after the disaster of the Great Leap Forward, aggravated by natural calamities and the withdrawal of Soviet aid, the leadership under Liu Shao-chi set China on a course which Mao feared would restore traditional bureaucratic and managerial class relationships—"taking the capitalist road." In unleashing the Great Proletarian Cultural Revolution upon China, Mao's primary objective undoubtedly was to complete the revolution as he conceived it. After the political and economic stages had been carried out, there remained, in C. P. Fitzgerald's paraphrase, "a further stage; the government had been changed and the economy transformed, but the Chinese themselves, their thoughts, their tastes, their outlook on life and their personal hopes and ambitions, remained largely unaltered. The last step was to be a cultural revolution, whereby these characteristics were to be remodelled, culminating in genuine socialists to whom the way of life and thought of his ancestors would be as alien as those, for example, of the pagan world to the Christian era which followed it."[98]

In the following years, Mao's resolve "to carry the revolution into the superstructure"[99] developed into a gigantic social experiment in "mobilising collective energies."[100] Incessant exhortation gave Mao's instructions, in the words of two Western sympathisers, "a hypnotic, even magical, character."[101] In an effort to replace material by moral incentives, financial rewards, such as bonuses and piecework, were abolished. Egalitarian zeal found expression in the abolition of ranks and insignia in the armed forces. Millions of young Red Guards, carrying the little red books of Mao's thoughts, rampaged through the country. A large proportion of the country's intelligentsia—party cadres, officials, and academics—were removed from their posts, often publicly humiliated and rusticated. Confucian books were burned, libraries ransacked, works of art of earlier centuries destroyed. Somewhere between eight and fifteen million young people were sent from the cities to work as agricultural labourers in communes, in what has been called "the largest forced transfer of population any government has tried since Stalin's mass deportations."[102]

As Mao's health gave way and power slipped from his hands, first the army and later a more pragmatic leadership under Teng Hsiao-p'ing took control, overcame the left-wing "Gang of Four," and gradually restored order. Denouncing the Great Leap Forward and the Great Cultural Revolution as enormous mistakes, the new leaders during the 1970s and early 1980s reversed course, restoring economic incentives in agriculture and industry and embarking on a more market- and export-oriented development strategy.

All through the 1960s and for some years into the 1970s,

"Maoism" exerted a powerful appeal among Western left-wing intellectuals, young and old. In the immediate aftermath of the Great Cultural Revolution, an Oxford historian had no hesitation in calling Mao "by far the greatest man in the world today—probably the greatest of this century,"[103] while a Cambridge economist, speaking of the less developed countries, thought that China was "one (perhaps the only one) where development is really going on."[104]

The appeal of "Maoism" was manifold. "For the young it's idealism; for the middle-aged nostalgia; for the worried an alternative lifestyle."[105] To young radicals in the West, the Cultural Revolution appealed as "an outbreak of revolutionary romanticism."[106] Many were repelled by the Soviet Union, where, it seemed, "a privileged group now holds power and seeks to perpetuate it by destroying revolutionary spirit and developing another self-interest and the consumer society."[107] The notion of a peasant revolution evoked echoes of Rousseau and Thoreau. "In peasant societies, revolution, followed by the construction of socialist values, is at least possible (even if Marx doubted it). This vision is Mao's contribution, and it helps to explain why leadership of the world socialist movement is passing in part from the Soviet Union to China and other peasant societies."[108] Middle-class puritans at odds with Western consumerism and materialism were attracted by "the moral element in Chinese socialism."[109] "Maoists deemphasize material incentives, for they are the very manifestation of a selfish, bourgeois society. . . . Maoists believe that each person should be devoted to 'the masses,' . . . should serve the world proletariat. . . . A selfish person is not an admirable person."[110] Maoism meant doing away with all the distasteful features of contemporary approaches to development in the Third World. "Maoists believe that economic development can best be promoted by breaking down specialization, by dismantling bureaucracies, and the undermining of centralising and divisive tendencies that give rise to experts, technicians, authorities and bureaucrats remote from or manipulating 'the masses.' . . . Maoists seem perfectly willing to pursue the goal of transforming man even though it is temporarily at the expense of some economic growth."[111]

Maoism was a phase in Western radicalism. The Great Cultural Revolution coincided with the Vietnam War and the student revolt on Western campuses. As D. S. Zagoria pointed out in his judicious summing up of Mao's achievements and failures in China, "many people who are alienated from contemporary society project their dissatisfaction on to China. They see in China virtues that America once had but lost, such virtues as self-discipline and self-sacrifice."[112] An Australian journalist, viewing the phenomenon of Western Maoism after a long spell as correspondent in Peking, commented sardonically: "I often used to wonder what the Chinese masses would think of the slavering adulation which vesterners have applied indiscriminately to their system. How they must have felt to see comfortable foreigners accepting the notion that there were no human problems in packing high school graduates off to the countryside or separating husbands and wives."[113]

For all its vogue in the West, Maoism made little impact in Third World countries. Throughout the 1960s and 1970s the Soviet Union and China bid for Third World support. "The barrage of revolutionary rhetoric was, of course, intended by each side to win over all revolutionary communists struggling for power."[114] But to revolutionaries in Latin America, Africa, and Asia, the Soviet Union and China were great powers, more important as suppliers of political and military support than as models of development, and here the Soviet Union had a decisive edge because it "was better able to supply money, arms and training facilities than the Chinese."[115] "The Maoist splinter parties that appeared in some Latin American countries and the guerilla movements that claimed Chinese inspiration, proved ineffective."[116] The circumstances which made it possible for Mao Tse-tung to impose on China, in a spirit of romantic puritanism, "a revolution taking place under an already established dictatorship of the proletariat,"[117] were not remotely replicated in any other country. In Cuba, Angola, and Vietnam, "the guerilla leaders, once in power, would prefer Soviet big battalions to Chinese doctrinal attractions."[118]

There was another way in which radical, if not necessarily

Marxist, ideology, with its egalitarian emphasis on redistribution and its hostility to capitalism and imperialism, during the 1970s came to influence Third World thinking much more powerfully than it did in its Maoist manifestation. This was the formulation by Third World spokesmen of demands for a New International Economic Order. Although not, in itself, a strategy of development, it formed so important an ingredient in Third World thinking about development that it demands some attention; and although not necessarily radical in its implications for the domestic structure of society in developing countries, it had so many surface affinities with left-wing radical thought about development that it is best dealt with here.

A New International Economic Order

When Western economists, such as Singer and Myrdal, in the 1950s demanded action by the West, through aid and technical assistance, to help the less-developed countries to develop and thus narrow the gap between rich and poor nations, they were in effect advocating internationalisation of the welfare state. When Prebisch in the 1960s argued that the old order of free trade between the "centre" and the "periphery" did not meet the trade needs of the developing countries, he was in effect advocating internationalisation of protection. When in the 1970s spokesmen of the Third World demanded a new international economic order, they—or at least some of them—introduced into the debate an element best described as internationalisation of class conflict.

The concerns of the Nonaligned Movement, formed in the 1950s by Nkrumah, Nasser, Nehru, Sukarno, and other leaders of the newly independent countries of Africa and Asia, had been political rather than economic—decolonisation of the remaining dependent territories and an international role and voice for the Third World independent of the First and Second Worlds and their Cold War. As decolonisation was substantially accomplished, incidentally giving Third World countries majority control of the UN General Assembly, and as detente between the two superpowers lessened the force of "nonalignment" as a unifying slogan,[119] the emphasis shifted to economic issues. In the preparations for UNCTAD I, the "Group of 77" Third World member countries of the United Nations formed themselves into an effective bargaining unit which succeeded in turning the new organisation into a trade union of LDCs, with a program of demands on the developed countries ready-made by Raul Prebisch. But throughout the 1960s it remained a program of demands for concessions to be negotiated in international discussion.

The atmosphere changed quite suddenly in 1973 with the oil price increase of that year. The Club of Rome had prepared the ground with its dire predictions of early exhaustion of oil and other nonrenewable resources. The October 1973 war between Egypt and Israel, which galvanised the Arab members of the Organisation of Petroleum Exporting Countries (OPEC) into concerted action to raise the price of oil and to threaten to cut off oil supplies to countries branded as supporters of Israel, provided an object lesson. "The boycott and price rise clearly showed what power the oil states possessed when they could act in unison against the . . . industrialised countries."[120] The success emboldened the nonaligned countries at their Algiers meeting of that year to proclaim the principle of "unconditional right" to command natural resources. The host at that meeting, President Boumedienne, at the sixth special session of the UN General Assembly, which was called at his request, was even more explicit: "Nationalisation is a stage of development."[121] The successful OPEC cartel action suggested that the Third World was in a position not merely to request but to "force the industrialised countries to make concessions."[122]

It was here that neo-Marxist ideas about development provided valuable intellectual underpinning. Early in 1974, Denis Goulet, in the article "Development and the International Economic Order," gave three reasons for the view that "the workings of the international economic order are crucial to the domestic effort of poorer countries to achieve development." One is that the present international economic order blocks social justice not only by freezing the unjust division of the world's wealth but also by favouring privileged classes in the underdeveloped countries at the expense of the popular masses. A second reason, echoing Frank, is that it embodies "dependency and domination—and hence underdevelopment." The third is that "without reciprocity no international order can foster authentic development." "An international economic order controlled by a few rich countries . . . cannot be a just development order. All nations must have effective access to resources and a share in effective decisions governing their use."[123]

The "Declaration on the Establishment of a New International Economic Order" adopted by the sixth special session in April 1974 contained a list of twenty broadly formulated demands, largely taken from earlier UNCTAD programs, inspired by principles of "equity, sovereign equality, interdependence, common interest and cooperation among all States."[124] Among them were sustained improvement in the terms of trade for primary products; favourable conditions for transfer of financial resources to developing countries; reform of the international monetary system; promotion of transfer of technology to developing countries; improvement in the competitiveness of natural raw materials with synthetics; preferential and nonreciprocal treatment for developing countries, wherever feasible, in all fields of international economic cooperation; full permanent sovereignty of every state over its natural resources, including the right of nationalisation; and regulation and supervision of the activities of transnational corporations. The accompanying Program of Action spelled these out in more detail but did not add anything of substance.

The ideological high-water mark of the New International Economic Order (NIEO) as a radical movement was reached at the Nonaligned Conference held at Dakar in February 1975. The neo-Marxist ideas of the Latin American dependency theorists and of Samir Amin (here on his home ground) resounded in the document adopted at the conference. "In brief, the nonaligned countries argued that the development of the rich capitalist countries is intimately related to the colonial and neo-colonial exploitation of the periphery. . . . The Third World functions as a reservoir of raw materials and cheap labour power, contributing to the development of the center while indigenous social systems are disrupted and Third World societies are less able to satisfy their own basic needs than they were before the colonial period. Any 'development' that occurs is distorted and uneven, involving only a small part of the population and confining itself to sectoral and regional enclaves."[125]

In the following years, the NIEO campaign scored some successes, most conspicuously in the acceptance in principle by the developed countries of the chief plank of the NIEO commodities program, the creation of a UN Common Fund. But in most of the (nearly forty) issue areas gradually identified by its proponents,[126] North-South negotiations bogged down, and as a political force the campaign lost most of its momentum in the later 1970s. Among the reasons were political developments—stronger resistance in the North and weakening drive in the South. In the developed countries, increasingly beset with domestic economic and social problems as growth slowed down, arguments such as those of the Pearson Commission and the Brandt Report came up against more inward-looking policies and "aid weariness." In the developing countries, disillusion set in with the gradual realisation that the monopoly power which had been so effectively used by OPEC in the case of oil did not extend to any other significant commodities and was in danger of backfiring even in the case of oil. More important, the Third World lost its political cohesion, as the economic experience and interests of its members increasingly diverged. The rich Arab OPEC countries, the newly industrialising countries (NICs) of north and south east Asia, and for a time also some of the most advanced Latin American countries, such as Mexico and Brazil, found they had less and less in common with the least-developed countries of Africa or even with the low-income countries of South Asia. With more and more middle-income countries emerging in the Third World, the bipolar conception of a world divided into haves and have-nots which was fundamental to the class-war ideology declined in plausibility, much as its equivalent in capitalist societies, the worker-capitalist dichotomy, had done in the preceding decades. As a delegate of Singapore, a country which was doing very well under the existing international order, is said to have remarked, apropos of a Cuban draft at the Nairobi UNCTAD: "Who am I uniting with and for what objectives and purposes and against whom?"[127]

The notion that underdevelopment was due to the existing international economic order was bound to seem increasingly dubious during a decade which saw average per capita income in the developing countries of the Third World rise at an unprecedented rate and faster than in the developed countries, so that the "gap," which had been the focus of so much discussion in the preceding years for the first time narrowed. True, progress in the Third World was very uneven. But this very fact cast further doubt on the neo-Marxist interpretation since it posed the obvious question why, under the existing international order which presumably affected all developing countries in much the same way, some were doing so much better than others. The inference seemed inescapable that the problems of countries which were doing badly had much more to do with their domestic situation than with any external factors.

The basic dilemma from which no amount of rhetoric could extricate the NIEO campaign was that it demanded a better deal for poor countries, not poor people. "Equality of states, not people, is what the New International Economic Order is about."[128] The very first of the principles proclaimed in the 1974 declaration by the UN General Assembly was the principle of "sovereign equality of states." Thus, when in the following year the ILO advocated a basic needs strategy, the developing countries were at best lukewarm,[129] seeing it "as an attempt on the part of the rich countries to meddle in their internal affairs."[130] If the objective of development was, as the neo-Marxists insisted, to free the masses from poverty and exploitation, it was not obvious that massive transfers or other concessions to autocratic governments of whatever political complexion would promote development. The gibe that aid too often represented a transfer "from the poor in rich countries to the rich in poor countries" was not entirely without justification. In many of its manifestations, the NIEO campaign invited the suspicion that it was concerned, as has been said of the Brandt Report, "with something that appeals less to the bellies of the poor than to the hearts of the rulers of poor countries; namely, an increase in their power."[131]

But this appeal itself guarantees for the NIEO, or at least for demands for economic concessions by the developed countries to developing ones a continuing role in the United Nations and other international forums. For governments struggling with unmanageable domestic problems and enmeshed in domestic power struggles, the temptation to blame their troubles on forces beyond their control, whether the international economic order or the machinations of imperialists and neocolonialists, is hard to resist. And the left-wing ideological tinge of the NIEO campaign, born of past resentment of colonialism and sustained by the hold of socialist and other radical ideas on articulate public opinion and governments in much of the Third World, has exempted the Comecon countries from its strictures and ensured the sympathy and often active political support of the Soviet bloc for most of its demands in the continuing international debate.

Neo-Marxist Revisionism

As early as 1962, Paul Baran had pointed to "political troubles within the socialist camp"—Khrushchev's denunciation of Stalinism, the Sino-Soviet split, the setback suffered by China in the wake of the Great Leap Forward—and to the risk that people would lose faith in revolution.[132] By the late 1970s, the disintegration of the monolith was even more apparent. What had happened to Christianity after 1,500 years seemed to be happening to communism within a century. In China, Maoism had been swept away by a new leadership which, in the eyes of Western Maoists, appeared to put a "one-sided emphasis on production."[133] Countries professing Marxism were at loggerheads all over the world—Vietnam with China and Cambodia, Ethiopia with Somalia, Yugoslavia and Albania with all the others. It was evident that "the socialist camp . . . is far from united."[134]

Moreover, there was "much disagreement over what Marxian socialist development is supposed to be."[135] What Teng

Hsiao-p'ing was saying about Mao's rule did not sit well with the enthusiasms of Western Maoists, nor could the performance of Pol Pot please enthusiasts for the Khmer Rouge peasant revolution.[136] Some of the more open-minded among neo-Marxists began to concede that, *pace* Baran and Frank, capitalist development in the Third World was possible. Writers such as Bill Warren, "although speaking from a Marxist perspective," pointed out that "there have been tremendous increases in the forces of production in the postwar period, that development is indeed occurring in exactly the way Marx would have predicted."[137] Countries such as Brazil, Mexico, and Nigeria were going through a capitalist revolution. Gurley concluded from "sib-comparisons" of the relative performance of pairs of socialist and capitalist developing countries that they "challenge the fundamental notion of socialist superiority."[138] He suggested that "Marxists ought to look carefully at what conventional economists call success stories. . . . Circumstances have permitted many Third World countries to stand on their own feet and to pursue, in the name of nationalism, a more self-directed course toward industrialization and higher living standards."[139] None of this shook Gurley's belief in the "world transformation to socialism. . . . Socialism is bound to replace capitalism almost everywhere."[140] But at any rate, it was a Marxian, rather than a neo-Marxist, vision— development through a capitalist stage.

Latin American neo-Marxists tended to react to such evidence by amending Frank's formulation. "To the extent that today monopoly capital *does* promote a form of industrial growth, it makes more sense to speak of 'dependent development,' rather than of 'development of underdevelopment.'"[141] (Frank responded to this by designating oil-boom countries, such as Venezuela, as "ultra-underdeveloped" because they suffer "ultra-incorporation of their satellite into the metropolitan sphere";[142] but this terminology did not commend itself even in neo-Marxist circles.)

Others reacted by adopting what might be called a neutralist position: "A look at the postwar record indicates that countries prospered and stagnated regardless of social system or development strategy. Brazil and Mexico grew while their poor suffered. Costa Rica grew and Cuba failed to grow while their poor prospered. Both China and Taiwan are cited as 'models' of development. Both Tanzania and Peru are floundering. Capitalism has not brought freedom to Chile or South Korea and socialism has not brought liberation to Cambodia or North Korea."[143]

Some neo-Marxists, while conceding that rapid economic development of some sort was going on in much of the Third World, objected that it fell far short of the socialist ideal. "What is important is an understanding of the essence of contradiction . . . between technocratic elitism and a vision [of] . . . a state capable of seeking socialist forms for the social organization of the future."[144] Others interpreted the widely divergent experience in different parts of the Third World as evidence that "the development process is a dialectic one."[145] Others again, initially sympathetic to the neo-Marxist position, were led to a completely agnostic conclusion. "There are no general patterns of development just as there is no general definition of development. Each people must write its own history."[146]

6

Radical Counterpoint
The Right

The Sceptics

Towards the end of the colonial era some colonial administrators had become very sceptical about the benefits of Western material progress for the native peoples and pessimistic about their future. I quoted Furnivall's assessment of the situation in Burma: "There is good reason to believe that the cultivators, as individuals, were vastly better off from a material standpoint under British than under Burmese rule." But "the mere maintenance of law and order set free economic forces which dissolved the village into individuals. . . . The annexation destroyed the Burmese social order and probably nothing less catastrophic would have cleared the way for reconstruction; but the destruction of a civilisation is in itself an offence against humanity."[1]

Like Marx, Furnivall appears to have thought the destructive impact of Western capitalism a necessary stage in the economic development of Burma. Some went much further. J. H. Boeke, disillusioned by the failure of the "ethical policy" in the Dutch East Indies, came to the conclusion that Eastern and Western society differed so profoundly that Western-type economic development was impossible in the East. "There is no question of the eastern producer adapting himself to the western example technologically, economically or socially."[2]

Boeke's theory of "dualism" postulated that people in traditional Eastern societies do not behave as "economic men." Their "needs are very limited."[3] "Social needs, determined by a man's social standing, are of much greater importance than individual or "economic" needs.[4] The result is a pervasive "inverse elasticity of supply" (backward sloping supply curve).[5] This, he thought, was "one of the essential differences between western and eastern economies,"[6] another being a "greater or lesser immobility of the factors of production."[7] Between them, these rendered the price mechanism largely inoperative as an allocative system and thus made Western economic theory inapplicable to Eastern economies.

Nor did he see any prospect of the gulf being narrowed, with gradual capitalistic development of the traditional sector. "The particular dualistic situation to be found in such societies is not the temporary result of closer contact with the Western elements to be found in most of them, but is permanent."[8] "In Europe, capitalism, after a tumultuous and destructive period of transition, . . . has had a unifying effect on society. . . . And the Eastern societies—why has capitalism not exerted a similar influence there?" "The basic reason . . . was undoubtedly that there was no force for vigorous development operative in the cultures of such Eastern peoples."[9] "It is not possible to transform the operating forces into the opposite of what they are. The contrast is too all-inclusive, it goes too deep. We shall have to accept dualism as an irretrievable fact."[10]

The sad result of Boeke's final experience in the tropics, as one commentator put it, was that he "turned his back upon every ideal of economic welfare in the western sense even for the vigorous, energetic, better-educated rural element" and pinned what hopes he had for the rural masses of Asia on a vague notion of "village reconstruction" in which "an Eastern Heritage," revitalised, would form "the natural basis for the entire social structure."[11]

Boeke developed his view in the 1930s. By the time he consolidated them once more in English, in his last book published in New York in 1953, they had become distinctly unfashionable. In the postwar intellectual climate of optimism about economic development, few if any in the West held, let alone publicly avowed, Boeke's Kiplingesque image of East and West. But from the beginning there were voices raising questions about the emerging consensus on the means and ends of economic development, at least to the extent of warning against overoptimism and too rapid change, and this undercurrent of scepticism among a minority has continued through the years.

In the same year as Boeke's last book, 1953, a volume of essays under the title *The Economic Impact on Under-Developed Societies* was published by S. H. Frankel, an authority on colonial economics in Africa. The title was carefully chosen. Using "economic" where Boeke would have used "capitalist" (and A. G. Frank "imperialist"), Frankel identified the "economic impact" with the European expansion, the process culminating in the nineteenth century, when the West's world-economy expanded "in the peripheral areas, . . . economically penetrating, physically harnessing, and politically integrating those dormant regions."[12] The process was not planned by anyone. "The very notion of 'developing' a whole community, a whole people, . . . did not arise. What was meant by 'development' was the creation of political and economic institutions which would bring new regions and other peoples into the accepted framework of reference for economic action."[13] It was no accident that most progress was achieved in the "by and large 'empty' areas" of North America and Oceania, which were settled by emigrants from Europe, "people with the same habit patterns of thought, the same symbolism of accounting, the same aptitudes and broadly the same conscious and unconscious social heritage."[14] "Where, however, there were large indigenous populations with a different social heritage the provision of the Western framework did not by itself stimulate such development."[15]

Frankel was a Burkean conservative. He thought economic development of the underdeveloped regions necessary and desirable, but he warned that it was inevitably a slow process. "It is upon the shoulders of the new governments that there now rests the heavy burden of reconciling their peoples to the fact that structural and social change is inevitable if the burden of their poverty is to be eased; that the costs of change are heavy. . . . Development can be neither foreseen, nor enforced by a single will—be it the 'general will' or the will of a tyrant. . . . The real problem . . . is to achieve new goals of social action with the least unnecessary or premature social disintegration and disharmony. True economic growth is a many-sided individual and social process. . . . It consists in refashioning aptitudes and beliefs of individuals to give them new freedom in their multitudinous daily tasks. . . . The real task is not to force change but to induce it in a manner which will be meaningful to the members of the societies it affects."[16]

Another sceptical discussion of economic development, published in 1953, was by the American economist Jacob Viner. But Viner's concern was chiefly to debunk what he regarded as facile, superficial thinking in much of the burgeoning development literature, beginning with the identification of economic development with growth in per capita income. Viner had no doubt about "the world's greatest, most serious, economic problem: the problem of much over half the world's population living under conditions of acute poverty."[17] He merely questioned whether action by the developed countries, through aid or trade, could make more than a marginal difference. "The problem will not even begin to have a practical solution unless the underdeveloped countries dedicate their own resources, human, physical, and financial, to a sound, large-scale and persistent attack on basic internal causes of mass poverty."[18]

Much the same is true of the most persistent and articulate dissenter on development among Western economists, P. T. Bauer. Bauer was, and remains, all in favour of material progress for the people of the less developed countries. "Changes in general living standards are to me the principal criterion of material progress"[19] or of economic development—he uses the two terms interchangeably.[20] And, like W. A. Lewis, he thinks economic development desirable because it increases freedom. "The widening of the range of effective choice is the most valuable single objective of economic development as well as the best single criterion of its attainment."[21] His dissent has throughout been on means, not ends. His animus has been directed at the whole approach to development—voluntarist, welfarist, dirigiste—that seemed to him to characterise mainstream thinking in Western as well as developing countries.

Starting out from an ideological preference for "an economic system in which decision making is widely diffused and coordinated by market forces," not merely as a safeguard of political freedom but also because "in general this system secures an efficient deployment of resources and promotes the growth of resources,"[22] Bauer attacks what he sees as the static, zero-sum-game preoccupation of Western development enthusiasts and spokesmen of less developed countries with "domestic and international redistribution."[23] He rejects an egalitarian interpretation of social justice as philosophically groundless—"why is it obviously unjust that those who contribute more to production should have higher incomes than those who contribute less?"[24] (characteristically abstracting from other sources of inequality of wealth and income). He attributes support among Western intellectuals for the radical class-war interpretation of the North-South relationship to "the operation of widespread feelings of guilt in contemporary Western society." As adherence to Christian beliefs has declined, "collective guilt has replaced a sense of personal sin."[25] In evidence, he quotes Myrdal: "Not merely to save the world, but primarily to save our own souls, there should again be dreamers, planners, and fighters."[26]

His market orientation, however, also leads Bauer to reject Boeke's view of people in traditional societies as unresponsive to material incentives and limited in their wants: "At least at present there appears to be no ceiling to economic development imposed by inflexibility in habits of consumption."[27] The demonstration effect is favourable to economic growth: "throughout the underdeveloped world there is ample evidence of the importance of contact with foreigners in bringing about a revision of wants and needs."[28]

Bauer distances himself from laissez-faire. "I envisage an extensive range of appropriate and even essential government tasks in poor countries."[29] But he believes that "preoccupation with central planning has, paradoxically, contributed to a serious neglect of essential government tasks in many underdeveloped countries."[30] Somewhat like Frankel, he thinks it wrong to suggest that the problems of underdevelopment are "readily rectifiable."[31] He believes that "the potentialities of development economics for the promotion of material progress have been oversold to a credulous public. . . . Economic development is a major aspect of the historical process of entire societies, and is therefore not susceptible to general theory."[32] The dichotomy between a developed North and underdeveloped South is overdrawn. "The notion of the gap implies a distinct and substantial discontinuity in per capita incomes of developed and underdeveloped countries. In fact, there is no such appreciable gap. There is a continuous graduation in per capita income between different countries."[33] Some Third World countries have done extremely well, others have stagnated. "Progress has often been rapid and generally also uneven. . . . Economic advance always affects certain regions and activities first, from which it spreads outwards."[34]

Furnivall, Boeke, Frankel, Viner, Bauer—and there were no doubt other sceptics about development less outspoken and less well known—were Westerners viewing the problems of the less developed countries, sympathetically, from outside. It is not an attitude one would expect to find among their contemporaries in the Third World itself. The great majority of Third World intellectuals, and more generally of articulate public opinion in developing countries, took for granted the desirability of modernisation in some sense which embraced material progress, as well as national independence, very much in the image of the West. But there were minority voices which questioned the modernisation objective, and especially Western-type material progress, or rejected it outright. Insofar as they favoured economic development at all, their conception of it was very different. To some of these "antimodernisers" we now turn.

The Anti-Modernisers

We saw in chapter 2 how Gandhi, then a young Indian lawyer in South Africa, conceived a passionate hatred for Western civilisation in general and British capitalism in particular, how he railed against their manifestations—greed and profits, railways, machinery, cities, banks, doctors and all.

Gandhi's rebellion had two roots—nationalism and religion. British rule of India had to be overthrown because the

British were imposing on India a civilisation both alien and evil. "In order to restore India to its pristine condition, we have to return to it. In our own civilisation there will naturally be progress, retrogression, reforms and reaction; but one effort is required, and that is to drive out Western civilization."[35] Like Tolstoy, whom he greatly admired,[36] Gandhi rejected Western civilisation on quasi-religious moral grounds. Tolstoy, as an aged prophet, had not minced words: "The root of all evil is property. The rich who produce nothing and revel in vice, luxury and idleness, attract the poor to the towns and enslave them. . . . The State is a murderous vehicle devised by the violent to dominate the weak. . . . How to combat the evil to which mankind is sinking ever more deeply? First, by rejecting all the machinery on which society is now founded . . . give up money and land, abolish industry—a source of pauperism—flee the corrupting cities, tear the conceit of education out of your heart and return to a healthy rural existence."[37]

Gandhi's rhetoric, even in his youth, did not reach such extremes. But he sympathised with the general trend of Tolstoy's thinking. "This mad rush for wealth must cease." "True economics is the economics of justice. People will be happy in so far as they learn to do justice and be righteous." "Does progress clash with real progress? I take [progress to mean] material advancement without limit; and by real progress we mean moral progress."[38] Like Tolstoy, he saw urban industrial culture corroding the simplicity of village life. "Our cities are not India. India lives in her seven and a half lacs of villages and the cities live upon the villages."[39] Here lay Gandhi's appeal to Boeke, who saw him wanting "to abolish the effects of dualism on the village by cutting off the influence of the government . . . substituting for them the complete self-sufficiency of the village. . . . It is nothing more nor less," thought Boeke, "than a complete return to the situation in which the village found itself before Western capitalism began making its revolutionary inroads in the East."[40]

Gandhi felt deep compassion for the poor of India. But if he demanded social justice for them, it was, as has been said of his work for the untouchables, to make them "raise their head in pride and self-confidence"[41] as much as to improve their material condition. "To teach people to get rich by hook or crook is to do them an immense harm."[42] Since his primary concern was with social justice, he was less interested in economic development in any form than in an equal distribution, and "the real implication of equal distribution is that each man shall have the wherewithal to supply all his natural needs and no more. To bring this ideal into being the entire social order has got to be reconstructed."[43]

Boeke, however, much as he empathised with Gandhi's philosophy, saw in 1930 that it left one question unanswered: "Will it be possible to maintain such a programme in its entirety once Home Rule has been obtained? Now the people are united in the struggle against British domination. But once independence has been granted, who will come to power and lay down the law: the militant, advanced, politically trained, centralized, and organized western urban element or the peaceful, backward, weak, localized and unorganized Oriental rural masses?"[44] The question answered itself.

Gandhi himself, in his last years, as independence and responsibility for government dawned, adopted a less uncompromising attitude towards economic development and industrialisation. He admitted the usefulness of machinery in many fields and came to accept it, especially for rural industry. "We have to concentrate on the village being self-contained, manufacturing mainly for use. . . . What I am against is large-scale production of things that the villages can produce without difficulty."[45] Indeed, "I visualize electricity, ship building, iron works, machine making, and the like, existing side by side with the village crafts." But "if the same work can be done by a small machine, a large one should not be employed";[46] and "I am socialist enough to say that such factories should be nationalized or state-controlled," they should work "not for profit, but for the benefit of humanity."[47]

Latter-day Gandhians have stressed these later, more moderate—and politically perhaps more realistic—views as against the youthful Gandhi of 1909, who, in his "urge to defend the best in Indian civilization," was inclined to "throw out the baby with the bathwater."[48] But they have continued to uphold the Gandhian ideals in the light of what they see as "the failure of non-Gandhian models of economic and political development in India," which "has caused frustration and bewilderment almost to the entire intellectual class, most particularly to those who have grown up in the liberal tradition of Nehru or under the strong influence of Marxist thought."[49]

Thirty years after Gandhi's death, a variant of his attack on Western civilisation, harsher and more strident, came to the fore in another part of Asia—Iran. Throughout the Islamic world, stretching in a long arc from Morocco to Mindanao, tension between modernisation and tradition had for some decades been reflected in intellectual ferment. "In our own time, the impact of industrial development, technology, urbanization, and secular values has had far-reaching consequences. . . . Along with the flood of Western technology have come new, and sometimes unwelcome ideas concerning individualism, materialism, sexuality, family and politics. To some, these ideas seem to threaten basic Islamic values. Furthermore, the outlook of most Muslims is strongly colored by a very recent emergence from a long period of foreign domination."[50] "The manifestations of this phenomenon include ferment, restiveness, a hunger for an Islamic renaissance . . . and new dichotomies between 'modernists' and 'tradionalists.' "[51] In Iran, a combination of circumstances—the Shah's attempt to modernise by resort to oil money and repression and an alliance of Shi'ite clergy with merchants and landowners who saw their interests threatened—brought to power an extreme fundamentalist regime led and inspired by the Ayatollah Khomeini. In the spring of 1980, "the regime of the clerics and their supporters launched, in the name of Islamic purity, a 'cultural revolution.' "[52]

Muslim modernists have argued that there is no necessary conflict between Islamic teaching and economic development. They quote the Koran: "It is He who has produced you from the earth and settled you therein to develop it."[53] "Development is an essential requirement, and participation in economic activity is obligatory on every Muslim."[54] Concern among leaders of Islamic opinion, according to the modernists, is directed "not against science education or technology-oriented education as such" but against "the divorce of education and training . . . from Islamic moral and spiritual values."[55] "With the help of science, technology, and economic power [man] has made impressive material progess, but has not been able to achieve fraternity, equity, and piety."[56]

The Ayatollah Khomeini's favourite quotation from the Koran was a different one: "The oppressed people must triumph over the oppressors."[57] The oppressors included the Shah and his associates at home, the superpowers, multinational corporations, "capitalist imperialism and socialist imperialism" and their "Zionist, Phalangist and Fascist" instruments.[58] With a ferocity which left even the Gandhi of 1909 entirely in the shade, Khomeini denounced "the poisonous culture of imperialism"[59] and its chief exponent, "the Great Satan," the United States. It is true that his hostility to the West was "an integral part of a deeper and wider rejection of such perceived Western values as the primacy of individualism, . . . and capitalism and materialism, as contrasted with Islamic welfarism and spiritualism."[60] Much of his venom was directed at moral vices he associated with the West—"those who have grown up with lechery, treachery, music and dancing, and a thousand other varieties of corruption,"[61] and against the "xenomaniacs"[62] in his own country, who were dazzled by the material progress of the imperialist countries.[63] But there was in his rhetoric also another element, much more reminiscent of A. G. Frank, Samir Amin, and other neo-Marxists.

"The superpowers of East and West are plundering all our material and other resources, and have placed us in a situation of political, economic, cultural and military dependence."[64] "Our country is being turned into a market for expensive, unnecessary goods by the representatives of foreign companies."[65] "The imperialists have also imposed on us an unjust economic order, and thereby divided our people into two groups: oppressors and oppressed."[66] "Are we to be trampled underfoot by the boots of America simply because we are a weak nation and have no dollar? America is worse than Britain; Britain is worse than America. The Soviet Union is worse than both of them. They are all worse and more unclean than each other. But today it is America we are concerned with."[67] Latin American neo-Marxists, of course, would not have bracketed the Eastern with the Western superpower, but they lacked the Ayatollah's grounds for opposing atheist communism and for fearing the Soviet Union. In Iran, Islamic fundamentalism was competing with Marxism for the souls of "young people, mostly urban, and the poorer classes, rural and urban, whose lives have not witnessed great improvement over the past years."[68] Hence the Ayatollah's constant concern, on the one hand, to refute Marxism, and, on the other, to claim that he, too, was an anticapitalist revolutionary.[69]

Like Gandhi, the Ayatollah Khomeini, once he attained power, took a kindlier—or more pragmatic—view of material progress for the Iranian people. "In all my approach to the Iranian people . . . I have always emphasised my country's social and economic development. . . . Our agriculture has been destroyed. . . . The Shah has destroyed our economy and squandered revenue from oil—the wealth of the future."[70] The government needed money to provide "for the needs of the people, for public services relating to health, education, defence, and economic development."[71] We cannot be complacent about "the hunger and poverty of our people, the bankruptcy of the bazaar, the unemployment of our educated youth, the sorry state of our agriculture and industry, the domination of the country's economy by Israel."[72] But central to his thinking, as well as Gandhi's, was social justice rather than material progress, distribution rather than economic growth. "If we obtain power," he said in 1979, "we will confiscate their [the landlords'] ill-gotten wealth and redistribute it equitably among the needy."[73] "The solution of social problems and the relief of human misery requires foundations in faith and morals; merely acquiring material power and wealth, conquering nature and space, have no effect in this regard." In the last resort, "the happiness [man] may enjoy in the world will not be confined to it, for his ultimate goal is a world that lies beyond the present one."[74]

A striking feature of the Ayatollah's teaching—if not his practice—is its close resemblance, in its combination of "traditional [religious] doctrines . . . with elements of modern radical ideologies,"[75] to contemporary teaching about economic development of the Christian churches. There may not be many stern Calvinists left who believe, with the Ayatollah, that "man's passions and covetousness are unlimited" and that "this animal that has broken its bridle" must be "tamed."[76] But spokesmen of the Christian churches, Catholic and Protestant alike, have spoken up as vigorously for social justice and against the pursuit of material progress.

Representatives of Christian churches in East Asia have demanded a "social revolution for justice" and condemned communism as an ideological error only because of its "militant atheism."[77] Papal encyclicals have presented the North-South problem in terms not very different from those of Islamic or Marxist radicals. The core of the problem is distribution, "the fairness in the exchange of goods and in the division of wealth between individuals and countries."[78] "The poor nations remain ever poor while the rich ones become still richer. . . . There is also the scandal of glaring inequalities not merely in the enjoyment of possessions but even more in the exercise of power."[79] "Very large numbers of people are unable to satisfy their primary needs" while "superfluous needs are ingeniously created"[80] by multinational enterprises responsible for "inhuman principles of individualism when they operate in less developed countries."[81] Like Gandhi, and like the Ayatollah Khomeini, the pope teaches that government must lay down the ends and means of development, for only government can be relied on to pursue the general welfare, rather than private profit.[82] "It always intervenes with careful justice and with devotion to the common good for which it holds final responsibility."[83]

In 1984, the Vatican, seriously alarmed by Marxist infiltration of the priesthood and laity in Latin America, issued an *Instruction on Certain Aspects of the "Theology of Liberation."* With the object of "drawing the attention of pastors . . . to the deviations, and risks of deviation, damaging to the faith and

Christian living . . . brought about by certain forms of liberation theology which use, in an insufficiently critical manner, concepts borrowed from various currents of Marxist thought,"[84] this carefully reasoned and phrased document set out where the Church agreed and where it disagreed with the theology of liberation.

It agreed that "mankind will no longer passively submit to crushing poverty with its effects of death, disease and decline"; that "the scandal of the shocking inequality between the rich and the poor—whether between rich and poor countries, or between social classes in a single nation—is no longer tolerated"; that "the gulf between the rich and the poor is ever widening"—hence the feeling of frustration among Third World countries "and the accusations of exploitation and economic colonialism brought against the industrialised nations"—and it concurred with the liberation theologians' "special concern for the poor and the victims of oppression, which in turn begets a commitment to justice."[85] If the Church agreed with so much, where did it differ?

Some of its objections to liberation theology, or at least to "certain forms" of it, were essentially theological. It warned against the temptation to emphasise liberation from servitude of an earthly and temporal kind; "the most radical form of slavery is slavery to sin." Or again, "God, and not man, has the power to change the situations of the suffering." For the rest, the differences were about means, not ends. Affirmation of class struggle and necessary violence was said to amount to "political amorality." The battle for justice must "be fought in ways consistent with human dignity. . . . The systematic and deliberate recourse to blind violence must be condemned."[86]

The outlook of even quite conservative churchmen of all denominations, Christian and Moslem alike, had a natural affinity, in substance though not in method, with that of neo-Marxists and liberation theology because their religion enjoined them to show compassion for the poor and to condemn self-seeking materialism while their church accustomed them to hierarchy and paternalism. Since the notion of economic growth had little place in their thinking, their concern for social justice naturally predisposed them to redistributive policies; and if there was to be economic development, their disapproval of many aspects of Western society and their professionally paternalistic viewpoint inclined them toward the socialist rather than the capitalist model. The Vatican document on liberation theology contains only one passing reference to economic progress—"thanks to the amazing advances in science and technology, mankind, still growing in numbers, is capable of assuring each human being the minimum of goods required by his dignity as a person"—but only in the context of underlining the "shocking inequality," which is thus presented as the cause of poverty. This same view has been even more sharply enunciated by organs of the Protestant churches, such as the World Council of Churches and its national affiliates. To cite one example among many, a recent document published under the aegis of the Australian Council of Churches advocates "a society in which the resources available are so fairly shared that no one is considered wealthy but all have some share in poverty."[87] It is therefore not surprising that, on issues relating to social policy, especially in the Third World, the Christian churches have tended to expound views which, in the conventional political spectrum of Western countries, would lie well to the Left. But for the fact that they lacked the nationalist motive for detestation of Western civilisation, their stand in relation to economic development might not have been very different from that of Gandhi and the Ayatollah Khomeini.

Towards the end of the previous chapter, we found neo-Marxism leading some to advocacy of nationalism and self-reliance, others to rejection of material goods and primary schools in favour of "liberation" as the purpose of development, others again to the transformation of selfish bourgeois man into moral socialist man. In this chapter we have found religious leaders being led by concern for social justice to advocacy of redistributive policies hardly less radical, except in method, than those neo-Marxist and other socialists and an implicit downgrading, if not total rejection, of the objective of material progress. Are we then to conclude that Adam Smith,

Karl Marx, Gunnar Myrdal and Peter Bauer, all proponents of material progress, must be regarded as "Right" and A. G. Frank, Dudley Seers, the Ayatollah Khomeini, and the pope as "Left"? Or is it the other way round? Clearly, there is something wrong, certainly in relation to economic development as a policy objective, with these labels.

7

Assessment

Almost everyone considers development—-even economic development—-a desirable objective for the countries and people of the Third World. But so diverse have the interpretations of "development" become that one sometimes wonders whether it now stands for anything more substantial than everyone's own utopia. Certainly, when development is identified with "the means to human ascent" and each country is told that it must "write its own history," the word seems to have all but lost any specific meaning. But this is carrying scepticism too far. Development still means something, as evidenced by the fact that some are against it. It is the purpose of this final chapter to distil some specific meanings of development, as a policy objective rather than a process, from the ferment of ideas surveyed in the earlier historical chapters.

Development as a process preceded development as a policy objective. It had been happening for centuries in Europe before anyone consciously put forward material progress as a desirable objective of state policy. Similarly, development, in the sense of an irreversible trend of economic and social change, happened outside Europe, under the impact of the European expansion, long before anyone conceived development policies for non-European people.

Economic development as a policy objective for what we now call the Third World does not, as we have seen, greatly antedate World War II. For Third World leaders, what mattered most was emancipation from colonial rule and catching up with the West in power and status. But modernisation through industrialisation and other forms of economic growth was desired as a means to these ends, as well as for the alleviation of poverty and more generally for material progress. Conversely, modernisation based on the absorption of Western science and technology, attitudes and behaviour, was seen as a necessary condition of economic growth. In Western countries, economic development of the Third World became a major policy objective because humanitarian as well as political-strategic considerations made it seem important to reduce the gap between the rich and poor countries by raising living standards in the latter.

There were some who, while accepting development—material progress and modernisation—as a desirable end, disagreed with the mainstream about means. When the mainstream argued about alternative reformist development strategies, some of the dissidents focused on power because they regarded a change in power relationships, nationally and internationally, as a prerequisite for development; others focused on morality because they believed that only through a transformation of human nature could development, or at least desirable development, be achieved. Others again, without necessarily rejecting development as an objective, attached little importance to it compared with the imperative, as they saw it, of social justice. Finally, there were some who altogether repudiated development as an objective, either because they condemned pursuit of material progress on moral grounds or because they considered development on the Western model as destructive of more important values.

In reviewing these various strands of thought about development, I will take them in reverse order.

Dissent from Development

It is doubtful whether there is now anyone who is out-and-out opposed to economic development of Third World countries—and this is in itself a striking fact. There are, to be sure, people who have turned their backs on the current pursuits and aspirations of their societies, monks and gurus in the East, alienated young idealists, hippies, and dropouts in the West. But they are not active opponents and in any case are at best fringe minorities without even potential influence on the course of events.

There have been, and continue to be, many articulate and

more or less active opponents of modernisation on anything like the Western model. The ferocity with which the young Gandhi denounced Western civilisation as a disease has its present counterpart in the Ayatollah Khomeini's condemnation of capitalism and communism alike as evil, corrupt, and unclean, and while pure Gandhianism is now uncommon in India, Islamic fundamentalism has a strong and probably still increasing hold on minds in many countries. Religious conceptions of man in society—the Buddhist ideal of extinction of desire, the Christian command to eschew selfishness, Gandhian resigned acceptance of the fact that "millions will always remain poor," Moslem precepts of godliness—all these are in fundamental conflict with worldly concern for material progress. Reinforced by nationalist and xenophobic resentments, some of these religious doctrines have inspired powerful political movements. But antimodernising zeal has nowhere long survived the attainment of power, the capacity to influence policy. By 1946, as we saw, Gandhi was all in favour of electricity, ship-building and factories, so long as they were state-controlled, small, and operated "not for profit, but for the benefit of humanity"; and the Ayatollah Khomeini, once in power, came to stress the importance of economic and social development, provided it had its "foundations in faith and morals."

The transformation of human nature from selfishness and greed to selfless service to others which religious leaders have sought through teaching and preaching, Mao Tse-tung tried to achieve through the political instrument of mass mobilisation. But Mao, even at his most millenarian during the Great Cultural Revolution, was never against development in some sense which included material progress. To him, the transformation of selfish bourgeois into moral socialist man was a necessary condition of development; and the same probably holds for his Western admirers who saw in Maoist China "virtues that America once had but lost."

Neither can outright opposition to development be attributed to the Western sceptics, such as Boeke and Furnivall. Boeke may have doubted whether capitalist development would ever take off among Eastern people, but only in moments of despair about the impact of colonialism on the Javanese did he wish the native people could be left alone. Similarly, Furnivall did not assert that the Burmese social order which was destroyed by the British annexation was better for the Burmese people than the material progress they enjoyed under British rule. When, having conceded that "nothing less catastrophic would have cleared the way for reconstruction," he added that "the destruction of a civilisation is in itself an offence against humanity," he was uttering a sigh of regret rather than making a policy pronouncement. In recent decades, as the West has lost some of its nineteenth-century self-confidence—its nerve or its arrogance, depending on the point of view—assertion of its "civilising mission" has virtually disappeared, to be replaced among guilt-stricken sections of Western opinion by a disarming cultural relativism. But this rarely extends to a rejection of economic development for the sake of preserving traditional culture and social order in Third World countries, and where it does it is shared by few in the Third World itself. Self-reliance may be recognised as a virtue in the abstract, but with a few partial exceptions Third World leaders have in practice been unwilling to forgo the advantages of aid and trade, transfer of technology, and access to Western civilisation for the sake of the ascetic virtues claimed for a strategy of "delinking" their countries from the world economy. (Even romantic neo-Marxists, such as A. G. Frank and K. Griffin, in claiming that underdevelopment was caused by the West, merely used this as a stick with which to belabour the hated imperialists. They never asked themselves the counterfactual question of what life for the people of Mexico or Peru or Nigeria or India would be like had they never been touched by Western civilisation.)

Social Justice

A much more formidable challenge to the primacy of development as a policy objective for the Third World has been the call for social justice. It has united, in uneasy and shifting alliance, Christian and other religious leaders, Marxists and neo-Marxists, advocates of a new international economic order and humanitarian intellectuals of various hues. What united them was compassion for the poor, resentment of the rich, and moral outrage at the "scandal" of inequality, in the Vatican's words. But they differed widely in the inferences they drew from this, explicitly or implicitly, for development as a policy objective.

At its most unsophisticated, the demand by churchmen, vulgar socialists (in Marx's sense), and idealistic men and women in the street for policies of redistribution—taking from the rich and giving to the poor—rather than development reflected thoughtlessness and lack of imagination. To an ill-paid factory worker, illiterate landless labourer, kindly village priest, or young student, the glaring contrast between rich and poor in front of their eyes is the obvious explanation of poverty; they naturally think in terms of what we have learned to call a zero-sum game. It simply does not occur to them that poverty can be alleviated more effectively by development than by redistribution, by increasing the size of the cake than by sharing it out more equally. The learned theologians who wrote the Vatican's 1984 instruction against liberation theology were not rejecting economic development as a way of reducing poverty in the Third World, the "shocking inequality" between rich and poor countries. They just did not think of mentioning it (and, to be fair, might not have impressed the theologians of liberation had they done so).

Gandhi's position was somewhat different. He had no wish to see India catch up with the West in material progress. When he demanded an equal distribution he probably believed that, given equal shares, there was enough to secure for everyone "the wherewithal to supply all his natural needs and no more," which was all he thought desirable. Similarly, the World Council of Churches' objective of a world in which "no one is considered wealthy, but all have some share in poverty" could, presumably in their view, be achieved without any further economic growth (depending on the desirable degree of poverty to be shared by all).

The almost universal lack of sympathy for economic development among religious leaders has another explanation, besides this tendency to think in zero-sum-game terms.

Economic development in its capitalist manifestation evokes among them distaste, if not revulsion, because they see it rooted in materialism—greed, competition, and the pursuit of profit—and "inhuman principles of individualism." Churchmen have little time for the mechanism by which a country's progress is maintained; that is, in Adam Smith's words, the mechanism of citizens' "universal, continued, and uninterrupted effort to better their own condition." Professionally, they see the moral dangers and social consequences of inequality of wealth and income more easily than the consequences of inequality of power. Thus, their sympathies tend naturally towards socialist ideals of cooperation, social welfare, and a government that "always intervenes with careful justice and devotion to the common good." They will concede that socialist governments do not in practice always conform to this ideal, and they will denounce atheist totalitarian communism. But this does not necessarily dispose them more favourably towards economic development.

Support for and thinking about economic development has also, and in quite a different way, been inhibited by demand for social justice where this demand has taken the form of advocacy of class war and revolution. Neither Marx nor Lenin can be accused of zero-sum-game thinking. No one has more wholeheartedly than Karl Marx proclaimed the virtues of economic development, which has "created more massive and more colossal productive forces than have all preceding generations together." But the emotional drive behind Marx's scholarly and political labours was hatred of an exploitative system and of its capitalist rulers and beneficiaries. For most of his life, he was too preoccupied with proving the inevitability of the revolutionary overthrow of capitalism, and with helping to bring it about, to give much thought to the objectives of the society that was to follow. Lenin was even more exclusively concerned with the strategy and tactics of winning power, and this has been true in varying degree of most Marxist and neo-Marxist revolutionaries. It was only when and where power had been won, and they confronted the tasks of government, that they began seriously to think about the forms that development should take. Neo-Marxists, in Latin America and elsewhere, thought much more about underdevelopment than about development.

The Marxist view that sustained economic development in Third World countries, and certainly equitable development, was impossible without a prior revolutionary change in power relationships—without holders of wealth and power being expropriated or expelled—had plausibility and appeal. In seventeenth-century Britain, in eighteenth-century France and in much of nineteenth-century Europe, violent social upheaval had preceded capitalist economic development, and in much of the Third World, even after the more or less peaceful departure of colonial rulers, revolution could readily be seen as the quickest, if not the only, path to a more dynamic as well as a more just society. But the historical evidence for the necessity of revolution was by no means clear-cut and, in any case, once victorious, communism soon lost its allure for Third World idealists. For a decade or two, the forced industrialisation and military prowess of Russia under Stalin evoked admiration, but by the 1960s few Third World revolutionaries looked to the Soviet Union as the model; nor, with the partical exception of the romantic image of Fidel Castro in Cuba, did Mao's China, Ho Chi Minh's Vietnam, or any of the lesser Marxist regimes in the Third World for long fill that role. The ideal socialist society after the revolution would invariably be different from all existing ones.

The campaign for a New International Economic Order which rode the crest of high oil prices during the 1970s was also ostensibly a call for social justice and in its more militant versions amounted, as we have seen, to internationalisation of class war. Its exponents, like the advocates of domestic revolution, claimed not only that the poor countries of the Third World would benefit directly from international redistributive policies but also that a drastic change in international power relationships between the Third and the First World—the Second World of Comecon was usually delicately left out of the argument—was a necessary precondition of effective economic development in Third World countries.

But the international version of the argument too often smacked of scapegoatism—blaming malign outside forces for domestic failures—to carry much conviction. Moreover, it was vulnerable to the charge that its concern was for "justice" among countries, not people, and therefore for prestige of the elites rather than the welfare of the poor in developing countries. As the Third World itself became increasingly heterogeneous in degree of development and prosperity, in ideology and policies, the underlying bipolar notion of two classes confronting each other came to seem as specious internationally as domestically.

Those who, in the 1960s and 1970s, began to think systematically about the relations between inequality and poverty and economic growth found themselves facing a series of dilemmas. Mere economic growth was not enough, for its benefits did not sufficiently "trickle down" to the poor to eradicate, or even markedly alleviate, poverty or to reduce inequality—or so some of the statistical evidence suggested. Granted that the objective had to be not just growth but the right kind of growth, was the chief task to reduce poverty or inequality? What was an acceptable poverty line, what an acceptable degree of inequality? What if economic growth was, after all, the surest way of raising the living standards of the bottom 20 percent? What if "some degree of inequality of incomes is an essential part of the structure of incentives in any growing economy," as Pitambar Pant emphasised in India in the 1960s and Teng Hsiao-p'ing took as the guiding principle of a new development strategy for the 1980s in China?

Were the unemployed to be the target group of the ideal development strategy, or the underemployed, or the working poor? Should development aim, in the first instance, at satisfying "basic needs"? Should it aim at protecting the people of the Third World from the demonstration effect of Western consumerism and at giving them what they "really want," whether they like it or not? Small was beautiful, but was it also sensible?

While these nostrums were being advanced by Western experts and advisers of international organisations, one by one in an apparent process of "accelerated slogan obsolescence"—the policy makers in Third World countries who carried the responsibility, bemused and not a little suspicious of

Western motives, held on to the development strategy which commanded the widest public support and was therefore most likely to keep them in power: aiming, within the constraints imposed by conflicting pressures of interest groups and by underdevelopment itself, at the highest attainable rate of economic growth.

Economic Growth and Modernisation

It was not caprice that made economic growth central to thinking about development, that put GNP on the throne and has, in the face of all the onslaughts and pinpricks, firmly kept it there. If poverty in the Third World was to be reduced, if living standards were to be steadily raised, a sustained rise in per capita income was essential and, given high rates of population growth due to Western technology for public health, this meant historically unprecedented rates of growth of GNP. If the gap between rich and poor countries was to be narrowed, the rate of growth of per capita income had to be higher in the less developed countries than in the more developed. Economic growth, in other words, was the only effective way of making the people of the Third World materially better off, of raising consumption standards.

In the West, the jaundiced view about "the kind of economical progress which excites the congratulations of ordinary politicians" that J. S. Mill had expressed a century earlier received widespread support during the 1960s and 1970s. Apart from heightened awareness of some of the environmental and other costs of economic growth and Club-of-Rome-sponsored anxieties about threatened exhaustion of nonrenewable resources, increasing numbers came to share the doubts long ascertained by a sceptical few whether there was any point in doubling per capita income every so many years, whether in the rich consumer societies there was any need or demand for an ever larger volume of consumer goods and services. Even in Western countries, these doubts did not deter voters and politicians from the pursuit of economic growth, although in various ways they probably contributed to slowdown and recession. The continuing incidence of massive poverty and the continuing wide gap between the great majority and the even moderately well-to-do minority in standards of comfort and of health, education, and other services made satiety ("bliss") still appear no nearer than it had seemed to Keynes in the 1930s when he contemplated the economic future of our grandchildren. A fortiori, any suggestion that economic growth was no longer urgent in the Third World because consumers would soon have all they wanted or needed was hardly persuasive.

In any case, the importance attached to economic growth as an ingredient in the development objective for Third World countries did not derive solely, or even primarily, from its role in making possible higher levels of consumer spending. Economic growth increases people's capacity to produce. At least in the longer run, they are free to use this capacity for household or government consumption, for private or public capital formation, for armaments or aid, and to distribute the output of goods and services as they think fit. By whatever social processes these choices are in practice made, the capacity to make them is severely limited in poor, underdeveloped societies and is enhanced by economic growth. It was the creation of unprecedented, colossal productive forces which Marx regarded as the great achievement of capitalism.

But it would be taking too narrow a view of what Marx had in mind, and of the significance of economic development to people in nineteenth-century Europe and in the Third World today, to focus merely on expanding capacity to produce goods and services as measured by GNP. For Marx, as for many Victorians, as we noted in the first chapter of this book, the essence of progress was the Promethean conquest of nature by man, "the development of the productive power of man and the transformation of material production into a scientific domination of natural agencies." His focus was on the role of the bourgeoisie in creating urban civilisation, in rescuing "a considerable part of the population from the idiocy of rural life."

Urban civilisation is one aspect of what leaders of opinion in less developed countries have meant by modernisation. Modernisation in this sense, which encompasses economic growth but goes much beyond it, comes closest to what economic development has meant and still means to those who think about it in the Third World. Myrdal, in *Asian Drama*, listed the "modernisation ideals" which he saw as the "official creed"—"almost a new religion"—of the people of south Asia, or at least "of the politically alert, articulate, and active part of the population—particularly the intellectual elite." Better even than his extensive list is Nehru's summary, in homely language, which Myrdal quoted in a footnote: "What is society in the so-called advanced countries like today? It is a scientific and technological society. It employs new techniques, whether it is in the farm or in the factory or in transport. The test of a country's advance is how far it is utilizing modern techniques. Modern technique is not a matter of getting a tool and using it. Modern technique follows modern thinking. You can't get hold of a modern tool and have an ancient mind."[1]

Modernisation, as we saw, was initially sought in Japan and China as necessary for national survival, to ward off the onslaught from the West, and its pursuit has continued to be motivated in the Third World in part by considerations of national power and status, of concern primarily to national elites. But modernisation has also been sought as necessary to economic growth and thus to alleviation of poverty and to higher living standards; for economic growth depends on modern technology, modern attitudes and institutions. Modernisation, however, is not merely a means to economic growth. The rationality, dynamism, and mobility of modern society, the scope for a fuller life and greater individual freedom for men and women, for the advancement of knowledge and cultivation of the arts offered by urban civilisation, all these are seen as aspects of modernisation valuable in themselves, apart from the contribution of modernisation to economic growth. Insofar as there is a common element in the diverse interpretations of development as the official creed of the Third World, it is this amalgam of economic growth and modernisation as interdependent ends.

Enough has been said in earlier chapters, and in the first pages of this one, to demonstrate that not everyone is unreservedly and continuously in favour of development in this sense. There are few thoughtful people anywhere who would not confess to reservations, to difficulties in weighing all the imponderables that must go into a design for living, for nations as for individuals. But the reservations about economic growth which have been so conspicuous in Western thinking about development have not been widely shared in the Third World; they have largely reflected First World rather than Third World tribulations.

The first of these broad conclusions from our survey was pointed out by Arthur Lewis when he ended his discussion of the desirability of economic growth—in 1955 he still used this term as virtually synonymous with economic development—by saying that "because economic growth has both its gains and its losses we are all almost without exception ambivalent in our attitudes towards economic growth."

The second conclusion is illustrated by two recent statements, one by a distinguished French colonial administrator, the other by a distinguished Indian development economist.

Jacques Binet can see little but harm coming to African people from economic growth and modernisation:

> Development is a complex enterprise. A civilisation is a more or less coherent combination of technology and law, of social organisations, beliefs, values, and insights. Thoughtless introduction of a new and strange element into such a mosaic can easily destroy it altogether. . . . If no conscious effort is made, the errors of the nineteenth century risk being repeated. Industrialisation will cause a rural exodus and proletarianisation. Social classes will crystallise and confront each other. Instead of a moneyed bourgeoisie, one will perhaps have a bureaucratic bourgeoisie, but the result will be similar. The cities will develop, the country stagnate. . . . Propelled by economism and the consumer society, materialism will engender unlimited greed and false wants. . . . Men will let themselves be dominated by egoism, the old social links of family and ethnic community will lose their force without being replaced by new communal ties. . . . Our generation has learned that development of consumption is not an end in itself,

that production has its limits, that the quality of life is important. Scientific progress has been put into question by Hiroshima. Many of the old certainties have been shattered.[2]

By contrast, R. M. Sundrum has no doubt that economic development is desirable and that modernisation is the way to promote it:

The central problem of development economics is to understand the nature of the process which has transformed the DCs in the past, why it has not occurred in the LDCs and what may be done to promote it in the future. . . .

What can be done is implicit in a definition of development in terms of

the pervasiveness of modern economic behaviour and the ability of people to absorb modern technology, based on education, infrastructure and institutions. On this view, a society can be considered more developed, the higher the education of its members, the greater the supply of infrastructure and the better its economic institution for encouraging modern technology.[3]

Perhaps the reader should be left to ponder the relative merits of these two sharply opposed points of view. But if I were asked to declare my own preferences more openly than I have already done between the lines in the preceding pages, I would once again quote the wisest of development economists:

The advantage of economic growth is not that wealth increases happiness, but that it increases the range of human choice. . . . The case for economic growth is that it gives man greater control over his environment, and thereby increases his freedom.

There will always be disputation about the uses to which our expanding productive forces should be put. But only an extreme pessimist about the folly of mankind would deny the benefit of the increased freedom to choose that comes with economic development.

Notes

Chapter Two

1. Gunnar Myrdal, *Economic Theory and Under-Developed Regions* (London: Duckworth, 1957), p. 80.

2. W. W. Rostow, *How It All Began: Origins of the Modern Economy* (London: Methuen, 1975).

3. W. W. Rostow, *Politics and the Stages of Growth* (Cambridge: Cambridge University Press, 1971), p. 54.

4. Lewis Mumford, *Technics and Civilization* (London: Routledge, 1934), p. 3.

5. Rostow, *Politics*, p. 26.

6. Quoted in J. B. Bury, *The Idea of Progress* (London: Macmillan, 1924), p. 52.

7. Rostow, *How It All Began*, p. 151.

8. Mumford, *Technics and Civilization*, p. 43.

9. Rostow, *How It All Began*, p. 145.

10. Mumford, *Technics and Civilization*, p. 3.

11. Ibid., p. 14.

12. Ibid., p. 19.

13. Ibid., pp. 28, 31.

14 R. H. Tawney, *Land and Labour in China* (London: Allen & Unwin, 1932), p. 11.

15. Rostow, *How It All Began*, p. 11.

16. Ibid., pp. 7f.

17. Ibid., p. 158.

18. Ibid., p. 105.

19. Ibid.

20. Adam Smith, *The Wealth of Nations*, first published 1776; ed. E. Cannan (London: University Paperbacks, 1961), vol. 1, p. 91.

21. Rostow, *Politics*, p. 63.

22. Ibid., p. 62.

23. Ibid., p. 63.

24. Ibid., p. 24.

25. Ibid., p. 62.

26. D. S. Landes, "Japan and Europe: Contrasts in Industrialization," in W. W. Lockwood, ed., *The State and Economic Enterprise in Japan: Essays in the Political Economy of Growth* (Princeton: Princeton University Press, 1965), p. 93.

27. E. S. Crawcour, "The Tokugawa Heritage," in Lockwood, *The State and Economic Enterprise*, p. 36.

28. J. W. Hall, "Changing Conceptions of the Modernization of Japan," in M. B. Jansen, ed., *Changing Japanese Attitudes Towards Modernization* (Princeton: Princeton University Press, 1965), p. 56.

29. Landes, "Japan and Europe," p. 93.

30. Rostow, *Politics*, p. 69.

31. B. K. Marshall, *Capitalism and Nationalism in Prewar Japan: The Ideology of the Business Elite, 1868–1914* (Stanford: Stanford University Press, 1967), p. 14.

32. A. H. Gleason, "Economic Growth and Consumption in Japan," in Lockwood, *The State and Economic Enterprise*, p. 393.

33. Quoted in ibid., p. 392.

34. Hall, "Changing Conceptions," p. 79.

35. Landes, "Japan and Europe," p. 112.

36. Marshall, *Capitalism and Nationalism*, p. 13.

37. Hall, "Changing Conceptions," p. 66.

38. Liu Kweng-ching, "The Emergence of a Policy, 1870–1875," in I. C. Y. Hsu, ed., *Readings in Modern Chinese History* (Oxford: Oxford University Press, 1971), p. 234.

39. Hsiao Kung-chuan, "The 'Hundred Day' Reform," in Hsu, *Readings*, p. 350.

40. Chow Tse-tung, *The May Fourth Movement* (Cambridge, Mass.: Harvard University Press, 1960), p.7.

41. Sun Yat-sen, "The Three Principles of the People," in K.-C. Hsiao, "The 'Hundred Day' Reform," p. 411.

42. See C. Martin Wilbur, *Sun Yat-Sen: Frustrated Patriot* (New York: Columbia University Press, 1976).

43. M. Gasster, *Chinese Intellectuals and the Revolution of 1911: The Birth of Modern Chinese Radicalism* (Seattle: University of Washington Press, 1969).

44. Wilbur, *Sun Yat-Sen*, pp. 25ff.; cf. also H. D. Fong, *Toward Economic Control in China* (Tientsin: China Institute of Pacific Relations, 1936), p.5.

45. Sun Yat-sen, *The International Development of China* (New York: Putnam, 1922).

46. Sun Yat-sen, in K.-C. Hsiao, "The 'Hundred Day' Reform," pp. 423f.

47. Sun Yat-sen, *The International Development of China*, p. 8.

48. Cf. J. B. Condliffe et al., *Honolulu Session* (Institute of Pacific Relations, 1925); J. B. Condliffe, *China Today: Economic* (Boston: World Peace Foundation, 1932); J. B. Condliffe, in A. Loveday et al., *The World's Economic Future* (London: Allen & Unwin, 1938).

49. Dadabhai Naoroji, *Poverty and Un-British Rule in India* (1901) (New Delhi: Government of India, 1962), p. 191; cf. also B. N. Ganguli, *Dadabhai Naoroji and the Drain Theory* (London: Asia Publishing House, 1965).

50. P. J. Jagirdar, *Studies in the Social Thought of M. G. Ranade* (Bombay: Asia Publishing House, 1963), p. 122.

51. M. G. Ranade, "Indian Political Economy" (1892), in *Essays on Indian Economics* (Bombay: Thacker, 1899), p. 24.

52. S. P. Aiyer, "Gandhi, Gokhale and the Moderates," in Sibnarayan Ray, ed., *Gandhi, India and the World* (Melbourne: Hawthorn Press 1970), p. 108.

53. Ganguli, *Dadabhai Naoroji*, p. 140.

54. Ranade, "Indian Political Economy," p. 20.

55. Ibid., p. 70.

56. Mahatma Gandhi, "Hind Swaraj" (1909), in *Collected Works*, vol. 10 (Allahabad: Government of India, 1963), pp. 21, 24, 26.

57. Ibid., p. 58.

58. Ibid., p. 37.

59. Jawaharlal Nehru, "Presidential Address at Lahore" (1929), in *India's Freedom* (London: Unwin Books, 1962), p. 15.

60. Jawaharlal Nehru, "Presidential Address at Lucknow" (1936), in ibid., p. 35.

61. Jawaharlal Nehru, "Whither India?" (1933), in ibid., p. 21.

62. Ibid., p. 24.

63. Ibid., p. 36.

64. Ibid., p. 35.

65. Jawaharlal Nehru, *Autobiography* (1936) (Bombay: Allied Publishers, 1962), p. 517.

66. Jawaharlal Nehru, *Speeches*, vol. 1 (New Delhi: Government of India, 1949), p. 91.

67. Ibid., p. 141.

68. C. Veliz, *The Centralist Tradition of Latin America* (Princeton: N.J.: Princeton University Press, 1979), chap. 8, p. 15.

69. C. W. Anderson, *Politics and Economic Change in Latin America* (Princeton, N. J.: Van Nostrand, 1967), p. 29.

70. Sarmiento, quoted in Veliz, *The Centralist Tradition*, p. 17.

71. Ibid., p. 21.

72. Anderson, *Politics and Economic Change*, p. 39.

73. Quoted in R. E. Betts, *Assimilation and Association in French Colonial Theory, 1890–1914* (New York: Columbia University Press, 1961), p. 145.

74. Quoted in K. E. Knorr, *British Colonial Theories, 1570–1850* (Toronto: Toronto University Press, 1944), p. 31.

75. Quoted in Eric Stokes, *The English Utilitarians and India* (Oxford: Clarendon Press, 1959), p. 34.

76. Ibid.

77. Ibid., p. 36.

78. H. J. Pedraza, *Borrioboola-Gha: The Story of Lokoja, The First British Settlement in Nigeria* (London: Oxford University Press, 1960), p. ix.

79. Betts, *Assimilation and Association*, p. 136.

80. Ibid., p. 11.

81. J. S. Furnivall, *Colonial Policy and Practice: A Comparative Study of Burma and Netherlands India* (Cambridge University Press, 1948), p. 6.

82. Stokes, *The English Utilitarians*, p. 31.

83. Ronald Robinson et al., *Africa and the Victorians: The Official Mind and Imperialism* (London: Macmillan, 1961), p. 1.

84. T. B. Macaulay, quoted in Stokes, *The English Utilitarians*, p. 43.

85. Quoted in ibid., p. 35.

86. Betts, *Assimilation and Association*, p. 11.

87. Stokes, *The English Utilitarians*, p. 38.

88. Quoted in ibid., p. 43.

89. Quoted in ibid., p. 39.

90. James Mill, quoted in ibid., p. 52.

91. James Mill, quoted in ibid., p. 69.

92. Sir Thomas Munro, quoted in ibid., p. 19.

93. James Mill, *The History of British India* (1820), ed. H. H. Wilson, 9 vols (London, 1848), 9:566.

94. Furnivall, *Colonial Policy and Practice*, p. 62.

95. Betts, *Assimilation and Association*, p. 144.

96. Furnivall, *Colonial Policy and Practice*, p. 6.

97. A. D. A. de Kat Angelino, *Colonial Policy*, vol. 1, *General Principles* (Chicago: University of Chicago Press, 1931), p. 23.

98. Furnivall, *Colonial Policy and Practice*, p. 64.

99. Ibid., p. 5.

100. Betts, *Assimilation and Association*, p. 120.

101. F. D. Lugard, *The Dual Mandate in British Tropical Africa* (Edinburgh: Blackwood, 1921).

102. L. C. A. Knowles, *The Economic Development of the British Overseas Empire* (London: Routledge, 1924), p. vii.

103. J. S. Furnivall, *An Introduction to the Political Economy of Burma* (1931), 3d ed. (Rangoon, 1957), p. i.

104. Betts, *Assimilation and Association*, p. 142.

105. W. K. Hancock, *Survey of British Commonwealth Affairs*, Part II, *Problems of Economic Policy* (London: Oxford University Press, 1942), p. 267.

106. J. H. Boeke, *The Evolution of the Netherlands India Economy* (New York: Institute of Pacific Relations, 1942), pp. 3, 18.

107. Furnivall, *Colonial Policy and Practice*, pp. 28, 51.

108. Furnivall, *Burma*, p. xii.

109. W. Arthur Lewis, "An Economic Plan for Jamaica," *Agenda*, November 1944, p. 154.

110. Adam Smith, *The Wealth of Nations*, 2:221.

111. Ibid., 1:73.

112. Ibid., 2:180.

113. J. S. Mill, *Principles of Political Economy*, 5th ed. (London: Parker, 1862), 2:324.

114. J. R. Hicks, "Growth and Anti-Growth," *Oxford Economic Papers*, November 1966, p. 260.

115. Ibid., p. 258.

116. A. Marshall, *Principles of Economics*, 9th ed. (London: Macmillan, 1961), 2:737.

117. A. Marshall, *Industry and Trade* (London: Macmillan, 1919), pp. 161f.

118. Ibid., p. 5.

119. A. C. Pigou, *The Economics of Welfare*, 2d ed. (London: Macmillan, 1924), p. 657.

120. F. W. Taussig, *Principles of Economics*, 2d ed. (London: Macmillan, 1916), 1:101.

121. Irving Fisher, *Elementary Principles of Economics* (London: Macmillan, 1915), pp. 476f.

122. J. M. Keynes, "Economic Possibilities for Our Grandchildren," in *Essays in Persuasion* (London: Macmillan, 1933), pp. 358, 361, 365f.

123. E. Cannan, *Economic Scares* (London: P. S. King, 1931), p. 92.

124. F. Benham, *Economics* (London: Pitman, 1938), p. 418.

125. League of Nations, *World Economic Survey, 1937/38* (Geneva, 1938).

126. P. A. Samuelson, *Economics*, 1st ed. (New York: McGraw-Hill, 1948), p. 67.

127. Ibid., p. 377.

128. Ibid., p. 563.

129. Cf., e.g., J. W. F. Rowe, *Markets and Men* (Cambridge University Press, 1936); P. Lamartine Yates, *Commodity Control* (London: Jonathan Cape, 1943).

130. Cf., e.g., H. Feis, *Europe, the World's Banker, 1870–1914* (New Haven: Yale University Press, 1920); Royal Institute of International Affairs, *The Problem of International Investment* (London: Oxford University Press, 1937); S. H. Frankel, *Capital Investment in Africa* (London: Oxford University Press) 1938.

131. Cf., e.g., I. Bowman, ed., *Limits of Land Settlement* (New York: Council on Foreign Relations, 1937).

132. See, especially, G. E. Hubbard, *Eastern Industrialization and Its Effects on the West* (London: Oxford University Press, 1938); Kate L. Mitchell, *Industrialization of the Western Pacific* (New York: Institute of Pacific Relations, 1942); Harold Butler, *Problems of Industry in the East* (Geneva: International Labour Office, 1938).

133. See, e.g., Institute of Pacific Relations, *Honolulu Session;* J. B. Condliffe, ed., *Problems of the Pacific* (Chicago: University of Chicago Press, 1928).

134. Colin Clark, *The Conditions of Economic Progress,* (London: Macmillan, 1940).

135. League of Nations Mixed Committee on Nutrition, *Final Report* (Geneva, 1937).

136. For an account, see *Social Policy in Dependent Territories* (Montreal: International Labour Office, 1944), p. iii.

137. Cf. E. Staley, *World Economy in Transition* (New York: Council on Foreign Relations, 1939), pp. 61ff.

138. Karl Marx, *Capital,* trans. E. and C. Paul, Everyman's Library, 2 vols, Preface to the First German Edition, 2:864.

139. Cf. H. W. Arndt, "Economic Development: A Semantic History," *Economic Development and Cultural Change,* April 1981.

140. See S. Avineri, ed., *Karl Marx on Colonialism and Modernization* (New York: Doubleday, 1968).

141. Karl Marx and Friedrich Engels, *The Communist Manifesto,* quoted in M. D. Kennedy, *A Short History of Communism in Asia* (London: Weidenfeld & Nicolson, 1957), p. 161.

142. Ibid., quoted in J. A. Schumpeter, *Capitalism, Socialism and Democracy* (London: Allen & Unwin, 1943), p. 7.

143. Karl Marx, "The Consequences of British Rule in India," quoted in Helene Carrère d'Encausse and S. R. Schram, *Marxism and Asia* (London: Penguin Press, 1969), p. 119.

144. Marx, *Capital*, 2:847.

145. *Communist Manifesto*, quoted in Schumpeter, *Capitalism, Socialism and Democracy*, p. 7.

146. Marx, *Capital*, 1:386.

147. *Communist Manifesto*, quoted in Schumpeter, *Capitalism, Socialism and Democracy*, p. 525.

148. Marx, *Capital*, 1:379.

149. Marx, "The Consequences of British Rule in India," p. 117.

150. Ibid.

151. Marx, *Capital*, 2:846.

152. Ibid., Preface to the First German Edition, p. 863.

153. Ibid.

154. A. Erlich, *The Soviet Industrialization Debate, 1924–1928* (Cambridge, Mass.: Harvard University Press, 1960), p. xviii.

155. Marx, *Capital*, 2:864.

156. Ibid., p. 846.

157. Carrère d'Encausse and Schram, *Marxism and Asia*, pp. 125, 131.

158. Ibid., p. 128.

159. Ibid., p. 130.

160. Ibid., p. 31.

161. Ibid., p. 27.

162. V. I. Lenin, *Imperialism*, quoted in R. Owen and B. Sutcliffe, eds., *Studies in the Theory of Imperialism* (London: Longman, 1972), p. 53.

163. Ibid.

164. Lenin, quoted in E. H. Carr, *The Bolshevik Revolution, 1917–23* (London: Macmillan, 1952), 2:32.

165. Ibid., p. 36.

166. Lenin, quoted in Erlich, *Debate*, p. 7.

167. Carr, *Revolution*, p. 376.

168. Ibid., p. 372.

169. Ibid., p. 373.

170. Erlich, *Debate*.

171. Ibid., p. xvii.

172. Ibid., p. 15.

173. Ibid,. p. 180; cf. also I. Deutscher, *Stalin: A Political Biography*, 2d ed. (New York: Oxford University Press, 1966), p. 326.

174. Deutscher, *Stalin*, p. 328.

175. Quoted in S. R. Schram, *The Political Thought of Mao Tse-Tung* (New York: Praeger, 1963), p. 57.

176. Quoted in Carrère d'Encausse and Schram, *Marxism and Asia*, p. 44.

177. Ibid., p. 48.

178. Ibid., p. 26; cf. also F. Schatten, *Communism in Africa* (London: Unwin, 1966), p. 57.

179. Carrère d'Encausse & Schram, *Marxism and Asia*, p. 151.

180. Quoted in P. Owen and B. Sutcliffe, *Studies in the Theory of Imperialism* (London: Longman, 1972), p. 111.

181. Schram, *Mao Tse-Tung*, pp. 25f.

182. Carrère d'Encausse and Schram, *Marxism and Asia*, p. 31.

183. Ibid., p. 36.

184. Owen and Sutcliffe, *Imperialism*, p. 103.

185. Ibid., p. 97.

186. Schatten, *Communism in Africa*, p. 19.

187. Carrère d'Encausse and Schram, *Marxism and Asia*, p. 37.

188. Ibid., p. 47.

189. Schram, *Mao Tse-Tung*, p. 55.

190. Cordell Hull, *Memoirs* (London: Hodder & Stoughton, 1948), pp. 1625ff.

191. F. S. Dunn, *Peace-Making and the Settlement with Japan* (Princeton: Princeton University Press, 1963), p. 5.

192. W. L. Neumann, *Making the Peace, 1941–1945* (Washington: Foundation for Foreign Affairs, 1950).

193. Heather Harvey, "War-Time Research in Great Britain on International Problems of Reconstruction," *Agenda*, April 1942, p. 164.

194. *The Annals*, July 1940, p. 24.

195. Staley, *World Economy*, p. 68.

196. Ibid., p. 70.

197. Ibid., p. 278.

198. Ibid., p. 282.

199. Ibid.

200. *International Conciliation*, no. 369, 1941, p. 141.

201. Cf., e.g., H. P. Jordan, ed., *Problems of Post-War Reconstruction* (Washington: American Council on Public Affairs, 1942), especially Jordan's own chapter on Latin America; P. E. Corbett, *Post-War Worlds* (New York: Institute of Pacific Relations, 1942); S. E. Harris, ed., *Postwar Economic Problems* (New York: McGraw-Hill, 1943); J. B. Condliffe, *Agenda for a Post-War World* (London: Allen & Unwin, 1943); *War and Peace in the Pacific*, Institute of Pacific Relations Conference, 1942 (London: Royal Institute of International Affairs, 1943);

E. Staley, *World Economic Development* (Montreal: International Labour Office, 1944).

202. Harris, *Postwar Economic Problems*, p. 364.

203. National Peace Council, *The Economic Basis of Peace* (London, 1942), p. 10.

204. Ibid., p. 26.

205. See the various surveys of research on postwar reconstruction in *Agenda*, 1944.

206. "Economic Development in South-Eastern Europe," *Planning*, 21 July 1944; *Economic Development in South-Eastern Europe* (London: Political and Economic Planning, 1945).

207. K. Mandelbaum, *The Industrialization of Backward Areas* (Oxford: Blackwell, 1947); mention should also be made of A. Bonné, *The Economic Development of the Middle East: An Outline of Planned Reconstruction* (London: Kegan Paul, 1945), and of the "Bombay Plan" for India, Sir P. Thakurdas et al., *A Plan of Economic Development for India* (London: Penguin, 1944).

208. P. N. Rosenstein-Rodan, "Problems of Industrialisation of Eastern and South-Eastern Europe," *Economic Journal*, June–September 1943; and "The International Development of Economically Backward Areas," *International Affairs*, April 1944.

Chapter Three

1. United Nations, *World Economic Report 1948* (New York, 1949), p. 251.

2. *The Work of the FAO*, Food and Agriculture Organisation (1945), quoted in G. Hambidge, *The Story of the FAO* (New York: Van Nostrand, 1955), p. 56.

3. P. T. Ellsworth, *The International Economy* (New York: Macmillan, 1950), p. 786.

4. United Nations, *Economic Report: Salient Features of the World Economic Situation, 1945–7* (New York, 1948), p. 271.

5. Gunnar Myrdal, *Asian Drama* (New York: Random House, 1968), 1:58.

6. United Nations, *Economic Development in Selected Countries: Plans, Programs and Agencies* (New York, 1947), p. 151.

7. Rosenstein-Rodan, "Problems of Industrialisation of Eastern and South-Eastern Europe," *Economic Journal*, June–September 1943; among many other examples that could be given, see the Nehru quotation, above, p. 20.

8. United Nations, *Economic Development in Selected Countries*, Introduction, p. xv.

9. Ellsworth, *The International Economy*, p. 796.

10. Gunnar Myrdal, *Economic Theory and Under-Developed Regions* (London: Duckworth, 1957), p. 80.

11. B. Okun and R. W. Richardson, eds., *Studies in Economic Development* (New York: Holt, Rinehart & Winston, 1962), p. 230.

12. Irma Adelman, *Theories of Economic Growth and Development* (Stanford: Stanford University Press, 1961), p. 1.

13. W. A. Lewis, *The Theory of Economic Growth* (London: Allen & Unwin, 1955).

14. J. R. Hicks, *The Social Framework* (Oxford: Clarendon Press, 1942).

15. Some of the first results were published in United Nations, *Economic Report, 1945–7*, referred to in n. 4 above.

16. E. Staley, *World Economic Development: Effects on Advanced Industrial Countries* (Montreal: International Labour Office, 1944), p. 2.

17. Ibid.

18. United Nations, *Formulation and Economic Appraisal of Development Projects*, 2 vols. (United Nations: [Lahore], 1951), 1:29.

19. Cf. H. W. Arndt, *The Rise and Fall of Economic Growth* (Melbourne: Longman Cheshire, 1978; reprint, University of Chicago Press, 1984).

20. J. Baster, "Recent Literature on the Economic Development of Backward Areas," *Quarterly Journal of Economics*, vol. 58, November 1954, p. 602.

21. H. W. Singer, "The Mechanics of Economic Development" (1952), reprinted in *International Development: Growth and Change* (New York: McGraw-Hill, 1964), p. 120.

22. Cf., e.g., Baster, "Recent Literature," p. 602.

23. J. Viner, "America's Aims and the Progress of Underdeveloped Countries," in B. F. Hoselitz, ed., *The Progress of Underdeveloped Areas* (Chicago: University of Chicago Press, 1952), p. 187.

24. G. Hakim, "Technical Aid from the Viewpoint of the Aid-Receiving Countries," in Hoselitz, *The Progress*, p. 259.

25. Quoted in S. Weintraub, *International Approaches to Problems of Underdeveloped Areas* (New York: Millbank Memorial Fund, 1948), p. 21.

26. UN Group of Experts, *Measures for the Economic Development of Under-Developed Countries* (New York: United Nations, 1951), p. 13.

27. Myrdal, *Asian Drama*, 1:59.

28. R. Nurkse, *Problems of Capital Formation in Underdeveloped Countries* (Oxford: Blackwell, 1953), p. 1.

29. Ibid.

30. Lewis, *The Theory of Economic Growth*, pp. 208, 226.

31. Nurkse, *Problems of Capital Formation*, p. 2.

32. Cf. Arndt, *The Rise and Fall*, p. 33.

33. G. M. Meier and R. E. Baldwin, *Economic Development: Theory, History, Policy* (New York: Wiley, 1957), p. 303.

34. C. Bekker, "The Point IV Program of the United States," in Hoselitz, *The Progress*, p. 242.

35. Singer, "The Mechanics of Economic Development."

36. UN Group of Experts, *Measures for the Economic Development*, chap. 11.

37. B. Higgins, *Economic Development* (London: Constable, 1959), p. 642.

38. Cf., e.g., R. B. Bryce, quoted above, p. 46.

39. See above, p. 16.

40. J. B. Condliffe, *Agenda for a Post-War World* (London: Allen & Unwin, 1943), p. 172.

41. United Nations, *Supplement to Economic Report, 1945–7, Discussion of Report* (New York: United Nations, February–March 1948), p. 36.

42. S. E. Harris, "Some Aspects of Foreign Aid and Development," *Economia Internazionale*, August 1950.

43. P. E. Corbett, *Post-War Worlds*, IPR Enquiry Series (New York: Farrer & Rinehart, 1942), p. 133.

44. United Nations, *Supplement to Economic Report, 1945–7*, p. 16.

45. Nurkse, *Problems of Capital Formation*, p. 3.

46. Cf. Arndt, *The Rise and Fall*, chap. 5.

47. A. Bonné, *The Economic Development of the Middle East* (London: Kegan Paul, 1943), p. 2.

48. Rosenstein-Rodan, "Problems of Industrialization."

49. H. W. Singer, "Economic Progress in Underdeveloped Countries," *Social Research*, March 1949, pp. 5, 10.

50. Ibid., p. 7.

51. Ibid., p. 6.

52. Ibid.

53. United Nations, *Formulation and Economic Appraisal of Development Projects*, 1:2.

54. Gunnar Myrdal, *Development and Under-Development* (Cairo: National Bank of Egypt, 1956), p. 24.

55. Nurkse, *Problems of Capital Formation*, p. 15.

56. United Nations, *Formulation and Economic Appraisal of Development Projects*, 1:2.

57. Condliffe, *Agenda*, p. 180.

58. E.g., Ellsworth, *The International Economy*, p. 796; A. K. Cairncross, "The Place of Capital in Economic Progress," in L. H. Dupriez, ed., *Economic Progress*, Papers and Proceedings of a Round Table held by the International Economic Association (Louvain: Institut de Recherches Economiques et Sociales, 1955); W. Salant, "The Domestic Effects of Capital Export under the Point Four Program," *AEA Proceedings*, May 1950, p. 514.

59. Cf., e.g., H. Myint, *The Economics of the Developing Countries* (London: Hutchinson, 1964), chap. 6; S. Enke, *Economics for Development* (Englewood Cliffs, N. J.: Prentice-Hall, 1963), chap. 9.

60. N. S. Buchanan, "Deliberate Industrialisation for Higher Incomes," *Economic Journal*, December 1946, p. 552.

61. Viner, "America's Aims," p. 192; also his *International Trade and Economic Development* (Oxford: Clarendon Press, 1953), pp. 114f.; Ellsworth, *The International Economy*, p. 797; Buchanan, "Deliberate Industrialisation," p. 537.

62. M. Fleming, "External Economies and the Doctrine of Balanced Growth," *Economic Journal*, June 1955.

63. H. Myint, *The Economics of Developing Countries* (London: Hutchinson, 1964), chap. 9.

64. A. O. Hirschman, *The Strategy of Economic Development* (New Haven: Yale University Press, 1958).

65. Higgins, *Economic Development*, p. 202.

66. H. W. Singer, "Education and Economic Development" (1961), reprinted in *International Development: Growth and Change* (New York: McGraw-Hill, 1964), p. 66.

67. M. Abramovitz, "Economics of Growth," in B. Haley, ed., *A Survey of Contemporary Economics*, vol. 2 (Homewood, Ill.: Irwin, 1951), p. 141.

68. Cf. C. Kennedy and A. P. Thirlwall, "Technical Progress," *Economic Journal*, March 1972; reprinted in Royal Economic Society, *Surveys of Applied Economics*, vol. 1 (New York: St. Martin's Press, 1973), p. 121.

69. Ibid.

70. Cf. J. Vaizey et al., *The Residual Factor and Economic Growth* (Paris: OECD, 1964); UN Economic Commission for Europe, *Some Factors in Economic Growth in Europe during the 1950s* (Geneva: United Nations, 1964), chap. 7, p. 5.

71. Kennedy and Thirlwall, "Technical Progress," p. 123.

72. J. Vaizey, in Vaizey et al., *The Residual Factor*, p. 5.

73. T. W. Schultz, *The Economic Value of Education* (New York: Columbia University Press, 1963), p. viii.

74. T. W. Schultz, "Investment in Man: An Economist's View," *Social Science Review*, June 1959; "Capital Formation by Education," *Journal of Political Economy*, December 1961; and G. S. Becker, *Human Capital* (1960) (Princeton University Press, 1964).

75. M. Blaug, in M. Blaug, ed., *Economics of Education: Selected Readings* (Harmondsworth: Penguin, 1968), 1:7; cf. also J. Vaizey, ed., *The Economics of Education*, International Social Science Journal, no. 5, 1962.

76. UN Group of Experts, *Measures for Economic Development*, p. 28.

77. Ibid.

78. Ibid., p. 30.

79. A. Maddison, *Foreign Skills and Technical Assistance in Economic Development* (Paris: OECD, 1965), p. 25; cf. also W. A. Brown and R. Opie, *American Foreign Assistance* (Washington, D.C.: Brookings Institution, 1953), p. 16.

80. R. E. Asher et al., *The United Nations and Promotion of the General Welfare* (Washington, D.C.: Brookings Institution, 1957), p. 584.

81. J. Bernstein, "Point Four and After," in *Technical Assistance and Development* (Jerusalem: Harry S. Truman Research Institute, 1970), p. 25.

82. Ibid., p. 24.

83. H. S. Truman, *Years of Trial and Hope, 1946–53* (London: Hodder & Stoughton, 1956), p. 247.

84. *Technical Assistance for Economic Development* (New York: United Nations, 1949), p. 6.

85. Quoted in Bernstein, "Point Four and After," p. 26.

86. Ibid.

87. Asher et al., *The United Nations*, p. 593.

88. Ibid., p. 594; cf. also David Owen, "The United Nations Expanded Program of Technical Assistance: A Multilateral Approach," *The Annals*, May 1959.

89. Cf., e.g., I. M. D. Little and J. M. Clifford, *International Aid* (London: Allen & Unwin, 1965), p. 35.

90. J. Kaplan, "Background Paper," in United Nations, *Technical Assistance*, p. 7.

91. Ibid., p.6.

92. Bernstein, "Point Four and After," p. 28.

93. D. Seers, "Why Visiting Economists Fail," *Journal of Political Economy*, August 1962.

94. Maddison, *Foreign Skills*, p. 9.

95. Singer, "Education and Economic Development," pp. 71f.

96. Maddison, *Foreign Skills*, p. 12.

97. For select bibliographies, see, e.g., J. Bhagwati and R. Eckaus, *Foreign Aid* (Harmondsworth: Penguin Books, 1970); and A. H. Boxer, *Experts in Asia* (Canberra: Australian National University Press, 1969).

98. Maddison, *Foreign Skills*, p. 9.

99. P. N. Rosenstein-Rodan, "International Aid for Underdeveloped Countries," *Review of Economics and Statistics*, May 1961.

100. R. W. Gable, ed., "Partnership for Progress: International Technical Co-operation," *The Annals*, May 1959, p. vii.

101. Bernstein, "Point Four and After," p. 28.

102. Cf., e.g., Arndt, *The Rise and Fall*, chap. 5.

103. F. Harbison and C. A. Myers, *Education, Manpower and Economic Growth* (New York: McGraw-Hill, 1964), p. 105.

104. Ibid., pp. 104ff.

105. H. S. Parnes, *Forecasting Educational Needs for Economic and Social Development* (Paris: OECD, 1962), p. 7.

106. Vaizey, ed., *The Economics of Education*, p. 622.

107. J. Vaizey, "The Labour Market and the Manpower Forecaster: Some Problems," in M. R. Sinha, ed., *The Economics of Manpower Planning* (Bombay: Asian Studies Press, 1965), p. 53.

108. P. J. Foster, "The Vocational School Fallacy in Development Planning" (1966), reprinted in Blaug, ed., *Economics of Education*, 1:411.

109. W. A. Lewis, "Education and Economic Development," in Vaizey, ed., *The Economics of Education*, p. 686.

110. Ibid.

111. Parnes, *Forecasting Educational Needs*, p. 9.

112. H. Myint, "Investment in the Social Infrastructure" (1962), reprinted in G. M. Meier, *Leading Issues in Development Economics*, 1st ed. (New York: Oxford University Press, 1964), p. 282.

113. Vaizey, "The Labour Market and the Manpower Forecaster," p. 54.

114. B. Thomas, "International Factor Movements and Unequal Rates of Growth," *Manchester School*, January 1961, pp. 18f.

115. Ibid., p. 19.

116. B. Thomas, "The International Circulation of Human Capital," *Minerva*, Summer 1967, p. 486.

117. H. G. Johnson, "The Economics of the 'Brain Drain': The Canadian Case," *Minerva*, Spring 1965, p. 299.

118. H. G. Johnson, "An 'Internationalist' Model," in W. Adams, ed., *The Brain Drain* (New York: Macmillan, 1968); Johnson changed his mind—he had earlier supported Brinley Thomas's view (cf. Vaizey et al., *The Residual Factor*, p. 223).

119. E.g., Johnson, "The Economics of 'Brain Drain'," p. 304; OECD, *Technical Assistance and the Needs of Developing Countries* (Paris, 1968), p. 15; Johnson, "An 'Internationalist' Model," in Adams, ed., *The Brain Drain*, p. 90.

120. D. Patinkin, "A 'Nationalist' Model," in Adams, ed., *The Brain Drain*, p. 106.

121. J. A. Perkins, "Foreign Aid and the Brain Drain," *Foreign Affairs*, July 1966, p. 608.

122. Patinkin, "A 'Nationalist' Model," p. 108.

123. H. Myint, "The Underdeveloped Countries: A Less Alarmist View," in Adams, ed., *The Brain Drain*, p. 240.

124. Perkins, "Foreign Aid and the Brain Drain," p. 617.

125. Myint, "The Underdeveloped Countries," in Adams, ed., *The Brain Drain*, p. 236.

126. *Science and Technology for Development*, vol. 6, *Education and Training*, United Nations Conference on the Application of Science and Technology for the Benefit of the Less Developed Areas (New York: United Nations, 1963), p. 2 (emphasis added).

127. R. B. Goode, "Adding to the Stock of Physical and Human Capital," *AEA Proceedings*, May 1959, p. 147.

128. See n. 74 above.

129. Johnson, in Vaizey et al., *The Residual Factor*; reprinted in G. M. Meier, *Leading Issues in Economic Development*, 3d ed. (New York: Oxford University Press, 1976), p. 542.

130. Ibid., p. 543.

131. Ibid.

132. Harbison and Myers, *Education, Manpower*, p. 12.

133. Ibid.

134. Schultz, *The Economic Value of Education*, p. viii.

135. Harbison and Myers, *Education, Manpower*, p. 12.

136. Ibid., p. 2.

137. H. G. Johnson, *Economic Policies Toward Less Developed Countries* (Washington, D.C.: Brookings Institution, 1967), p. 25; A. S. Friedeberg, *The United Nations Conference on Trade and Development of 1964* (Rotterdam: Rotterdam University Press, 1969), p. 10.

138. D. H. Robertson, "The Future of International Trade," *Eco-*

nomic Journal, March 1938, reprinted in American Economic Association, *Readings in the Theory of International Trade* (Philadelphia: Blakiston, 1949), p. 501.

139. J. Viner, "The Prospects for Foreign Trade in the Post-War World" (1946), reprinted in ibid.

140. H. W. Arndt, *The Economic Lessons of the Nineteen-Thirties* (London: Oxford University Press, 1944), p. 297; the flavour of the debate is well conveyed in the "Dissenting Note" by Sir Andrew McFadyen; cf. also T. Balogh, M. Kalecki, E. F. Schumacher, in "New Plans for International Trade," Supplement, *Bulletin*, Oxford Institute of Statistics, August 1943.

141. R. Nurkse, "'Balanced Growth' and Specialization," reprinted in G. Haberler, ed., *Equilibrium and Growth in the World Economy: Economic Essays by Ragnar Nurkse* (Cambridge, Mass.: Harvard University Press, 1962), p. 242.

142. United Nations Economic Commission for Latin America, *Economic Survey of Latin America* (New York, 1949), p. 56.

143. Dr. Singer has answered the priority question as follows: "Roughly speaking, I would say that throughout 1948 and early 1949, Prebisch and I worked independently, and without knowing each other, on terms of trade problems—Prebisch more theoretically and generally; and I more empirically and statistically, at first" (personal communication). In a paper given in New York in December 1948 and published under the title "Economic Progress in Underdeveloped Countries" in *Social Research*, March 1949, Singer gave an analysis of the problems of the underdeveloped countries strikingly similar to Prebisch's.

144. Cf. L. E. di Marco, *International Economics and Development: Essays in Honor of Raul Prebisch* (New York: Academic Press, 1972), a symposium in which most of the Latin American contributors declared their belief in the Prebisch thesis as firmly as most other contributors rejected it.

145. G. Myrdal, *Development and Underdevelopment* (Cairo: National Bank of Egypt, 1956), p. 47; cf. also his *The International Economy* (New York: Harper, 1956), and *Economic Theory and Underdeveloped Regions* (London: Duckworth, 1957).

146. G. Myrdal, *Development and Underdevelopment*, p. 51.

147. R. Nurkse, *Patterns of Trade and Development* (Stockholm, 1959), p. 26.

148. *Economic Survey of Latin America*, pp. 49, 83.

149. Ibid., p. 84.

150. G. Myrdal, *The International Economy*, p. 276.

151. Cf. P. N. Rosenstein-Rodan, "Problems of Industrialization of Eastern and South-Eastern Europe," *Economic Journal*, June–September 1943; R. Nurkse, *Problems of Capital Formation in Underdeveloped Countries* (Oxford: Blackwell, 1953).

152. Myrdal, *The International Economy*, p. 276.

153. A. O. Hirschman, *The Strategy of Economic Development* (New Haven: Yale University Press, 1958), pp. 112, 114.

154. J. N. Bhagwati and P. Desai, *India: Planning for Industrialization* (London: Oxford University Press, 1970), p. 18; cf. also H. W. Arndt, "The Balance of Payments Argument for Priority to Heavy Industry," *Sankhya*, Series B, Calcutta, February 1962.

155. J. H. Power, "Industrialization in Pakistan: A Case of Frustrated Take-Off?" *Pakistan Development Review*, Summer 1963, p. 201.

156. Cf., e.g., J. Viner, *International Trade and Economic Development* (Oxford: Clarendon Press, 1953); G. Haberler, *International Trade and Economic Development* (Cairo: National Bank of Egypt, 1959); A. K. Cairncross, "International Trade and Economic Development," *Economica*, August 1961; H. Myint, "Infant Industry Arguments for Assistance to Industries in the Setting of Dynamic Trade Theory" (1963), reprinted in *Economic Theory and the Underdeveloped Countries* (London: Oxford University Press, 1971); W. M. Corden, *Recent Developments in the Theory of International Trade*, Special Papers in International Economics (Princeton International Finance Section, Princeton University, 1965).

157. GATT, *Trends in International Trade* (Geneva: GATT, 1958), p. 1.

158. Cf. B. Balassa, *Trade Prospects for Developing Countries* (Homewood, Ill.: Irwin, 1964).

159. Cf. H. B. Chenery and A. M. Strout, "Foreign Assistance and Economic Development," *American Economic Review*, September 1966; V. Joshi, "Two-Gap Analysis," reprinted in G. M. Meier, *Leading Issues in Economic Development*, 3d ed. (New York: Oxford University Press, 1976), pp. 336ff; R. Findlay, "The 'Foreign Exchange Gap' and Growth in Developing Economies," in J. N. Bhagwati, ed., *Trade, Balance of Payments and Growth* (New York: North Holland, 1971).

160. GATT, *Trends in International Trade*, p. 125.

161. Quoted in GATT, *International Trade, 1959* (Geneva: GATT, 1960), p. 56.

162. United Nations Economic Commission for Europe, "Europe and the Trade Needs of the Less Developed Countries," in *Economic Survey of Europe in 1960* (Geneva, 1961), pp. 4ff., 50.

163. United Nations Economic Commission for Latin America, *Economic Survey of Latin America for 1956* (New York, 1957), p. 151.

164. Ibid.

165. R. Prebisch, "Commercial Policy in Underdeveloped Countries," *AEA Proceedings*, May 1959, p. 253.

166. Ibid., p. 267.

167. Ibid., p. 264. Prebisch argued that there was no need for reciprocal tariff cuts by LDCs since the latter would in any case spend any additional export earnings on imports of industrial goods from the developed countries.

168. A. S. Friedeberg, *The United Nations Conference*, pp. 5–7.

169. Between 1955 and 1959, twenty-three new member countries were admitted to the United Nations, another seventeen in 1960; by 1963, GATT also had a majority of LDC member countries (ibid., pp. 8, 16).

170. Ibid., pp. 6ff.

171. H. G. Johnson, *Economic Policies*, p. 25.

172. Ibid., p. 29.

173. Raul Prebisch, *Towards a New Trade Policy for Development*, UNCTAD Proceedings, vol. 2 (New York: UNCTAD, 1964), p. 14.

174. G. Haberler, *International Trade*.

175. H. G. Johnson, *Economic Policies*, p. 28.

176. The North-South debate will be discussed in a later chapter.

177. I. Little, T. Scitovsky, M. Scott, *Industry and Trade in Some Developing Countries: A Comparative Study* (London: Oxford University Press, 1970).

178. B. Balassa, *Economic Growth, Trade and the Balance of Payments in Developing Countries, 1960–65* (Washington, D.C.: IBRD, March 1968).

179. Established 1968; see especially its series of *Thames Essays*.

180. Cf. K. Kojima, *Japan and the Pacific Free Trade Area* (London: Macmillan, 1971); S. Okita, ed., *Measures for Trade Expansion of Developing Countries* (Tokyo: Japan Economic Research Center, 1966); and subsequent proceedings volumes of the Pacific Trade and Development Conference series.

181. J. H. Power, "Industrialization in Pakistan."

182. Ibid., p. 198.

183. Ibid., p. 201.

184. Little, Scitovsky, Scott, *Industry and Trade*, pp. xviiiff.

185. R. Nurkse, *Patterns of Trade and Development*, p. 38.

186. H. Myint, "International Trade and Developing Countries"

(1969), reprinted in *Economic Theory and the Underdeveloped Countries* (London: Oxford University Press, 1971).

187. D. B. Keesing, "Outward-looking Policies and Economic Development," *Economic Journal*, June 1967, p. 303.

188. Ibid., p. 305.

189. Asian Development Bank, *Southeast Asia's Economy in the 1970s* (London: Longman, 1971), p. 232.

190. Ibid., p. 255.

191. Kojima quoted Harrod as an advocate of "agreed specialisation" but suggested that the idea was first expressed by Myrdal in *The International Economy* (Kojima, *Japan*, p. 51).

192. Kojima, *Japan*, p. 9.

193. Asian Development Bank, *Southeast Asia's Economy*, p. 255.

194. Ibid., pp. 19ff.

195. W. A. Lewis, "The Slowing Down of the Engine of Growth," *American Economic Review*, September 1980, pp.557–80.

196. I. B. Kravis, "Trade as a Handmaiden of Growth: Similarities between the Nineteenth and Twentieth Centuries," *Economic Journal*, December 1970, p. 850.

197. J. Riedel, "Trade as the Engine of Growth in Developing Countries, Revisited," *Economic Journal*, March 1984.

198. Helen Hughes and Anne O. Krueger, "Effects of Protection in Developed Countries on Developing Countries' Exports of Manufactures," in R. E. Baldwin, and A. O. Krueger, eds., *The Structure and Evolution of Recent U.S. Trade Policies* (Chicago: University of Chicago Press, 1985).

199. Ibid., pp. 401–3.

200. Cf., e.g., W. A. Lewis, "Employment Policy in Underdeveloped Areas" (1958), reprinted in G. M. Meier, *Leading Issues in Economic Development*, 1st ed. (New York: Oxford University Press, 1964), p. 379.

201. Little, Scitovsky, Scott, *Industry and Trade*, p. xix.

202. Myrdal, *The International Economy*, p. 257.

203. Bhagwati and Desai, *Trade, Balance*, p. 486.

Chapter Four

1. H. W. Singer, "Social Development: Key Growth Sector," *International Development Review*, March 1965, p. 5.

2. United Nations, *The United Nations Development Decade: Proposals for Action*, Report of the Secretary-General (New York, 1962).

3. For a full account, see UNRISD, *The Quest for a Unified Approach to Development* (Geneva, 1980).

4. United Nations, *Report on the World Social Situation* (New York, 1957), p. 4.

5. Ibid., p. 1.

6. UNRISD, *Studies for Social Change: An Account of UNRISD's Approaches and Activities* (Geneva, n. d.), p. 3.

7. Ibid., p. 6.

8. United Nations, *The United Nations Development Decade*, p. 2.

9. Marshall Wolfe, "An Assessment," in UNRISD, *The Quest for a Unified Approach*, p. 67.

10. H. W. Singer, "Debate on the Next Development Decade," *Ceres* (FAO, Rome), July–August 1968, p. 51.

11. H. W. Singer, "Social Development: Key Growth Sector," p. 5.

12. Ibid.

13. Dudley Seers, "The Meaning of Development," *International Development Review*, December 1969, pp. 2–3.

14. Mahbub ul Haq, "Employment and Income Distribution in the 1970s: A New Perspective," *Development Digest*, October 1971, pp. 5, 7.

15. R. Jolly, "Changing Views on Development," in J. J. Nossin, *Surveys for Development* (Amsterdam: Elserin, 1977), p. 21.

16. D. A. Morse, "The Employment Problem in Developing Countries," in R. Robinson and P. Johnston, eds., *Prospects for Employment Opportunities in the 1970s* (London: HMSO, 1971), p. 8.

17. Ibid., p. 6.

18. *Employment Objectives in Economic Development* (Geneva: International Labour Office, 1961), p. iii.

19. Cf. H. W. Singer, "A World Employment Programme," *Rural Life*, Third Quarter 1970.

20. *Employment Growth and Basic Needs* (Geneva: International Labour Office, 1976), p. 2.

21. Dudley Seers, "New Approaches Suggested by the Colombia Employment Program," *International Labour Review*, October 1970, p. 379.

22. *Towards Full Employment: A Programme for Colombia* (Geneva: International Labour Office, 1970), p. 14.

23. Dudley Seers, "The Dimensions of the Employment Problem: The Employment Mission to Colombia," in Robinson and Johnston, *Prospects*, p. 28.

24. *Towards Full Employment*, p. 15.

25. D. Turnham and I. Jaeger, *The Employment Problem in Less Developed Countries: A Review of Evidence* (Paris: OECD, 1971), p. 17.

26. J. White, "Economic Planning for Employment: Personal Impressions of the Conference Discussion," in R. Robinson and P. Johnston, *Prospects*, p. 19.

27. H. W. Singer, "Poverty, Income Distribution and Levels of Living: Thirty Years of Changing Thought on Development Problems," in C. H. Hammamantha Rao & P. C. Joshi, eds., *Reflections on Economic Development and Social Change: Essays in Honor of V. K. B. V. Rao* (Oxford: Martin Robertson, 1979), p. 34.

28. *Employment, Incomes and Equality: A Strategy for Increasing Productive Employment in Kenya* (Kenya Report) (Geneva: International Labour Office, 1972), pp. 62f.

29. Ibid., p. 1.

30. D. G. Davies, "A Critical Discussion of the ILO Report on Employment in Kenya," *Pakistan Development Review*, Autumn 1973; see also R. M. Sundrum, "Development, Equality and Employment," *Economic Record*, September 1974.

31. *Towards Full Employment*, p. 57; cf. E. Thorbeke, "The Employment Problem: A Critical Evaluation of Four ILO Comprehensive Country Reports," *International Labour Review*, May 1973, p. 422.

32. Kenya Report, p. 3.

33. Dudley Seers, in R. Robinson and P. Johnston, *Prospects*, pp. 145–47.

34. *Towards Full Employment*, pp. 145–47.

35. Ibid., p. 138.

36. Kenya Report, p. 3.

37. Ibid., p. 21.

38. *Towards Full Employment*, p. 157.

39. D. Turnham and I. Jaeger, *The Employment Problem*, p. 12.

40. Ibid., p. 97.

41. D. T. Healey, "Development Policy: New Thinking about an Interpretation," *Journal of Economic Literature*, September 1972, p. 773.

42. Helen Hughes, "The Scope for Labor Capital Substitution in the Developing Economies of Southeast and East Asia," in L. White, ed., *Technology, Employment, and Development* (Bangkok: Council for Asian Manpower Studies, 1974), p. 32.

43. D. T. Healey, "Development Policy," p. 794.

44. Mahbub ul Haq, "Employment and Income Distribution," p. 3.

45. Helen Hughes, "The Scope," p. 38.

46. E. F. Schumacher, *Small Is Beautiful: Economics as If People Mattered* (New York: Harper & Row, 1973).

47. R. S. McNamara, *Address to the Board of Governors* (Washington, D.C.: World Bank, 25 September 1972), p. 8.

48. R. S. McNamara, *Address to the Board of Governors* (Nairobi, Kenya, 24 September 1973), p. 10.

49. Cf. his speech to the American Society of Newspaper Editors of 18 May 1966, reprinted as chapter 9 in R. S. McNamara, *The Essense of Security* (London: Hodder & Stoughton, 1968).

50. The proceedings of the conference were published in Barbara Ward et al., *The Widening Gap: Development in the 1970s* (New York: Columbia University Press, 1971).

51. R. S. McNamara, *Address to the Columbia University Conference on International Economic Development* (New York: World Bank, 20 February 1970), p. 4.

52. Cf. J. L. Maddux, *The Development Philosophy of Robert S. McNamara* (New York: World Bank, June 1981).

53. R. S. McNamara, *Address to the Board of Governors* (Washington, D.C.: World Bank, 1971), p. 14.

54. R. S. McNamara, *Address to UNCTAD III* (Santiago, 1972).

55. R. S. McNamara, *Address to the Board of Governors* (Washington, D.C.: World Bank, 25 September 1972), p. 16.

56. R. S. McNamara, *Address to the Board of Governors* (Nairobi, Kenya, 24 September 1973), p. 27.

57. R. S. McNamara, *Address to the Board of Governors* (Washington, D.C.: World Bank, 30 September 1974), p. 2.

58. Dudley Seers, "The Meaning of Development," in Robinson and Johnston, *Prospects*, p. 4.

59. J. White, *Technology*, p. 17.

60. H. Chenery et al., *Redistribution with Growth* (Oxford: Oxford University Press, 1974), p. xii.

61. R. Jolly, "The World Employment Conference: The Enthronement of Basic Needs," *ODI Review*, 1976, no. 2, p. 40.

62. H. W. Singer, "Thirty Years," p. 36.

63. Ibid., pp. 36f.

64. Ibid., p. 37.

65. Reprinted in T. N. Srinivasan and P. K. Bardhan, eds., *Poverty and Income Distribution in India* (Calcutta: Statistical Publishing Society, 1974).

66. Ibid., p. 11.

67. Ibid., p. 14.

68. Kenya Report, pp. 111f.

69. R. S. McNamara, *Address to the Board of Governors* (1972), p. 16.

70. Cf., e.g., *Analysis of Distributional Issues in Development Planning*, World Bank Workshop, Bellagio, April 1977; symposium on "Meeting Basic Human Needs," *Economic Impact*, Washington, D.C., 1978, no. 3; Paul Streeten, *Development Perspectives* (London: Macmillan, 1981), Part IV; and other references given below.

71. Dudley Seers, "The Meaning of Development," p. 2; Mahbub ul Haq, "Employment and Income Distribution," p. 7.

72. *Employment, Growth and Basic Needs: A One-World Problem* (Geneva: International Labour Office, 1976), pp. 4–8.

73. F. Lisk, "Conventional Development Strategies and Basic-Needs Fulfilment," *International Labour Review*, March 1977, p. 185.

74. Ibid., p. 182.

75. Cf., e.g., M. Yudelman, "Agriculture in Integrated Rural Development: The Experience of the World Bank," *Food Policy*, 1976, no. 5; R. H. Retzlaff, "Problems of Aid for Rural Development," in R. T. Shand and H. V. Richter, eds., *International Aid: Some Political, Administrative, Technical Realities* (Canberra: Australian National University, 1979).

76. H. W. Singer, "Thirty Years," p. 40.

77. P. Streeten and S. J. Burki, "Basic Needs: Some Issues," *World Development*, 1978, no. 3, p. 418.

78. R. Jolly, "The World Employment Programme," p. 36.

79. *Employment, Growth and Basic Needs*, pp. 4, 9.

80. H. W. Singer, "Thirty Years," pp. 39f.

81. Development Assistance Committee, *Development Co-operation, 1977 Review* (Paris: OECD, 1977), p. 94.

82. R. S. McNamara, *Address to the Board of Governors*, (Manila: World Bank, 1976), p. 2.

83. R. S. McNamara, *Address to the Board of Governors* (Washington, D.C.: World Bank, 1977), p. 4.

84. Nancy Baster, ed., Special Issue on Development Indicators, *Journal of Development Studies*, April 1972, p. 1.

85. The report was published in *International Social Development Review*, 1971, no. 3.

86. M. Wolfe, "An Assessment," pp. 74f.

87. B. and J. D. Higgins, "The Reluctant Planner: An Overview," in W. D. Cook and T. E. Kuhn, eds., *Planning and Development Processes in the Third World*, TIMS Studies in Management Science (New York: North Holland, 1980) p. 26.

88. B. Higgins, "Economics and Ethics in the New Approach to

Development," in A. S. Rosenbaum, ed., *Philosophy in Context* (Cleveland: Cleveland State University, 1978), p. 18.

89. Cited in M. Wolfe, "An Assessment," pp. 76f.

90. Ibid., p. 77.

91. Ibid., p. 137.

92. Ibid., p. 91.

93. *Premises and Implications of a Unified Approach to Development Analysis and Planning* (Bangkok: ESCAP, 1976).

94. M. Wolfe, "An Assessment," p. 91.

95. S. L. Barraclough, Preface, in *The Quest for a Unified Approach to Development*, p. ii.

96. R. Dore, "Scholars and Preachers," *IDS Bulletin*, June 1978, p. 13.

97. Ibid.

98. Dudley Seers, "The Meaning of Development," p. 2.

99. D. A. Morse, "The Employment Problem," pp. 6f.

100. R. S. McNamara, *Address to the Board of Governors* (1972), p. 8.

101. R. S. MNamara, *Address to the Board of Governors* (Nairobi, Kenya, 24 September 1973), p. 10.

102. I. Adelman and C. T. Morris, *Economic Growth and Social Equity in Developing Countries* (Stanford: Stanford University Press, 1973), p. 192.

103. J. White, *Technology*, p. 18.

104. Deepak Lal, "Distribution and Development," *World Development*, 1976, no. 9, p. 729.

105. I. M. D. Little, review of Adelman and Morris, and Chenery et al., *Journal of Development Economics*, 1976, no. 3, p. 101.

106. H. Chenery et al., *Redistribution*, p. xiv.

107. I. M. D. Little, *Economic Development: Theory, Policy and International Relations* (New York: Basic Books, 1982), p. 212.

108. R. Jolly, "Changing View on Development," p. 19.

109. D. Lal, "Distribution and Development," p. 726.

110. R. S. McNamara, *Address to the Columbia University Conference* (1970), p. 6.

111. Cf. H. W. Arndt, *The Rise and Fall of Economic Growth* (Melbourne: Longmans, 1978), chaps. 7–9.

112. Dudley Seers, "The Meaning of Development," p. 4.

113. K. Griffin, *The Political Economy of Agrarian Change* (London: Macmillan, 1974), p. xi.

114. Cf. V. M. Dandekar and N. Rath, *Poverty in India* (New Delhi:

Ford Foundation, 1970); B. S. Minhas, *Planning and the Poor* (New Delhi: S. Chand, 1971).

115. [P. Pant], *Development and Environment*, Report of Founeux Panel of Experts (Stockholm: United Nations, 1971), p. 9.

116. D. Turnham and I. Jaeger, *Employment Problem*, p. 99.

117. R. Jolly, "The World Employment Programme," p. 42.

118. J. White, *Technology*, p. 21.

119. T. N. Srinivasan, "Development, Poverty and Basic Human Needs," *Food Research Institute Studies*, 1977, no. 2, p. 24.

120. Soedjatmoko, "National Policy Implications of the Basic Needs Model," *Prisma* (Jakarta), March 1978, p. 21.

121. Ibid.

122. G. Donald, "Some Trends in Thinking about Development in the 1970s," *Development Digest*, July 1981, p. 128.

123. R. Dore, "Scholars and Preachers," p. 13.

124. Ibid., p. 14.

125. J. W. Mellor, "Lessons from Experience," in *Economic Impact*, 1978, no. 23, p. 25.

126. G. Myrdal, *Asian Drama: An Inquiry into the Poverty of Nations*, 3 vols. (New York: Pantheon, 1968).

127. Ibid., 1:529.

128. Ibid., 2:743.

129. Ibid., 1:54.

130. Ibid., 1:57.

131. Ibid., 1:65.

132. Ibid., 1:67.

Chapter Five

1. P. M. Sweezy and L. Huberman, eds., *Paul Baran (1910–1964): A Collective Portrait* (New York: Monthly Review Press, 1965), p. 46.

2. P. Baran, "On the Political Economy of Backwardness," *The Manchester School*, January 1952.

3. Ibid., p. 75.

4. Ibid., p. 80.

5. Ibid., p. 86.

6. Ibid., p. 78.

7. Ibid., p. 86.

8. Ibid., p. 90.

9. Ibid.

10. P. Baran, *The Political Economy of Growth* (New York: Monthly Review Press, 1957; New York: Penguin, 1973).

11. A. Foster-Carter, "Neo-Marxist Approaches to Development and Underdevelopment," in E. de Kadt and G. Williams, eds., *Sociology and Development* (London: Tavistock, 1974), p. 80.

12. Sweezy and Huberman, *Paul Baran*, p. 58.

13. Ibid., pp. 126, 128.

14. Ibid., p. 459.

15. Ibid., p. 119.

16. Ibid., p. 305.

17. A. Foster-Carter, "Neo-Marxist Approaches," p. 80.

18. Ibid., p. 402.

19. P. Baran, *The Political Economy of Growth*, p. 120.

20. Ibid.

21. Ibid.

22. Ibid., p. 121.

23. Ibid., p. 123.

24. Ibid., p. 294.

25. Ibid., p. 403.

26. See above, p. 73–74.

27. C. Furtado, *The Economic Growth of Brazil* (Berkeley: University of California Press, 1963).

28. C. Furtado, "The Concept of External Dependence in the Study of Underdevelopment," in C. K. Wilber, ed., *The Political Economy of Development and Underdevelopment* (New York: Random House, 1973), pp. 120ff.

29. O. Sunkel, "National Development and External Dependence in Latin America," *Journal of Development Studies*, October 1969, p. 32.

30. O. Sunkel, "Transnational Capitalism and National Development in Latin America" (mimeo.), Santiago, 1970, quoted in N. Girvan, ed., *Dependence and Underdevelopment in the New World and the Old*, Social and Economic Studies, vol. 22, no. 1, (Jamaica: University of West Indies, March 1973), p. 22.

31. Ibid.

32. Ibid.

33. I. M. D. Little, *Economic Development: Theory, Policy and International Relations* (New York: Basic Books, 1982), p. 20.

34. Cf. H. W. Arndt, "The Origins of Structuralism," *World Development*, vol. 13, no. 2, 1985, pp. 151–54.

35. Cf. W. Leontief, "Postulates: Keynes' General Theory and the

Classicists," in S. E. Harris, ed., *The New Economics* (New York: Knopf, 1947).

36. Cf. D. M. Bensusan-Butt, *On Economic Man* (Canberra: Australian National University Press, 1978).

37. Cf. J. H. Boeke, *Economics and Economic Policy in Dual Societies* (New York: Institute of Pacific Relations, 1953); B. Higgins, *Economic Development* (London: Constable, 1959).

38. T. Wilson and P. W. S. Andrews, eds., *Oxford Studies in the Price Mechanism* (Oxford: Clarendon Press, 1951).

39. H. W. Arndt, *The Economic Lessons of the Nineteen-Thirties* (London: Oxford University Press, 1944), p. 293.

40. Cf., e.g., J. E. Meade, *Planning and the Price Mechanism* (London: Allen & Unwin, 1948), and references given there; also W. A. Lewis, *The Principles of Economic Planning* (London: Dobson, 1949).

41. Exceptions are J. Viner, S. H. Frankel, P. Bauer; see chapter 6 below.

42. G. Myrdal, *Economic Theory and Underdeveloped Regions* (London: Duckworth, 1957), p. 49.

43. R. de O. Campos, "Two Views of Inflation in Latin America," from A. O. Hirschman, ed., *Latin American Issues* (New York: Twentieth Century Fund, 1961), quoted in G. M. Meier, *Leading Issues*, p. 211.

44. J. Noyola Vazquez, "El desarollo economico y la inflacion en Mexico y otros paises latino-americanos," *Investigacion Economica*, 1956, pp. 603–48.

45. O. Sunkel, "La inflacion chilena: un enfoque heterodoxo," *El Trimestre Economico*, 25 (4), English translation in *International Economic Papers*, no. 10 (London: Macmillan, 1960), p. 110.

46. H. B. Chenery, "Development Policies and Programmes," *Economic Bulletin for Latin America*, March 1958, pp. 51f.

47. Cf. T. Balogh, "Economic Policy and the Price System," *Economic Bulletin for Latin America*, March 1961; D. Seers, "Inflation and Growth: A Summary of Experience in Latin America," *Economic Bulletin for Latin America*, February 1962, and "A Theory of Inflation and Growth in Underdeveloped Economies Based on the Experience of Latin America," *Oxford Economic Papers*, June 1962.

48. F. H. Cardoso and E. Faletto, *Dependency and Development in Latin America* (Berkeley: University of California Press, 1971, English translation, 1979), p. ix.

49. P. J. O'Brien, "A Critique of Latin American Theories of De-

pendency," in I. Ozaal et al., eds., *Beyond the Sociology of Development* (London: Routledge, 1975), p. 9.

50. Ibid., p. 51.

51. Ibid., p. 64.

52. A. G. Frank, *Capitalism and Underdevelopment in Latin America* (Monthly Review Press, 1969; Harmondsworth: Penguin Books, 1971), p. 11.

53. Ibid.

54. Ibid., p. 33.

55. Ibid.

56. Ibid., p. 30.

57. A. Foster-Carter, "Neo-Marxist Approaches," p. 69.

58. K. Griffin, "Underdevelopment in History," from *Underdevelopment in Spanish America* (London: Allen & Unwin, 1969), quoted in C. K. Wilber, *The Political Economy*, p. 69.

59. Ibid., p. 70.

60. Ibid., p. 75.

61. P. J. O'Brien, "A Critique," p. 66.

62. A. G. Frank, *Lumpenbourgeoisie, Lumpendevelopment* (New York: Monthly Review Press, 1972).

63. A. Foster-Carter, "Neo-Marxist Approaches," p. 84.

64. H. Seton-Watson, *The Imperialist Revolutionaries: World Communism in the 1960s and 1970s* (London: Hutchinson, 1980), p. 81.

65. Western Marxists, however, applied it assiduously to countries such as Indonesia after the 1965/66 change of regime; cf., e.g., R. Mortimer, ed., *The Showcase State: The Illusion of Indonesia's Accelerated Modernization* (Sydney: Angus and Robertson, 1973).

66. Samir Amin, *Neo-Colonialism in West Africa* (Harmondsworth: Penguin, 1973); *Unequal Development* (Delhi: Oxford University Press, 1979; trans. of 1973 French ed.).

67. Samir Amin, *Unequal Development*, p. 141.

68. Cf. on this, I. M. D. Little, *Economic Development*, p. 220.

69. Samir Amin, *Neo-Colonialism*, p. 384.

70. K. P. Jameson and C. K. Wilber, eds., *Directions in Economic Development* (Notre Dame, Ind.: University of Notre Dame Press, 1979), p. 19.

71. A. Foster-Carter, "Neo-Marxist Approaches," p. 80.

72. Jameson and Wilber, *Directions*, p. 27.

73. P. Baran, *The Political Economy of Growth*, p. 462.

74. A. Foster-Carter, "Neo-Marxist Approaches," p. 78.

75. Ibid., p. 92.

76. Ibid.

77. Samir Amin, *Neo-Colonialism in West Africa*, p. xii.

78. Samir Amin, *Unequal Development*, p. 200.

79. A. Foster-Carter, "Neo-Marxist Approaches," p. 77.

80. Dudley Seers, "The New Meaning of Development," *International Development Review*, 1977 (3).

81. Ibid., p. 4.

82. Ibid., p. 5.

83. Ibid.

84. Ibid., p. 6.

85. Ibid., p. 7.

86. C. W. Bergqvist, *Alternative Approaches to the Problem of Development: A Selected and Annotated Bibliography* (Durham: Carolina Academic Press, 1979), p. xii.

87. Ibid., p. xiv.

88. D. Goulet, " 'Development' . . . or Liberation," *International Development Review*, September 1971, p. 6.

89. Ibid.

90. Ivan Illich, "Outwitting the 'Developed Countries' " from *Celebration of Awareness* (New York: Doubleday, 1969), quoted in C. K. Wilber, *Directions*, p. 405.

91. D. Goulet, " 'Development' . . . or Liberation," p. 8.

92. H. Schram, *The Political Thought of Mao Tse-Tung* (New York: Praeger, 1963), p. 54.

93. J. G. Gurley, "Mao and the Building of Socialism," in *Challengers to Capitalism* (San Francisco: San Francisco Book Company, 1976), p. 115.

94. Ibid., p. 119.

95. H. Schram, *The Political Thought*, p. 54.

96. Ibid., p. 52.

97. Ibid., p. 55.

98. C. P. FitzGerald, *Mao Tse-Tung and China* (London: Hodder & Stoughton, 1976), p. 110.

99. E. L. Wheelwright and B. McFarlane, *The Chinese Road to Socialism: Economics of the Cultural Revolution* (New York: Monthly Review Press, 1970), p. 8.

100. D. Goulet, " 'Development' . . . or Liberation," p. 9.

101. Wheelwright and McFarlane, *The Chinese Road*, p. 18.

102. D. S. Zagoria, "China by Daylight," *Dissent* (New York, 1975), reprinted in *Quadrant* (Sydney), November 1978, p. 10.

103. A. L. Rowse, quoted in C. P. FitzGerald, *Mao Tse-Tung*, p. v.

104. Joan Robinson, quoted in Wheelwright and McFarlane, *The Chinese Road*, p. 8.

105. Yvonne Preston, "Australian Public Opinion and China," *Quadrant* (Sydney), November 1978, p. 41.

106. Wheelwright and McFarlane, *The Chinese Road*, p. 213.

107. Ibid., pp. 214f.

108. Ibid., p. 213.

109. Joan Robinson, quoted in ibid., p. 8.

110. J. G. Gurley, "Maoist Economic Development: The New Man in the New China," from *Center Magazine* (May 1970), quoted in C. K. Wilber, *The Political Economy*, p. 311.

111. Ibid., p. 310.

112. D. S. Zagoria, "China by Daylight," p. 6.

113. Yvonne Preston, "Australian Public Opinion," p. 41.

114. H. Seton-Watson, *The Imperialist*, p. 127.

115. Ibid.

116. Ibid.

117. Joan Robinson, quoted in Wheelwright and McFarlane, *The Chinese Road*, p. 7.

118. H. Seton-Watson, *The Imperialist*, p. 127.

119. L. Anell and B. Nygren, *The Developing Countries and the World Economic Order* (London: Methuen, 1980), p. 87.

120. Ibid., p. 102.

121. Ibid., p. 97.

122. Ibid., p. 103.

123. D. Goulet, "Development and the International Economic Order," *International Development Review*, 1974 (2), pp. 10f.

124. Anell and Nygren, *The Developing Countries*, p. 187.

125. Ibid., p. 108.

126. Cf. E. Laszlo et al., *The Objectives of the New International Economic Order* (New York: Pergamon Press, 1978).

127. Anell and Nygren, *The Developing Countries*, p. 110.

128. Cf. I. M. D. Little, *Economic Development*, p. 326.

129. Ibid.

130. Anell and Nygren, *The Developing Countries*, p. 156.

131. K. Minogue, "Between Rhetoric & Fancy," *Encounter*, December 1980.

132. P. Baran, *The Political Economy of Growth*, p. 47.

133. J. G. Gurley, "Economic Development: A Marxist View," in Jameson and Wilber, *Directions*, p. 233.

134. Ibid., p. 239.

135. Ibid.

136. Cf. M. Caldwell and L. Tan, *Cambodia in the Southeast Asian War* (New York: Monthly Review Press, 1973).
137. Jameson and Wilber, *Directions*, p. 29.
138. J. G. Gurley, quoted in ibid., p. 220.
139. Ibid., pp. 194, 210.
140. Ibid., p. 247.
141. P. J. O'Brien, "A Critique," p. 75.
142. Ibid., p. 76.
143. Jameson and Wilber, *Directions*, p. 31.
144. Cordoso and Faletto, *Dependency*, p. 216.
145. Gurley, quoted in Jameson and Wilber, *Directions*, p. 201.
146. Jameson and Wilber, *Directions*, p. 31.

Chapter Six

1. Above, p. 29.
2. J. H. Boeke, *Economics and Economic Policy in Dual Societies* (New York: Institute of Pacific Relations, 1953), p. 103.
3. Ibid., p. 39.
4. Ibid., p. 37.
5. Ibid., p. 40.
6. Ibid.
7. J. H. Boeke, "Dualistic Economics," in W. F. Wertheim, ed., *Indonesian Economics: The Concept of Dualism in Theory and Practice* (The Hague: W. van Hoeve, 1961), p. 179.
8. Ibid., p. 174.
9. Ibid., p. 172.
10. J. H. Boeke, "Three Forms of Disintegration of Dual Societies," cited in B. Higgins, *Economic Development* (London: Constable, 1959), p. 277.
11. J. H. Boeke, Letter (1931), cited in W. F. Wertheim, *Indonesian Economics*, p. 45.
12. S. H. Frankel, *The Economic Impact on Under-Developed Societies* (Oxford: Blackwell, 1953), p. 70.
13. Ibid., p. 71.
14. Ibid., p. 72.
15. Ibid.
16. Ibid., pp. 74 ff.
17. J. Viner, *International Trade and Economic Development* (Oxford: Clarendon Press, 1953), p. 119.
18. Ibid., p. 120.

19. P. T. Bauer, *Dissent on Development* (London: Weidenfeld & Nicolson, 1971), p. 26.

20. Ibid., p. 25.

21. P. T. Bauer and B. S. Yamey, *The Economics of Underdeveloped Countries* (Cambridge University Press, 1957), p. 149.

22. Ibid., p. 154.

23. P. T. Bauer, *Reality and Rhetoric: Studies in the Economics of Development* (London: Weidenfeld & Nicolson, 1984), p. 83.

24. Ibid., p. 80.

25. Bauer, *Dissent on Development*, p. 21.

26. G. Myrdal, *An International Economy*, p. 322, cited in Bauer, *Dissent on Development*, p. 470.

27. Bauer and Yamey, *The Economics*, p. 86.

28. Ibid., p. 88.

29. Bauer, *Dissent on Development*, p. 27.

30. Ibid., p. 90.

31. Ibid., p. 24.

32. Ibid., pp. 20, 23.

33. Ibid., p. 52.

34. Ibid., p. 41.

35. Quoted in J. D. Sethi, *Gandhi Today* (New Delhi: Vikas, 1978), p. 7.

36. H. Troyat, *Tolstoy* (Harmondsworth: Penguin, 1970), p. 879.

37. Ibid., p. 636.

38. Quoted in Sethi, *Gandhi*, p. 64.

39. Quoted in Boeke, "Dualistic Economics," p. 181.

40. Ibid., p. 185.

41. Sethi, *Gandhi*, p. 18.

42. Quoted in Sethi, *Gandhi*, p. 64.

43. Quoted in ibid.

44. Boeke, "Dualistic Economics," p. 185.

45. Quoted in Sethi, *Gandhi*, p. 66.

46. Quoted in ibid., p. 66.

47. Quoted in ibid., p. 10.

48. Sethi, *Gandhi*, p. 8.

49. Jayaprakash Narayan, in Foreword to Sethi, *Gandhi*, p. vii.

50. P. H. Stoddard et al., *Change in the Moslem World* (Syracuse: Syracuse University Press, 1981), p. 9.

51. Ibid., p. 15.

52. Ibid., p. 16.

53. Islamic Council of Europe, *Islam and Contemporary Society* (London: Longman, 1982), p. vii.

54. Ibid., p. 262.
55. Muh. Kamal bin Hassan, "Education and Family Life in Modernising Malaysia," in Stoddard, *Change*, p. 67.
56. Islamic Council of Europe, *Islam*, p. 259.
57. Rouhollah K. Ramazani, "Iran: the Islamic Cultural Revolution," in Stoddard, *Change*, p. 42.
58. Ibid.
59. Imam Khomeini, *Islam and Revolution: Writings and Declarations* (Berkeley: Mizan Press, 1981), p. 195.
60. Stoddard, *Change*, p. 42.
61. Imam Khomeini, *Islam*, p. 172.
62. Ibid., p. 38.
63. Ibid., p. 35.
64. Ibid., p. 276.
65. Ibid., p. 115.
66. Ibid., p. 49.
67. Ibid., p. 185.
68. Stoddard, *Change*, p. 39.
69. N. R. Keddie, ed., *Religion and Politics in Iran* (New Haven: Yale University Press, 1983), p. 147.
70. Quoted in S. A. A. Rizvi, *Iran: Royalty, Religion and Revolution* (Canberra: Ma'rifat, 1980), p. 313.
71. Imam Khomeini, *Islam*, p. 45.
72. Ibid., p. 190.
73. Quoted in Rizvi, *Iran*, p. 325.
74. Imam Khomeini, *Islam*, p. 331.
75. N. R. Keddie, *Religion*, p. 165.
76. Imam Khomeini, *Islam*, p. 331.
77. East Asian Christian Conference, *The Church in East Asia* (Bangkok, December 1949), p. 7.
78. *Octogesima Adveniens* (1971), quoted in Bauer, *Reality and Rhetoric*, p. 74.
79. *Populorum Progressio* (1968), quoted in Bauer, *Reality and Rhetoric*, p. 75.
80. *Octogesima Adveniens*, quoted in Bauer, *Reality and Rhetoric*, p. 76.
81. *Populorum Progressio*, quoted in Bauer, *Reality and Rhetoric*, p. 76.
82. Ibid., p. 78.
83. Ibid.
84. Cardinal Ratzinger, *Instruction on Certain Aspects of the "Theology of Liberation"* (Vatican, 6 August 1984).

85. Ibid.
86. Ibid.
87. Anglican Social Responsibilities Commission et al., *Changing Australia* (Blackburn, Vic.: Dove Communications, 1983), p. 19.

Chapter Seven

1. G. Myrdal, *Asian Drama*, 1:58.
2. Jacques Binet, "Développement. Transfer de technologie. Transfer de culture," *Diogene* (Paris), April–June 1984 (my translation).
3. R. M. Sundrum, *Development Economics: A Framework for Analysis and Policy* (London: Wiley, 1983), p. 78.

Index of Names

215